HOLY GRAIL AND HOLY THORN

Glastonbury in
the English Imagination

RICHARD HAYMAN

FONTHILL

Fonthill Media Limited
Fonthill Media LLC
www.fonthillmedia.com
office@fonthillmedia.com

First published in the United Kingdom and
the United States of America 2014

British Library Cataloguing in Publication Data:
A catalogue record for this book is available from the British Library

ISBN 978-1-78155-049-6

Typeset in Sabon 10/13.5
Printed and bound by CPI Group (UK) Ltd, Croydon, CRO 4YY

Contents

Acknowledgements

I would like to thank various people for help in finding illustrations and for permission to reproduce them, specifically Ian Rutland Boughton of the Rutland Boughton Music Trust; Cecilia Nicholson of the John Michell Club; and Paul Fletcher of the Chalice Well Trust.

1

The Holiest Earth in England

Glastonbury is to England much like Delphi is to Greece. From road signs reminding you that you are entering the Isle of Avalon, its mythical status is something that you are never allowed to forget. Glastonbury is the home of Avalon Plastics, Avalon Motors, Avalon Tyres, Isle of Avalon Caravan Park and so on, but in fact the name of no other town in England has inspired so many authors to wax lyrical. It has been called Heaven on Earth, a Paradise Garden, cosmological world-centre, earthly paradise in the Western Seas, the first ground of God, the English Jerusalem, the holiest earth in England and more. This book explains how and why Glastonbury has acquired that special status in English, British and international culture.

How could such a thing happen to a small Somerset town? I grew up less than twenty miles from Glastonbury and my image of it is a slightly down-at-heel town of sheepskin coat factories, a place where Somerset occasionally played their Sunday League cricket matches. True, it has the magnificent Tor, but for us the magical mystery tour had started much earlier because we travelled to Glastonbury across Sedgemoor, so we passed Athelney where Alfred burned the cakes, and Burrow Mump which, although smaller than Glastonbury Tor, easily equals it in strangeness. But I have met many people who think mine is just a prosaic image of a landscape in which some great primeval mystery resides.

I acknowledge these feelings about Glastonbury. They are not new and they are not the preserve of alternative or youth culture, the people they are now most associated with. G.K. Chesterton, in his short history of England written in 1917, thought that Glastonbury was a place of universal sanctity. That is why Joseph of Arimathea, the man who buried Jesus, settled there.

> Something of rich rains and warmth in its westland meadows, or something in lost pagan traditions about it, made it persistently regarded as a kind of Earthly Paradise. Arthur, after being slain at Lyonesse, is carried here, as if to heaven.[1]

John Cowper Powys (1872–1963) grew up at Montacute, within sight of Glastonbury Tor on a clear day, and the place haunted him as he grew to middle age and had made his life elsewhere. He understood why people went to Glastonbury and what a transforming effect it could have on them. They are 'attracted by a magnetism too powerful to resist, but as different people approached it they changed its chemistry, though not its essence, by their own identity'.[2] This book is about the many individuals captured by those words, who have found in Glastonbury 'an immaterial fountain of life'.

It is often said that there are two Glastonburys. In the 1930s Dion Fortune divided the townsfolk into Glastonburians and Avalonians, which was more or less a distinction between natives and incomers. It remains valid. Walk up the High Street today and there are people there who think they are in Glastonbury, while others think they are in Avalon. It seems entirely appropriate that the town has secular and sacred names. Its parallel worlds can be seen in the shops on the main streets, where Psychic Pig, Yin Yang and the The Goddess and Green Man rub shoulders with Boots the Chemist, Enchanted Florals and Burns the Bread.

The town thrives on its heritage, but popular interest in its past developed spontaneously. It is not sustained by heritage branding and marketing and would thrive quite happily without it. The attraction of the place is not immediately obvious, however. The town has an air of lived history but is not conventionally beautiful in a county where there is no shortage of such things. It lacks the superficial elegance of Bath, while for architecture it is outclassed by its near neighbour and erstwhile chief rival, the city of Wells. Of course, Glastonbury has some very fine historic buildings to complement the Tor and abbey ruins—St John's church, the magnificent abbey barn, the Tribunal among them—but they are scattered in streets of Victorian and later buildings which have their usual quota of sash windows but are otherwise unexceptional. The Tor looms over the town but is only accessible from the town centre through a Victorian suburb. This haphazard dispersal of the past beneath the imprint of modern life gives the place its authenticity and vitality. But Glastonbury is much more than that. It is a place of stories, of Joseph of Arimathea, King Arthur, the Holy Grail, Celtic saints, a place of miraculous trees and numinous waters. The Glastonbury thorn trees, although they are only descendants of the original tree that was cut down in the seventeenth century, are still something to stop and look at. Their potency has been sufficient to attract the vandals (to dignify them with the status of iconoclasts is hardly justified) who cut down the thorn tree on Wearyall Hill, just south of the town, in 2010.

Glastonbury has been studied by archaeologists and historians ever since those disciplines were formulated, and all of them have had to accommodate the rich mythology of the place, some of whom have been able to achieve it more comfortably than others. Even before that, the history of Glastonbury was a subject that preoccupied the monks of Glastonbury, for reasons different from the academic agenda of today, although many people would argue that the commercial agenda has remained unchanged. The lure of Glastonbury is irresistible, a mixture of fact and fable in a place where the past has never been a matter of local history. Christopher Hollis wrote in 1927 that 'a version of English history that does not mention Glastonbury is nonsense', like writing a history of the Flood without mentioning Noah.[3] Its place in the English imagination was also acknowledged in the opening ceremony of the London Olympic Games in 2012, when a model of the Tor was used to display the flags of all the competing nations. As we will see, even in the middle ages the history of England could not be written without Glastonbury.

The status of Glastonbury rests upon two contentious claims, otherwise known as legends. First, that Joseph of Arimathea, after he had buried the crucified Christ, travelled to England and founded in Glastonbury the first church of Christendom. Second, that King Arthur was buried at Glastonbury, which identifies the town as the mythical Isle of Avalon. We will find out later that these legends are intimately connected. They should certainly not be underestimated. Legends have determined much of what Glastonbury is today, as the unofficial capital of New Age Britain. They explain why the Church of England purchased the ruins of a Roman Catholic monastery that was so criminally destroyed by the head of its own church. If a visit to Glastonbury in the summer is a town full of pilgrims searching for spiritual enlightenment or a path to a better life, then it is a Glastonbury tradition that goes back centuries.

But for scholars who deal in hard evidence Glastonbury's legends have always been problematical. One of the reasons why the legends have flourished is that it is particularly difficult to find sources of evidence that are not legends. For example, archaeological excavation would be an obvious place to look for the early Christian settlements at Glastonbury. There have in fact been excavations at the abbey but they have not yielded evidence of the early-Christian period, and for good reasons. The oldest of the known structures at Glastonbury was destroyed in the serious fire of 1184. It was replaced by the Lady Chapel of the Norman abbey church which enclosed the entire extent of the earlier church. Some archaeological evidence for this early church would have survived if, in the early sixteenth century, the floor was not dug away to create a crypt below the chapel. So the most crucial of potential archaeological evidence has been destroyed. Compare this with its illustrious neighbour only five miles away at Wells, where excavations have revealed a remarkable sequence of sacred structures, beginning with a late Roman mausoleum, through to the Anglo-Saxon minster church and then cathedral, all of which was preserved archaeologically because a new cathedral church begun in the mid twelfth century was constructed on a slightly different site to the earlier churches there. Glastonbury's past, in this respect, has been particularly unlucky.

Historians and archaeologists have paid a price when they have divided their material into fact and fiction, often undermining their own claims for Glastonbury's importance when they champion one but disdain the other. Most of the blame for Glastonbury's legends has been directed at Glastonbury Abbey. For example, the nineteenth-century antiquary John Skinner dismissed the monks of Glastonbury as 'great proficients in milking the foolish and the rich', and yet he saw excavations of their church a project of great importance. If Glastonbury Abbey really was a conspiracy of cynical fraudsters then it makes a study of them seem rather pointless. On the contrary, to be interested in Glastonbury but disinterested in its myths is to miss the point. No one can understand Glastonbury past and present without reference to Arthur and Joseph of Arimathea.

In a recent survey of Glastonbury mythology Philip Rahtz and Lorna Watts go further than to state that the Glastonbury myths are not true, but are worth only a curt dismissal: they are 'wholly the product of medieval and later invention, for pecuniary, political or prestige motives; their continued exposition as fact degrades real scholarship and historical truth'.[4] The view expresses some of the irritation of academics when trying to piece together what actually happened at Glastonbury so many centuries ago. It is also at one of the polar extremes in the treatment of medieval and later literature about Glastonbury. This contends that the monks simply fabricated their evidence in a shameless desire to promote their institution, enhance its prestige, and live off the profits generated by gullible pilgrims. At the other extreme, and we will meet this in the twentieth century with the Reverend Lewis who was vicar of the town's churches, is the view that anything written in an ancient text has an unassailable authenticity. This point of view embraces the notion of ancient wisdom and that all sages of the past operated untainted by society, unlike modern academics who have competitive and overbearing egos, or who lack the moral courage to err from fashionable theories.

This book takes issue with both of these approaches. To pick one example amongst many, in the work of historian Geoff Doel, who is normally perfectly equitable in his treatment of sources, the tone is markedly judgmental when sources emanate from the monks of Glastonbury. The discovery of Arthur's grave in 1191 'appears to have been one of the great medieval forgeries at which the Abbey of Glastonbury was so adept' and with its success, 'the prosperity of the Abbey flourished, aided by other forged and faked celebrity connections'.[5] When historical sources are dismissed so gratuitously it is time to pause and reassess them. By dismissing these stories we also miss the opportunity to understand something of the culture that created them. The bones of Arthur will tell us much about how the past was remembered in the twelfth and subsequent centuries. Glastonbury Abbey is central to anyone's understanding of what Glastonbury was and is. After all, Glastonbury is not a town that acquired an abbey, but an abbey that acquired a town. Even if the conservative interpretations of the historians are correct, and the monastery at Glastonbury was not founded until the late seventh century, it gives the monastery a life of over 800 years, far far longer than the alternative institutions like the druids and the Glastonbury Goddess Temple and Chalice Well Trust put together.

Opinions about the Glastonbury monks come down ultimately to how we should read medieval literature. It is not fruitful to read these works in the same way that we read modern scholarship and its insistence on rigorous analysis of the evidence. Medieval historians always had their critics. Geoffrey of Monmouth, for example, was accused of being a notorious liar in his biased accounts of British history, but it would be mistake to think that the voices of medieval sceptics are the voices of our own generation. Like in any age, if there were biased writers in the middle ages, there were also biased readers. Geoffrey of Monmouth, who established Arthur in the mainstream of English culture in the twelfth century, was popular because he gave readers what they wanted or expected. The monks of Glastonbury, who developed the stories of Joseph and Arthur at Glastonbury, did exactly the same.

One of the principal aims of this book will be to rehabilitate the monks of Glastonbury. Accusations that they operated a crude propaganda for their own ends are exaggerated and unfair. When compared with work by other monastic and secular historians, the claims made for Glastonbury were not outrageous. Much of their concern was with land charters and establishing the right to ownership of land on which their subsistence as a community was based. Other monasteries were doing the same thing. Another of their obsessions was writing hagiographies, biographies of saints. Legends gave the impression that many monasteries were founded by saints and accounts of their lives inspired monks. They also remind us that monastic literature could be an internal conversation, and was not produced solely as a gift for posterity. This is well illustrated in the work of Thomas Burton, who in the later middle ages was commissioned to write the history of Meaux abbey in Yorkshire, and expressly intended to contrast the outstanding achievements of its previous abbots with the sloth and negligence of the monks in his own day. Hagiographers could use local legends, inscriptions on tombs and older written sources to illuminate a place by their pious presence. Such works could also be used to inspire the faithful. In a world where God was found in nature, and the actions of God explained things like the properties of holy wells, the association of the Holy Grail with Glastonbury was not as far-fetched as it seems in a secular society. Nor are the legends of Glastonbury unique to that institution. St Albans and Westminster Abbeys also claimed foundation by imaginary saints. Ultimately, all of the claims that hail Glastonbury as an important centre of pagan spirituality and Celtic Christianity rely on the beliefs of Anglo-Saxon monks, the very people that some of the mystical modern writers have seen as usurpers of the special place. It is one of the many ironies in Glastonbury's reputation.

This book is not about advancing a new theory of Glastonbury. It could plausibly be argued that we have enough of them already. It is a history of ideas, concerned about how the mysteries of Glastonbury have been explained over the centuries, and what has given it its special status as the holiest ground in Britain to Christians and pagans alike. Although it describes numerous theories and versions of the past, it is not my intention to then pick them apart. I am more interested in what made people think that Joseph of Arimathea founded a church at Glastonbury, that Christ himself came to Glastonbury as a child, that Glastonbury is the Arthurian Avalon, that it is the repository of miraculous trees, a gateway to the underworld and the storehouse of terrestrial power. This is quite a range of grand claims and yet they will be found to be interconnected in the minds of people who have visited or studied Glastonbury. And the emphasis here is on visitors, for Glastonbury's status has always been the creation of outsiders. The last local man to make an enduring impact on spiritual Glastonbury was St Dunstan in the tenth century.

Past explanations of the past can seem perverse, naïve, disingenuous and ignorant and they are easy to dismiss, but with a little contemporary context it is quite feasible to explain why people thought in the way they did. Our quest for the past is more than about what actually happened—the oversimplified idea of 'historical truth'. What people *thought* had happened and, yes, what people *wanted* to have happened, is just as relevant as what really did happen. That is especially true of Glastonbury.

Glastonbury has been especially prone to diverse interpretations, a trend that seems to have accelerated in recent decades as the data for the past has become more plentiful. It therefore challenges the expectation that the accumulation of evidence will lead to a consensus view of the past. Perhaps the reverse is the case. Nobody can incorporate all the evidence of the past. As evidence accumulates, historians and archaeologists have to select the data that they think is important and in doing so weight their arguments in different directions, with widely differing results. Instead of an ever narrowing consensus we live in an age of multiplying theories.

Glastonbury has an assured place in the national mythology because it provides us with one of our essential origin myths. We need to know where we have come from. Just as Roman civilisation was founded by refugees from Troy, in Geoffrey of Monmouth's twelfth-century history Britain was founded by the grandsons of those Trojan men. In Rome, emperors were descended from the Gods, but that was not possible in Christianity. The next best thing was descent from the saints and, if possible, the first generation of them, the apostles of Christ. Spain has its mythology of St James, Scotland the myth of St Andrew, but in England the equivalent myth is of Joseph of Arimathea at Glastonbury.

2

The Richest Monastery in England

According to the Domesday Survey of 1086, Glastonbury Abbey was the richest monastery in England. The terms 'monastery' and 'wealth' may seem on the face of it contradictory, and the perception of monks living a life of comfort and ease at the public's expense has earned them a good deal of opprobrium. But Domesday says as much about the Norman conquerors as it does about the abbey, that they were more interested in its financial than in its spiritual capital. In the historical record the role of abbey as landowner often seems to over-shadow its religious calling. Again, that does not necessarily reflect the priority of the abbey, but illustrates the importance of land and wealth in medieval society. The wealth of Glastonbury Abbey obviously contributed to its success, but it would also play a part in the manner of its downfall.

The monks who lived in closed communities were not economically productive and lived in a society where higher things than making money were respected and revered. They were able to support themselves only by the revenues they could accrue from land that they owned. Without land, the community of monks and lay brothers who worked at abbeys like Glastonbury could not have survived, and their churches could not have been built and maintained. Gifts of land by the elite were an act of piety, especially prevalent between the tenth and thirteenth centuries, but had an earlier pedigree too. Many of England's great monasteries were founded by kings, notably Westminster Abbey. Many kings and nobles gave land to Glastonbury, but it was not necessarily valuable. Monasteries set about improving their land, to the extent that a significant proportion of economic development in medieval England was achieved on monastic estates. Glastonbury Abbey was wealthy at the twilight of Anglo-Saxon England because it was a large and successful monastery of long standing.

Landscape is an important part of the Glastonbury story, especially the land to the west of the town that we now know as the Somerset Levels. This is a land-scape that has changed dramatically over the last three millennia. Even today the landscape of Glastonbury is striking, with the unmissable shape of its Tor rising purposefully on the skyline of the Levels. Fifteen hundred years ago it was a marginal place, making Glastonbury in many respects a classic place for the establishment of a religious community.

Once, this land was a plain over which many rivers, like the Brue, Yeo and Parrett, flowed into the River Severn. After the end of the last Ice Age the sea level slowly rose, so that the lower valley of the River Severn was eventually drowned by the sea to create what we now call the Bristol Channel. The rise in sea level impeded the flow of rivers over the plain and, eventually, salt water began to wash over it with the tides. The Levels became a place of freshwater and saltwater marshes. The area seems to have been well-populated in prehistory, as there is much evidence of people moving over the landscape. The remarkably preserved prehistoric wooden trackways across the Somerset Levels are the first sign that the sea was beginning to affect drainage of this former plain. The oldest of them, named the Sweet Track after its discovery in 1970 by a peat-digger named Ray Sweet, is dated at approximately 3,800 BC. Near Glastonbury and Meare small settlements were discovered in the late nineteenth century that had been established at the edge of what were probably fresh water lakes. These are known as the 'Lake Villages', although they have now been re-interpreted as small temporary settlements or meeting places, inhabited intermittently from about 200 BC until their abandonment in about 50 BC when the rising sea level made them too vulnerable to flooding. By the time of the Roman colonisation, the sea had risen to its modern level.

The Levels are low lying, much of it only 10 metres above sea level. Glastonbury is on slightly higher ground, a peninsula that juts out into the Somerset Levels, dominated by two hills, Wearyall and the Tor. In the middle ages, Glastonbury enjoyed something of an island character as it could be reached by water at high tide. Hills like Burrow Mump and Glastonbury Tor must have been useful as navigational aids. The small island of Athelney was the refuge to which King Alfred retreated from the Danes in 878. And from here he sailed off to launch his successful counter attack against them. And if today Glastonbury seems a long way from the sea it is not. In the tsunami-like flood that devastated the Somerset coastline in 1607 the flood water rose as far as St Benedict's church in the town.

Medieval churches are a prominent feature of the landscape because they occupy the slightly higher ground, which once were islands known as *soys*—hence Chedzoy, Middlezoy, Weston Zoyland. On Athelney King Alfred founded a monastery in gratitude for English deliverance from the marauding Danes. The most striking church site is just east of Athelney, on the conical hill known as Burrow Mump. Like Glastonbury Tor, the presence of a ruined church has transformed a natural hill into a place of mystery and imagination. From the top of

Burrow Mump the pattern of the landscape is perfectly illustrated. The Somerset Levels have retained their own special character, a place defined by the grids of drains (or rhynes) and canalised rivers, often outlined by pollarded willows. In its present form it is a landscape created mainly over the last four centuries in an effort to control the mingling of river water flowing from the south and the salty sea water advancing from the north. The project began in the middle ages. Beside the road that leads straight from Burrow Mump is a high bank that acted as the medieval sea wall in the time of Glastonbury Abbey. The draining of the Somerset Levels to produce the farmland that we are now familiar with was begun by neighbouring landowners—abbeys such as Glastonbury, Athelney and Muchelney, and the bishops of Bath and Wells. When land was first granted to them, swathes of these ecclesiastical estates were swampy wasteland. By the seventeenth century much had been achieved. According to Sir William Brereton, who passed through Glastonbury in 1635, the town was:–

> seated upon the lower part of a hill, which is rich in corn land; and on the other hand are very large, capacious, fruitful marshes, and very spacious, dainty, fruitful meadows as I ever saw, wherein, near the ditches, willows are planted in good order, which prosper excellently, and yield a very pleasing prospect.[1]

No archaeological evidence has been found to suggest that Glastonbury was a special place during the four centuries of Roman administration. But it was the Romans who introduced Christianity to Britain and throughout the Empire. Constantine was the first Christian Emperor and issued a proclamation in AD 313 to the effect that persecution of Christians in the Empire should henceforth cease. There were certainly Christians in Somerset and the remainder of Roman Britain in the fourth century, although the evidence is not always of churches, but includes personal items like the engraved tablets found in the baths at Bath and the cross on a pendant found in a settlement near Shepton Mallet. The possibility that Christianity was practised continuously from the time of Roman rule has never found much favour, although that may be because the early history of Christianity has been written from the perspective of south-east England. The prevailing view has always been that Christianity died out and was reintroduced in Anglo-Saxon times.

What we know for certain about the origins of Christianity in Glastonbury is as unsatisfactory to modern historians as it was to the medieval monks. The possibility that Christianity has been practised continuously from Roman times is not outlandish, since there is some indication of continuity at other important religious centres in the west of England, such as Gloucester and Worcester. Near Glastonbury is Leigh, known from the seventh century as Lantocai, which seems to be an anglicised version of *Llan*, the Welsh prefix that denotes a religious enclosure or community. So Lantocai could mean the church of St Cai, evidence of a British Christianity earlier than the Anglo-Saxon church.

Excavations on Glastonbury Tor in the 1960s uncovered remains of timber buildings that were constructed on the Tor in the sixth century. These could have been part of a defensive stronghold, but the preferred interpretation of Philip Rahtz, the archaeologist who excavated the site, is that it was a British monastery.[2] Later, in Anglo-Saxon times, a small but separate monastery was also constructed on the Tor, which remained in use as the abbey in the town flourished, perhaps as a hermitage or retreat for the monks. On the summit was an Anglo-Saxon cross that, although it was only five feet tall, would have been visible from some distance. The ruined church tower on the Tor is much later, all that remains of the church built during the abbacy of Adam of Sodbury (1323–34). If we can prove continuity from Celtic to Anglo-Saxon Christianity on the Tor, why should it not have happened on the site of the abbey itself?

According to the *Anglo-Saxon Chronicles*, Glastonbury Abbey was founded by King Ine of Wessex, who reigned from 688 to 726. Ine established full Anglo-Saxon control of the area, adopted Christianity as its religion and founded other important churches, notably the minster at Wells that was later elevated to cathedral status. However, evidence of charters suggests that a monastery was in existence a few years earlier, in the reign of Centwine who gave land to the abbey in 678.[3] Some evidence of the early Anglo-Saxon church at Glastonbury was found in excavations in the 1920s. It began as a church with a simple nave and presbytery, but was later expanded by the addition of side chapels, known as porticus (single and plural), and a tower at the eastern end over one of these porticus. This was the Anglo-Saxon monastery that was replaced by a new church in the twelfth century, which was in turn replaced by the much larger abbey church of the thirteenth century, the foundations of which remain visible today.

The most important figure to be associated with Anglo-Saxon Glastonbury Abbey was Dunstan (909–988). He was born at Baltonsborough in Somerset, entered the monastery at Glastonbury at a young age, and while in his twenties was appointed to the court of Athelstan, first king of all England, and then was chaplain to his successor, King Edmund. In approximately 940 he was appointed abbot of Glastonbury and in 958 was appointed Archbishop of Canterbury. During his time at Glastonbury he is credited with having revived the abbey, suggesting that it was in a moribund state at this time, and reorganised its life to follow the strict rules of St Benedict, which brought it into line with the international church. The monastery evidently enjoyed royal favour since two of the kings that Dunstan served, Edmund I (939–46) and Edgar (959–75), were buried there. As archbishop he was instrumental in the revival of other English monasteries that had declined or perished in the time of the Danish invasions. His cult emerged soon after his death and he became one of the more revered of Anglo-Saxon saints. But it was with Canterbury that he was most closely associated, and where his body was buried, much to the chagrin of the Glastonbury monks who would have liked such a venerable saint to be a figurehead of their own institution. As we will see, they made up for this loss in other ways.

Almost as soon as they were established, Anglo-Saxon monasteries became interested in their origins. In the developing practice of hagiography the works of the saints were identified with specific places, which gave those places an enhanced sanctity. Glastonbury Abbey was no different from any other monastery in this respect. In fact one of the first historians of England, the Venerable Bede, actively promoted the early foundation in 674 and the special sanctity of his own monastery at Monkwearmouth, and of its founder, Benedict Biscop. In periods when monastic communities were re-forming themselves in the tenth century stories such as these boosted the morale of the community. Communities also revered their founders because they had established the faith in places where it did not previously exist, and their achievements were a role model for later generations. Concern for the origins of Glastonbury Abbey is apparent in the first life of St Dunstan, written *c.* 1000, the author of which is known only by his initial 'B'.

That Glastonbury had a prominent place in the birth of Christianity in Britain has been accepted almost since the origin of Christianity has interested scholars and churchmen. That is to say, almost since the church was founded in Britain. But not quite. One of the first historians to write about the arrival of Christianity in Britain was Gildas, the monk who was later said to have ended his days at Glastonbury Abbey and died *c.* 570. His work, *The Ruin of Britain*, however, says nothing of Glastonbury. He claimed that Christianity arrived in Britain 'in the last years of the emperor Tiberius [ruled AD 14–37], at a time when Christ's religion was propagated without hindrance'. This was before the Roman invasion of Britain in AD 43. Christians apparently worshipped freely until their persecution began under the Emperor Diocletian (284–305). During this time Britain had its first martyrs, the soldier Alban at Verulamium, and Aaron and Julius at Caerleon. After the persecution was over the Christians 'rebuilt churches that had been razed to the ground; they founded, built and completed chapels to the holy martyrs, displaying them everywhere like victorious banners'.[4] Could one of these early churches have been built at Glastonbury?

Gildas was writing when the pagan Anglo-Saxons were establishing their supremacy over Britain. He described the retreat of the Britons back into the Celtic territories. The English therefore had to be converted to Christianity, the story of which is told in the *Ecclesiastical History of the English People* by the

Venerable Bede, completed *c.* 731. In 597 Pope Gregory I sent an official mission under Augustine to convert the English, which was successful largely because it was able to convert the Anglo-Saxon kings of Wessex, Essex and Northumbria. That date would become a pivotal one in arguments for and against the English and their Christianity. But that date was meaningless when it was applied to Glastonbury in the west of England, because that part of England did not come under Saxon rule until the following century. So Glastonbury did not fit into the official narrative of the conversion of the English, and if it was Christian in the sixth century it was British or Celtic Christianity.

Bede acknowledged that there was Christianity before Augustine because he also rewrote the story of how Christianity first came to Britain, based on a source unknown to Gildas. According to Bede, the faith reached Britain in AD 166, when King Lucius of the Britons implored Pope Eleutherius to send missionaries to Britain. Bede described them as the first 'neophites of the catholic law', a story repeated in the *Anglo-Saxon Chronicles*. There was, of course, no King Lucius of the Britons, since Britain was part of the Roman Empire at that time, but the mistake was not of Bede's making. Bede's source was the *Liber Pontificalis* (The Book of Popes), in which a scribe copying the work *c.* 530 added to the entry for Eleutherius that he received a letter from the British king Lucius. Lucius was in fact King Lucius Aelius Septimus Megas Abgarus VIII, the first Christian king of Edessa (modern Urfa in southern Turkey). The Latin name for his citadel was Britium, which seems to have been the root of the confusion.[5] It was a minor error, perhaps, but would come to have far-reaching consequences.

As far as Bede knew, he had it on literary authority that there had been a British Lucius. Bede did not mention any specific places, but a link between the neophytes of the Catholic law and Glastonbury appeared in the life of Dunstan written by 'B'. He was the first to claim that Dunstan was far from being the founder of the abbey at Glastonbury. Using a source that is no longer known, he concluded that the disciples sent to Britain had found a church at Glastonbury that, in an intriguing phrase, had been 'built by no human skill'. Later this church was claimed as not only the oldest church in Britain but the oldest church in Christendom. This should not be dismissed as fabrication or fantasy. There was a building at Anglo-Saxon Glastonbury Abbey that the monks thought was older than the Anglo-Saxon church and which could have been this first church. We will return to it in due course.

One of the reasons Glastonbury was thought to have a Celtic origin was its association with numerous Celtic saints. The abbey's history was embodied in its shrines and graves in the abbey burial ground, a fair proportion of which were Celtic. By the tenth century it already celebrated the cults of Patrick and Indracht. Both of them were buried in the abbey church. That the Irish venerated

Glastonbury because Patrick was buried there is first mentioned in the 'B' Life of Dunstan, and perhaps he was referring to the legend of St Indracht mentioned below. Patrick had been converted in Ireland but travelled to Britain where he found anchorites living at Glastonbury, who elected him as their superior. The claims for St Patrick were not universally accepted in the middle ages, however. It was said that the apostle of the Irish had become confused with an unrelated namesake who had been abbot. A Life of St Indracht was prepared at Glastonbury in the tenth century, but he was a comparatively recent martyr. In the version propagated by the monks of Glastonbury this son of an Irish king had travelled from Ireland to Rome with a group of friends and, on his return, decided to visit the shrine of St Patrick at Glastonbury. When his party rested for the night nearby, traditionally at Shapwick, they were murdered in the mistaken belief that they were carrying gold. Miraculous signs followed the murder, to which King Ine responded by ordering the remains to be buried in the abbey cemetery. In an alternative version, Indracht was an abbot murdered in England on his way to Rome in 854, an event recorded in the Irish Annals. Other Celtic saints would be added to the Glastonbury roster later, notably Gildas and St Benignus. Benignus was the fifth-century disciple and successor of Patrick who was also said to have been abbot of Glastonbury. But Benignus is the Latinised form of a name that could refer to Benen the famous Irish saint, or to an Anglo-Saxon man, Beonna. So the remains that were transferred to the abbey in 1091 from a shrine at Meare, which stood among the saltwater marshes near Glastonbury, may have been the bones of the local Anglo-Saxon holy man and not the Irish saint.[6]

The other source of early history for the monks was the memorials in the graveyard. Chief among these were two 'pyramids' or tapering obelisks, similar to the memorials used to mark the graves of Indracht and Patrick inside the church. By the twelfth century they were badly weathered but William of Malmesbury made an attempt at deciphering them. One was 26 feet high, the other 18 feet high. Several names were legible or semi-legible, and appear to refer to individuals from the late seventh century onwards. They included Bishop Hedde or Haeddi (bishop of Winchester *c.* 676–705) and Bregored, who was also apparently a British bishop and an abbot of Glastonbury. Other names are Anglo-Saxon, such as Winethegn, Wulfred, Eanfled and Beorhtwald, who was abbot in the early eighth century.

Not unreasonably, the Anglo-Saxon monks would have talked of a Celtic past, but Glastonbury Abbey did not make any grand claims for its origins until it needed to. History began to matter to the church and its individual foundations after the Norman Conquest, when English society needed to heal its wounded pride. In the tradition of Anglo-Saxon historiography it had been God's will that the Anglo-Saxons triumphed over the Britons. It followed, therefore, that their defeat at the hands of the Duke of Normandy was punishment for their spiritual failings. This was also the reasoning adopted at the court of William I and it therefore made it imperative that the conquered rescue their heritage from the condemnation of posterity.

Native churchmen had plenty of reason to feel aggrieved. Anglo-Saxon bishops and abbots were in due course replaced, mainly by men from Normandy, which meant that ambitious Anglo-Saxon monks were suddenly career-blocked. Monasteries owned land and the Norman barons often had their eye on it. A monk from Worcester, known as Hemming, complained that the Normans 'by force, guile and rapine have unjustly deprived this church of its lands, villages and possessions, until hardly anything is safe from their depradations'.[7] At Glastonbury the monastery compiled a *Liber Terrarum*, or 'Landbook', listing the charters of land granted to Glastonbury Abbey from the time of Centwine (*c.* 670) to the time of Aethelred (978–1016). The book has been lost but it was at Glastonbury in the 1120s when the first comprehensive history of the monastery was written. It was probably compiled as evidence that these landholdings were genuine and of ancient derivation. The most important of its landholdings were the Twelve Hides, mentioned in the Domesday Book as never paying tax. Henry I issued a charter in 1121 confirming these privileges. The Twelve Hides probably derive from six hides given by Centwine in 678 and six by Baldred in 681.[8] A hide was a unit of land sufficient for an individual to subsist on, so twelve hides suggested twelve monks.

The Normans, including Archbishop Lanfranc of Canterbury, were openly sceptical of Anglo-Saxon saints, whose sanctity was founded entirely upon local traditions. For example, the first Norman abbots of Malmesbury in Wiltshire alienated the Saxon monks, were sceptical of their saints and relics, and threatened the peaceful privileges enjoyed by the monastic community in pre-conquest times. One of them, Warin, threw out the remains of revered saints, the kind of disdainful treatment that the Anglo-Saxons would not forget.

Glastonbury also suffered in this respect, in especially dramatic fashion. Abbot Thurstan, from Caen, was appointed abbot of Glastonbury in 1082. According to William of Malmesbury, writing fifty years later, Thurstan:–

> removed many ancient and favoured customs from the convent, [and] changed certain practices according to the custom of his own country. ... Among other things he even rejected the Gregorian chant and began to force the monks to abandon it and learn to sing the chant of a certain William of Fécamp.[9]

Simmering tensions eventually boiled over. The monks refused to bend to his will and Thurstan lost his patience, ordering his armed guards into the church.

Neither reverence for that place nor for its saints could hinder them until they had transfixed one monk with a lance as he was embracing the holy altar, killed another at the base of the altar by piercing him with arrows, and seriously wounded fourteen others.[10]

Three dead and eighteen wounded were the casualties recorded in the *Anglo-Saxon Chronicles*. The monks complained to William I and achieved a partial victory when the king relieved Thurstan of his duties, but he was reinstated on the accession of William II in 1087.

A Norman abbot much more sympathetic to Glastonbury's ancient traditions and privileges was Henry of Blois, who was elected in 1126. He remained abbot until his death in 1171, although it was not his only job. In 1129 Henry was elected to the see of Winchester, and performed the dual roles of bishop and abbot. He was the son of Adela, sister of Henry I, which made him grandson of William the Conqueror. He was also brother of the next king of England, Stephen of Blois (1135–54), and through his influence he obtained a commission as papal legate, which ranked him above the Archbishop of Canterbury.

Abbot Henry decided that the reputation and prestige of Glastonbury was in need of restoration. He claimed that the abbey had suffered during the eleventh century (so much for being England's richest monastery). Thurstan's troubled abbacy has been described above, but accusations that the abbey and its estates had been poorly managed even before the Norman Conquest were also levelled. By the time of Henry of Blois, the reputation of abbots Aethelweard (1027–1053) and Aethelnoth (1053–1078) had declined. The conquerors had also apparently deprived the abbey of many of its possessions and in its weakened state it attracted the interest of the Bishop of Bath, who sought to transfer some of the abbey's privileges to himself, beginning a fractious relationship with the diocese that ended only when the abbey was dissolved at the Reformation.

Skilled historians provided the most eloquent defence of the English church against its Norman critics. Glastonbury's past needed to be set down on paper and it was done in two ways—a history of the monastery itself, and the history of various individuals associated with it. William of Malmesbury (*c.* 1095–1143) was commissioned in 1129 to write a history of Glastonbury Abbey and Lives of Saints Dunstan, Patrick, Indracht and Benignus. A contemporary monk, Caradog of Llancarfan in South Wales, was later commissioned to write a Life of St Gildas.

Since William of Malmesbury was writing at a time when the Anglo-Saxon monastic communities felt besieged and disrespected, he was naturally tempted to write church history as a continuum, and not one disrupted and corrected by the conquest. For William it was a familiar agenda. One of his previous subjects had been St Wulfstan, the Anglo-Saxon bishop of Worcester who was the last

Saxon incumbent of an English cathedral. William had already completed the first editions of his major works, *Gesta Regum Anglorum* and *Gesta Pontificum Anglorum*, which were intended to bring up to date English history since Bede. The *Gesta Regum Anglorum* was commissioned by Queen Matilda and covered the secular history, while the *Gesta Pontificum Anglorum* was a companion ecclesiastical history. Both stressed the continuity from Anglo-Saxon times into the Norman era. Other communities were also engaged in establishing the credibility of native saints. Ailred of Rievaulx was commissioned to write Lives of the saints of Hexham Abbey and of Edward the Confessor by Westminster Abbey, with evident success since Edward the Confessor remained England's national saint until the fourteenth century. Osbert of Clare wrote a Life of St Edmund for the abbey at Bury St Edmunds. Caradog of Llancarfan wrote a life of St Cyngar for Wells Cathedral.

William's history of Glastonbury does not survive, but parts of it appear in later versions of the *Gesta Regum*, and the work was later incorporated, with embellishments, into a longer history of the abbey written *c.* 1247 and later extended up to 1342. William's account of the early history of Glastonbury Abbey has been credited as being closest to the ideals and methods of modern scholarship. It seems restrained and cautious compared to authors of the later middle ages. This is only a partial appreciation, however. William's interest in history was not academic. He was a deeply religious man who recognised that, although the Bible furnished the precepts and examples of right living, men are nevertheless 'incited more by hearing examples than exhortations'. His work was a gift intended to inspire the brethren of Glastonbury. All saints are revered, but there is something especially inspiring about local saints: men are:–

> seized by a keener joy if the life of any saint who was their countrymen is set forth … for the affinity adds to the pleasure of the report and no-one despairs of being able to do himself, through the grace of God, what he hears has been done by another from his part of the world.[11]

William's more mundane purpose is made clear in the prefatory address to Henry of Blois. He wanted to 'rescue from suspicion the antiquity of your church'. In describing the virtues of his patron, William revealed other contemporary talking points of a more worldly nature: Henry excelled in patrimony—'you both recover holdings earlier lost and by your able skills amass new ones'. He protected the peace of the monastery—'you expose the chicanery of litigants by the good sense of your words'. And the community flourished under him—'you do not terrify [the monks] with a sneer but receive them joyfully when they come, treat them kindly and, like a father, wish them well when they leave'.[12]

William deals with the principal Glastonbury cults. Indirectly he showed that other Celtic and Northumbrian saints—Gildas, Benedict Biscop, Aidin, Ceolfrid, Bridget, David—as well as Patrick were associated with Glastonbury, which he probably gleaned from existing shrines and the liturgical calendar used by the monks. It all reminded themselves and the Norman barons that the church in England was already a venerable institution in 1066. He also describes how the relics of Northumbrian saints like Benedict Biscop and Aidan were deposited at Glastonbury in the time of the Danish invasions. The latter part of the book deals with the record of individual abbots and kings, lists many donations of land to the abbey and gives details of miracles that had occurred there. King Edgar was especially favoured because of the generous privileges he bestowed upon the abbey, and because it was Edgar who recalled Dunstan from exile and made him Archbishop of Canterbury. One of the privileges was that no man should become abbot unless he was already a Glastonbury monk, and in the event that there was no suitable candidate an abbot could only be consecrated with the blessing of the brothers. As the church 'long ago attained the highest dignity in my kingdom, [it] should be honoured by us with a special and singular liberty and privilege', to wit that it should be free of all taxes. More contentious was that 'neither the Bishop of Wells nor his servants shall have any power at all over this monastery'.[13] The monks would often cite these privileges in their dealings with bishops and kings, but they were not always able to put them into practice.

The most interesting part of William's history comes nearer the beginning. The hagiographer 'B' had noted that when the pope's missionaries had travelled to Britain at the request of Lucius they had found at Glastonbury an earlier church. William suggested then that the church was probably built by disciples of Christ himself. The notion was not as far fetched as it sounds, because it was said in the *Chronicle* of Freculf, written in Gaul *c.* 830 by the bishop of Lisieux, that St Philip had preached to the Gauls and could easily have sent a missionary party across the English Channel.

This was the church that William called the *vetusta ecclesia* or the *Ealde Cyrce*, the old church. It was apparently recognised and revered beyond Glastonbury. William described a conversation that took place in his own time between a Glastonbury monk named Godfrey and a monk of St Denis near Paris. The French monk had asked whether the *vetusta ecclesia* was still standing and, when he was told that it was, replied that:–

> this church here of the most glorious martyr Denis and that which you claim
> is yours share the same honour and privilege the one in France, the other in
> Britain; they both arose at the same time and each was consecrated by the

highest and greatest priest. Yet in one degree yours is superior, for it is called a second Rome.[14]

The most incredible thing about this second Rome, the church built by no human skill, discovered by the missionaries of Eleutherius in 166, was that a building existed at Glastonbury that seemed to fit the bill. William of Malmesbury saw, described and was in awe of the *vetusta ecclesia* at Glastonbury. A seal attached to a charter of the 1170s seems to depict it. This is the most convincing evidence that there was a church at Glastonbury before the time of King Ine, but it is not quite proof. If there was a continuous Christian presence at Glastonbury then it is reasonable to assume that the old building was indeed the first church. If the original foundation lapsed, it is possible that when it was revived the old building was merely assumed to have been the original church. Alas, archaeology can tell us nothing about this building because all physical traces of it were removed in the sixteenth century. The *vetusta ecclesia* certainly existed and is the one reason why no one can say definitively that there was not a monastery at Glastonbury before the Saxon colonisation. The origin and original purpose of the *vetusta ecclesia* are forever up for discussion.

The *vetusta ecclesia* was a wooden building that stood to the west of the abbey church. Its exact position is well known and so is the fact that it, the abbey church, the later chapel of St Dunstan and the parish church of St Benedict all stand on a common east-west axis. Patrick and Indracht were buried either side of its altar and, although William did not know it at the time, no less a person than Gildas was said to have been buried in front of its altar, at least according to the Life of St Gildas that Caradog of Llancarfan wrote for the abbey, slightly after William's time. The very existence of the building and the traditions associated with it were compelling enough for William to assume it was the church built by the disciples of Christ. The monks clearly thought so too.

William could not resist a rhetorical flourish when describing it, indicating the degree to which it was revered in the twelfth century. The church had been built of brushwood, 'yet from the very beginning it possessed a mysterious fragrance of divine sanctity, so that, despite its mean appearance, great reverence for it wafted throughout the whole country'.[15] The church was visited by Paulinus, the first bishop of York, who was a member of the mission headed by Augustine that had been sent by Pope Gregory to convert the pagan Saxons. Paulinus, acknowledging that Christianity here had a more ancient pedigree than his own momentous arrival, strengthened the original wattle church 'with a layer of boards and had it covered from the top down with lead'.[16] It was never a work of architecture, but in the time of William the interior had been laid with 'floor stones, artfully interlaced in the forms of triangles or squares and sealed with lead; I do no harm to religion if I believe some sacred mystery is contained beneath them'.[17]

The abbey cemetery was on the south side of *vetusta ecclesia*, not the Anglo-Saxon abbey church, which is yet another hint that it was an earlier church. And it was in this church that the abbey's treasures were stored:–

> In it are preserved the bodily remains of many saints ... and there is no part of the church that is without the ashes of the blessed. The stone-paved floor, the sides of the altar, the very altar itself, above and within, are filled with relics close-packed. Deservedly indeed is the repository of so many saints said to be a heavenly shrine on earth.[18]

It attracted its own superstitious aura. No building was built so close as to cast a shadow on the old church, or it was sure to decay.

> No one has brought a hunting bird within the neighbouring cemetery or led a horse thither and left again without himself or his possessions being harmed. Within living memory everyone undergoing ordeal by iron or water who has offered a prayer there has, with one exception, rejoiced in his salvation'.[19]

The repository of so many saints invested the building with its own divine powers; it had inspired heathens to take up the faith just like a miracle-working saint. The *vetusta ecclesia* was Glastonbury Abbey's most prized asset, and proof that ancient tradition was a powerful influence even in Anglo-Saxon Glastonbury, well before it attracted the names that helped to make it famous in history.

Among the relics of other saints in the old church were those of the third-century pope, St Urban. It was on his feast day, 25 May 1184, that a disaster all too common in medieval life struck. There was a fire at the abbey, and the old church, with all its sacred treasures and a good deal of the abbey's prestige, was burned to the ground. Not for the last time one of the physical manifestations of Glastonbury's holiness was destroyed, only for it to rise up again and be more alive in memory than it had ever been when it was a mere building.

3

Avalon

In his study of Glastonbury Abbey William of Malmesbury never mentioned the name Avalon, but since the end of the twelfth century it has been inextricably linked with the place. Two names is in its nature—Glastonbury its secular name, Avalon its mythological name—perhaps contrasting the real with the imagined. But at the end of the twelfth century the issue that concerned the monks was the chronology of its English and Welsh names—Glastonbury and Ynyswitryn. By the thirteenth century the monks had finally settled on an official version to explain it.

The monks assumed that the Welsh name came first. According to the thirteenth-century tweaking of William's history, the first disciples established their church in 'a place surrounded by woods, bramble bushes and marshes' known as Ynyswitryn. It was said to have derived its Anglo-Saxon name from another source, a man named Glasteing, one of twelve brothers from northern Britain. Glasteing was 'following his sow through the kingdom of the inland Angles' and found her 'suckling her piglets under an apple tree' beside the church at Glastonbury, where he settled with his family and lived out his days.[1]

The monastic historians seem to have got it the wrong way round. In reality it acquired its English name first and Welsh name later. The place may well have been named after an individual, to which was added the common suffix 'bury' meaning a monastery (or stronghold)—hence 'Glaston's monastery'. Glastonbury, in Latin *Glastonie*, was the name known to Anglo-Saxon monks, and remained so beyond the time of William of Malmesbury. Ynyswitryn was first used by Gerald of Wales in the late twelfth century and is usually translated as the Glass Island, which was presumably suggested by the reflective nature of its watery location. It was later on that monks decided that its Welsh name must have come first, but it seems more probable that Ynyswitryn is just a rendering in Welsh of Glastonbury. Whatever its origin, Ynyswitryn was not commonly used in medieval Welsh literature. Most Welsh authors who referred to Glastonbury used its English name.[2]

The name Avalon appears for the first time at Glastonbury in 1191. Welsh authors adopted this name too, accepting all the Arthurian baggage that went with it, but rendered it Ynys Afallach in Welsh. Once the name Avalon was accepted, a retrospective explanation was needed to explain its origin. One version was that Glasteing named it *Avallonie*, meaning Apple Island, because he found his pig under an apple tree in such a fortuitous location. An alternative was that it could have been named after an early hermit by the name of Avalloc.

With Avalon comes King Arthur. William of Malmesbury makes no mention of King Arthur, but contemporary with his work at Glastonbury was the completion of one of the most influential stories of ancient Britain, the *History of the Kings of Britain* by Geoffrey of Monmouth. Geoffrey had created a mythic origin of the British monarchy, descending ultimately from Aeneas of Troy, founder of Rome, culminating in the emergence of Arthur at the time of the Saxon invasions. It harked back to a golden age, not as it had been but what it should have been, when Britain was united by a single leader. English kings were attracted to the story and also came to like the idea of Britain united under a single leader.

Arthur had not hitherto been prominent in English history. He emerges first in Welsh literature, but not until the ninth-century *Historia Brittonum*, a work written in Gwynedd *c.* 830 that is often attributed to the Welsh monk Nennius. With regard to Arthur it writes of events three centuries past. Like all medieval histories, the work was in large part political, written for people on the losing side of the Anglo-Saxon settlement, when the prospect of Mercian colonisation of Wales was a real threat. It names the leader who was most successful in halting the Anglo-Saxon advances in Britain, who won the great battle at Badon that had been mentioned in the sixth century by Gildas. In doing so it created a national hero around whom the Welsh could unite, and offered a providential history that countered any idea that God had favoured the Anglo-Saxons. It told his audience, King Merfyn of Gwynedd and his followers, what they wanted or needed to hear. Arthur is mentioned again a century later in the *Annales Cambriae*, a work written in south-west Wales during the Viking Age and after England had been united under a single king. The *Annales* covers a paschal cycle of 532 years plus one, from 444 to 997. In the year 72 (i.e. AD 516), was 'the battle of Badon, in which Arthur carried the cross of our Lord Jesus Christ for three days and three nights on his shoulders and the Britons were victors'. It was inspired by a Bible passage in which Simon the Cyrenian carried the cross for Jesus.[3] The warrior hero depicted in the *Historia Brittonum* had now developed into a leader of a heroic Christianity under the protection of God. It is also the first work to mention his death at the battle of Camlann.

Arthur subsequently appears in other literature from Wales. In a poem in the Black Book of Carmarthen is the first mention of his knights Kay and Bedivere, but he soon became more than just a Welsh hero. And it was Welsh authors who made Arthur an international figure. Glastonbury is first brought into Arthurian literature by Caradog of Llancarfan who, subsequent to William's work at Glastonbury, was invited by the monks to write a *Life of St Gildas*. William of Malmesbury had mentioned that Gildas had once lived at Glastonbury. Now we learned that Gildas wrote his famous *Ruin of Britain* at the monastery, died there and was buried in front of the altar in the old church. According to Caradog, Arthur was king of all Britain and had a connection with Glastonbury. Guinevere was abducted by Melwas, king of Somerset, and held prisoner at Glastonbury, protected by the rivers and marshes that surrounded it. Battle was avoided only because Gildas brokered a peace between them. In *Culhwch and Olwen*, one of the earliest of the tales that makes up *The Mabinogion*, Arthur is seen fighting on the continent. This idea was taken further in the early twelfth century by Geoffrey of Monmouth, in which Arthur is lord of a broad swathe of Europe and its oceans from Iceland to Scandinavia to the Alps, and even challenges the power of Rome. Geoffrey of course was writing a political work, a story of power and self-esteem, of defiance in the face of outside intervention, including that of Rome. Geoffrey, probably a Welshman himself, is also enacting the first stage by which Arthur was taken off the Welsh. For all his appearances in Welsh literature, Arthur's elevation to a legendary of figure of international standing came when he was lionised in the work of Geoffrey of Monmouth, who was writing for an English audience.

The manuscript was completed *c.* 1138, at the beginning of the civil war that dogged Stephen's reign. Geoffrey is important not just because he was pivotal in spreading the legend of Arthur throughout England, but because he introduced the notion that the Norman conquerors of England should identify themselves with a British past. The isle of Avalon is mentioned twice by Geoffrey. It is the place where his peerless sword Caliburn (Excalibur) was forged. Later, following the Battle of Camlann in 542, Arthur was 'mortally wounded and was carried off to the Isle of Avalon, so that his wounds might be attended to'.[4] He handed the crown to his cousin Constantine, but there is no mention of Arthur's death and burial, suggesting the 'once and future king' myth that would later be challenged at Glastonbury. Geoffrey does not mention Glastonbury. In fact his geography is to us a mixture of the known and unknown, and was perhaps always a combination of the real and mythical. Many places in the south west of England are named, such as Gloucester, River Severn, Bath, Cornwall, Stonehenge, but other places are mysterious, such as Avalon and the scenes of various battles like Camlann. Monmouth is likely to have been Geoffrey's birthplace, which might help to explain his knowledge of places within the Severn basin, in which case failure to mention Glastonbury by name is a curious omission.

The cult of Arthur spread quickly among Anglo-Norman aristocrats. In the 1150s Geoffrey's work was rendered in French verse by Robert Wace. The first English translation of Geoffrey was by Layamon, made in the early thirteenth century after the discovery of Arthur's grave at Glastonbury. Both adapted rather than translated Geoffrey's work. And yet both faithfully report that Caliburn was forged in Avalon and that Arthur was taken there when mortally wounded, where he sleeps, awaiting his second coming. Because their sources were literary and not archaeological, neither mentions Glastonbury.

Everything changed at Glastonbury after the fire of 1184. The abbey had been able to boast of many saints who had an association with Glastonbury, but many of its sacred relics had been consumed by the fire and the loss of the *vetusta ecclesia* was irreversible. In straitened times the abbey needed to raise its profile and assert its ancient traditions. Over the next half century the abbey church was rebuilt and a suspiciously impressive haul of discoveries was made, such as the relics of St Dunstan, the charter of St Patrick and the grave of Arthur and Guinevere.

The most bizarre claim was to have discovered the relics of St Dunstan. When the contents of the old church were being salvaged the monks came across a box marked conveniently with an 'S' and a 'D', which was opened with witnesses present. The problem was that, as everybody knew, Dunstan's relics were at Canterbury Cathedral, but the monks developed a story to explain how they could have found their way to Glastonbury. In 1012 a Danish incursion had overwhelmed Kent, Archbishop Aelfheah was murdered and Canterbury Cathedral burned. The Glastonbury monks pleaded successfully with the king for Dunstan's relics to be transferred for safekeeping to the church where his gifts were first nourished. Canterbury Cathedral was deserted when the Glastonbury monks entered its church and they were able to complete their mission unchallenged. They knew, however, that when a new archbishop was enthroned and the church was restored they would want the relics back. So the Glastonbury monks hid Dunstan's relics and ensured that their whereabouts were entrusted only to a chosen few for the next 172 years. Needless to say, the story never gained much credibility beyond Glastonbury.

As a consequence of the fire, Glastonbury saw fit to enlarge on what it knew of the foundation of the abbey. Geoffrey of Monmouth had already identified Phagan and Deruvian as the two missionaries that Bede said had been sent to Britain by Pope Eleutherius, B's 'neophites of the catholic law'. He did not say that they went to Glastonbury, however. William of Malmesbury had suggested tentatively that these men went to Glastonbury at the behest of St Philip, but the monks were able to clarify this by reference to a new discovery, the Charter of St Patrick, written by the saint himself between his arrival at Glastonbury in

AD 433 and his death at the age of 111 in 472. A copy was apparently stored in a chest in the old church. It reinforced the apostle of Ireland's association with Glastonbury, by describing how he had come to Glastonbury and been its first abbot, and encouraged pilgrims to visit by offering them indulgences. It also stated that Saints James and Philip had sent twelve disciples into Britain who, as instructed by the Archangel Gabriel, had built the original church of Glastonbury. Britain was therefore converted at the same time as France and Spain and Glastonbury could claim to be one of the earliest churches of Christendom.

The reputation for the monks' mendacity rests heavily on the events of these years. But the claims regarding Saints Dunstan and Patrick have been over-shadowed, at least in the popular imagination, by the discovery in 1191 of the grave of Arthur and Guinevere. The argument runs that, despite its associations with several important saints, in every case there were other institutions that had rival claims, or were in possession of their relics. St Dunstan is a case in point—because he had been appointed Archbishop of Canterbury, Glastonbury Abbey no longer had a monopoly on his memory. Glastonbury lacked a patron saint. The martyrdom of Archbishop Thomas Becket in 1170, and the subse-quent creation of a shrine, had quickly made Canterbury Cathedral the most popular destination for pilgrims in England. The bones of king Arthur were the best Glastonbury could offer in response, an attempt to replicate the success of Becket's cult at Canterbury in the hope that it could attract funds for the rebuild-ing of the abbey church. In the wake of terrible disasters many monasteries made claims that stretched credulity, but evidence of the discovery of Arthur at Glastonbury is for many historians the acme of bogus history.

There were reasons to expect that the body of Arthur lay at Glastonbury, as well as good reasons for wanting him to be. In his *History of the Kings of Britain* Geoffrey of Monmouth had recounted that after being mortally wounded at the Battle of Camlann Arthur's body was taken to the Isle of Avalon. Geoffrey's account of the English kings had been popular and had enhanced the reputation of Arthur, especially west of Offa's Dyke. The mortal remains of Arthur would therefore be a prize worth having. According to Gerald of Wales, Henry II had been told by a Welsh bard that the body of Arthur lay between two pyramids (i.e. the two weathered obelisks that William of Malmesbury took pains to decipher) on the south side of the old church, the *vetusta ecclesia*. The king had apparently encouraged the abbot to search for the remains of Arthur so that he could be given a worthy burial and memorial. According to Adam of Domerham, writing in the thirteenth century, his successor Richard I had also urged that a more fitting memorial for Arthur should be made. Henry II's motive had been under-standable: he could bolster the power of the Plantagenet dynasty if he could appropriate some of the glorious British past embodied in stories of Arthur, and some of the credit for his discovery could rub off on himself. After all, Henry was from Anjou and had spent little of his reign in England. Wales was a thorn in the side of Henry II and the Norman kings. These kings had established the Marcher lordships in eastern Wales, a buffer zone ruled by barons that protected England from attack by the Welsh, but it was an imperfect solution. Welsh rebellion continued to worry and irritate the king. Arthur was their hero, the once ruler of all the Britons that inspired Welsh belief that their cause of independence was right. If Arthur's remains could be found in England it would silence Welsh claims that their once and future king could rise up again and challenge the English ascendancy, and undermine their claim to ownership of his legend. An English monastery with a Celtic ancestry would fit the bill perfectly.

There are two near contemporary accounts of the discovery of Arthur's grave, written by Ralph of Coggeshall, writing *c.* 1194 in his *Chronicon Anglicanum*, and by Gerald of Wales in his *De principis instructione* (On the Education of a Monarch) written in the 1190s. Gerald returned to the subject in his later work *Speculum Ecclesiae*, but without adding any new information. Ralph said that the remains were found by chance when the grave was being dug for one of the monks, whereas Gerald claimed that the excavation was carried out specifically to locate Arthur's grave. The latter account was more popular in the middle ages, and was the official line taken by the Abbey. According to John of Glastonbury's *Chronicle*, written a century and a half after the event, the abbot was admonished by Henry II:–

> to bury King Arthur in a more fitting place and to transfer him from the depths of the earth to a worthier condition; for he had rested for 648 years next to the Old Church [i.e. the *vetusta ecclesia*], between two stone pyramids which had once been nobly carved out. And so one day the abbot surrounded the spot with curtains and ordered an excavation.[5]

This may have been true, and it is likely that the abbey had been looking for Arthur even before Henry II died in 1189.

What they found was impressive and seemingly incontrovertible. The remains were found deep in the ground (plausibly so, as the ground level had been raised in Dunstan's time) under a stone. The greater part of the tomb was taken up with the bones of Arthur, who was clearly giant in stature and bore battle wounds. The bone of the upper arm was found to be three inches above the knee of the tallest man present at the exhumation. The bones of Guinevere were also found in the tomb, which were identified by the perfectly preserved tress of blond hair. This, alas, disintegrated as soon as it was handled by an over-eager monk. The remains were transferred into individual chests, adorned with images and arms.

Ralph and Gerald agreed that the remains were identified by a small lead cross fixed to the underside of the grave slab. It was inscribed with the legend 'Here lies buried the famous King Arthur in the island of Avalon'. Analysis of the Latin words employed, and the style of lettering used, has led to a rare thing in Glastonbury studies, a virtual consensus. The cross was cast in the twelfth century but was made to look like an antique. Therefore it was not the actual grave marker, but what the grave marker should have been like. An alternative explanation, put forward by Ralegh Radford in the 1960s, was that the original grave marker was lost in Dunstan's time when the ground level was raised, and that the lead cross was made in the tenth century to replace it. The lead cross remained in the possession of the abbey, and an engraving of it was published by William Camden in the late sixteenth century. The real thing was probably much smaller than Camden's engraving suggests, only about 7 inches high. After the abbey was closed down its ownership can be traced as far as the early eighteenth century, when it was the property of William Hughes, an official employed at Wells Cathedral. Thereafter it disappears from historical record and presumably has long been melted down.

The events of 1191 have been discussed exhaustively, and few people give any credibility to the discovery. It has been claimed that Gerald of Wales 'swallows a forgery ... hook, line and sinker', but this is surely overstating it.[6] Memorials for the dead were and are one of the chief ways by which we connect to the past. Discovery of the grave of an important king was not so incredible in the context of the late twelfth century. As we have seen, Glastonbury Abbey already had the bones of various kings, saints and popes. The twelfth and thirteenth centuries was the time of the Crusades, a particularly fertile period for the trade in relics. When compared to the items that were brought back from the Near East, including splinters from the cross on which Christ was crucified, fragments of the crown of thorns and congealed blood from Christ's wounds, the discovery of Arthur and Guinevere was not so incredible. That the trade in relics could be and often was abused in an unscrupulous manner, and that the medieval world always had its share of doubters, does not diminish the religious significance of saintly relics or the political significance of the bones of warrior kings. People believed that they could hold history in their hands, and the grave at Glastonbury was not the only source of Arthurian artefacts in circulation. A few months after Arthur's grave was discovered, Richard I took Excalibur with him when he set off for the Third Crusade. On his way there he exchanged gifts with the (Norman) king of Sicily. He gave Excalibur in exchange for four large transport ships and fifteen galleys and probably thought he had done well out of it.

It is usually assumed that Arthur's bones were drafted in to boost Glastonbury's pilgrim trade, which historians regularly demean as the 'tourist trade', a phrase that merely reveals the prejudices of modern minds. That pilgrimage was a lucrative business is simply taken for granted. True, Canterbury Cathedral had successfully promoted the cult of Thomas Becket after his martyrdom in 1170, and contributions from pilgrims are thought to have helped in the rebuilding of the cathedral after a fire there in 1174. But it is not obvious that the monks expected that Arthur could do the same for Glastonbury. After all, Becket was a saint, Arthur was not. He did not even merit the pious esteem accorded to Edward the Confessor, the English king who was canonised in 1163. Pilgrims sought intercession with the divine through the offices of the saints. Arthur could not do that. Moreover, we do not know how profitable pilgrimage was in the late twelfth century, although we do know that Glastonbury never competed with the principal centres of pilgrimage in England, such as Walsingham, Canterbury and Westminster, which were in more populous districts.

The monks made less of their discovery than is often supposed. Adam of Domerham said that the remains were placed in a 'magnificently carved' tomb but subsequent events surrounding the visit of Edward I in 1278 suggest that the Arthurian relics and/or shrine had not been displayed prominently enough. When William of Malmesbury's history of the abbey was updated in the mid thirteenth century, the burial of Arthur and Guinevere, and other Britons that proved how venerated the church of Glastonbury had been, was passed over 'for fear of being tedious'.[7] This is in contrast to the Anglo-Saxon kings, who remained more honoured at Glastonbury because they had granted lands and privileges to the abbey, which Arthur did not.

If the motive for discovering Arthur, Dunstan and the Charter of St Patrick was indeed financial it is more likely that they hoped to rekindle royal interest in the abbey, since a wealthy patron would more likely answer their short-term needs than humble pilgrims. During Henry II's reign Glastonbury Abbey had enjoyed his royal patronage. King Richard, his successor, was cooler on the subject of Arthur and Glastonbury, preferring to devote his attention to the Crusades. It is ironic that this most legendary of English kings seems to have been so uninterested in the legends of Glastonbury and so casually traded away Arthur's sword. However, in 1189 Richard I appointed his nephew, Henry of Sully, as Abbot and it was during his abbacy that Arthur was discovered. Significantly, Richard named another nephew, Prince Arthur of Brittany, as his heir. The abbey might therefore have been under pressure to bestow a more fitting memorial to his illustrious namesake than an unmarked grave in the abbey cemetery.

There were other reasons why the bones were important that had nothing to do with money or status. Relics of kings and saints allowed their owners to claim ownership of the past. It was a feature of medieval life that the bones of the long-dead retained some of the virtue of the living person, and was a way in which the living could be connected with the most edifying characters from history. They made the deeds of the past more real. We underestimate the extent to which artefacts were part of the story of the past, perhaps because their modern counterpart, the market for memorabilia, is far more trivial than the medieval veneration of relics. Relics associated with other illustrious warriors were safeguarded and revered in the middle ages, and so the presence of Arthur's bones at Glastonbury was not unique. The skull of Sir Gawain could be found in Dover Castle. The heart of Robert the Bruce was interred in Melrose Abbey. On his induction into the Order of the Garter in 1416 Sigismund, the king of the Romans, gave Henry V a reliquary containing the heart of St George. In each case memorialisation benefited from the actual physical presence of the person who was remembered. It focused the memorialisation in that one particular place. Even if they were not real, the bones attributed to Arthur and Guinevere still represented an acknowledged truth and made Glastonbury a special place in the cultural memory of Arthur. And it is worth remembering that just as places needed to associate themselves with individuals, individuals needed places where their memory could flourish. Glastonbury may have needed Arthur, but Arthur also needed Glastonbury. In his preface to the first printed edition of Arthurian literature in English, William Caxton acknowledged that 'divers men hold opinion that there was no such Arthur, and that all such books be made of him be but feigned and fables'. He answered these critics by pointing to the physical remembrances that were found in England, chiefly 'ye may see his sepulture in the Monastery of Glastonbury'.[8] When so little of the past, be it documents or artefacts, survived, objects that did survive enjoyed an enhanced value as testament.

Veneration of physical remains assisted in Christian devotion and allowed worshippers to become closer to God, especially as saints were intercessors between human and divine. The bones of king Arthur were a secular version of that, embodying the virtues of great kingship and somehow proving that such a thing existed. Sacred and secular cults derive from the same notion of the hero cult, and the discovery and veneration of the king's bones was a medieval version of hero worship. As a mnemonic, bones could help in remembering the great deeds of Arthur's life, and perhaps the monks thought that they could bring the community good fortune in a broad sense. Furthermore, the claim that Arthur was buried at Glastonbury was not wholly an invention of the Abbey, but was suggested by other credible sources. The discovery of the grave may not therefore have been a forgery in the modern meaning of the term. The monks were convinced they had the bones of Arthur and Guinevere because they expected to find them. The lead cross was the memorial that they thought should have accompanied the tomb.

The abbey's discovery was never challenged by a rival claim and so Glastonbury became the undisputed place of memorial. Arthur's cult at Glastonbury also gained currency within Wales, as in the late fourteenth-century works *Claddedigaeth Arthur* (the Burial of Arthur) and the *Llyfr Arfau* attributed to Siôn Trefor. Based on Gerald of Wales, *Claddedigaeth Arthur* describes sixteen wounds on Arthur's head and relates how Arthur came earlier to Glastonbury and set the image of the Virgin Mary within his shield. In *Llyfr Arfau*, a treatise on heraldry, this happened after 'he saw the miracles in the monastery at Glastonbury'.[9]

If the discovery of Arthur was a crock of gold, this wealth should have been reflected in the splendour and rapidity of the rebuilding. In fact the new abbey was no phoenix rising from the ashes of 1184 like the fabled rebuilding of Chartres Cathedral in the twelfth century. Building work started at Glastonbury immediately after the fire, beginning with the most important part of the complex. The Lady Chapel, built around the *vetusta ecclesia*, is an ambitious design that lacks nothing in the way of scale or decoration. It was consecrated as early as 1186, although that does not mean that it had been completed by then. The remainder of the abbey church and cloisters were rebuilt slowly during the thirteenth century, in a building programme that seems unremarkable by medieval standards. Its near neighbour, the cathedral church at Wells, underwent reconstruction over the same extended period but was finished sooner and achieved an architectural greatness that Glastonbury would never equal. At Glastonbury the nave of the new church was not vaulted until the early fourteenth century, more than a hundred years after the building was begun.

What is striking about the history of Glastonbury Abbey for the two decades following the discovery of Arthur is the struggle of the monks to be masters of their own house. They had more serious things to think about than cashing in on forgeries and fabrications. The discoveries relating to Dunstan and Patrick may have owed more to their defence against episcopal ambition than to a rebuilding programme. Abbot Henry of Sully saw Glastonbury only as a stepping stone in his career, and left in 1193 when he was elected Bishop of Worcester. He was replaced by the equally ambitious Savaric Fitzgeldewin, an Englishman but also cousin of the Holy Roman Emperor Henry VI, and the last person that the monks would have wanted. Savaric did not have to travel far, as the previous year he had been elected Bishop of Bath.

The shifting headquarters of the diocese during this period is a story in which Glastonbury became entangled, and demands a slight diversion to explain. It is a period that looks confusing after a long passage of time, but it was in these difficult and uncertain years that the great churches of Wells and Glastonbury were built. Wells had been a cathedral since 909, but following the Norman

Conquest the older Anglo-Saxon sees sometimes fell out of favour at the expense of larger towns and cities. The first Norman bishop of Wells, John de Villula, therefore moved the see to Bath Abbey in 1090, and there it stayed in the twelfth century even when Wells reverted to being the *de facto* cathedral. From 1195 Savaric called himself Bishop of Bath and Glastonbury, with the blessing of Pope Celestine III, and moved the see to Glastonbury Abbey. The monks complained about their loss of independence and initially persuaded Richard I to appoint one of their own, William Pica, as abbot. Savaric dealt swiftly with claims that the monks had a right to elect their own abbot—William Pica was excommunicated. The monks sent a deputation to the Pope to plead their case, but Savaric's rule prevailed because the Pope was convinced that only way to settle the rivalry between monastery and diocese was to unite them under a single leader.

Jocelyn, a canon at the church in Wells, succeeded Savaric as bishop and abbot in 1206. He seems to have been instrumental in the rebuilding of both Wells and Glastonbury. However, his tenure included the five years from 1208 when the Pope imposed an Interdict on all churches in England, until his dispute with King John could be resolved. Churches remained closed, and services were forbidden, until Christmas 1213. At the same time, building work on churches ceased. Not until 1219 did Pope Honorius III dissolve the union of Bath and Glastonbury. Jocelyn therefore lost his position as abbot at Glastonbury, where William of St Vigor was elected to replace him. Jocelyn's official title remained Bishop of Bath until his death in 1242, although it was in this period that the building of the cathedral church at Wells ceased. His successor, Roger of Salisbury, became officially Bishop of Bath and Wells in 1245, when the cathedral status of Wells was finally recognised again by the Pope. The monks of Glastonbury would have been mistaken, however, if they thought they had seen off the diocese. Cathedral and abbey remained jealous of each other throughout the middle ages.

There is no question that the recovery of Arthur's bones gave Glastonbury Abbey a national political profile. English kings varied in their enthusiasm for the cult of Arthur and Glastonbury's part in it, but were not shy to take advantage when they needed it. To name a prince after the hero of the Britons turned out to be the kiss of death, however. Prince Arthur of Brittany was a grandson of Henry II and had a strong claim to the throne following Richard I's death in 1199. He was murdered by his uncle King John, reversing Geoffrey of Monmouth's story in which Arthur dies by the treachery of his nephew. Nearly three centuries later Henry VII traced his ancestry back to Arthur as part of his claim to the English throne, and in 1486 named his first-born son Arthur, the Prince of Wales who died in 1502. Edward I was one of the great enthusiasts of Arthurian tradition, and understood its political symbolism. It was he who commissioned the round table at Winchester Castle, made for an Arthurian pageant in 1289. His grandson, Edward III, had it hung on the wall, transforming it into a symbolic icon, and it was Henry VIII who had it painted in about 1516. Six years later he was able to show it off to Charles V, Emperor-elect of the Holy Roman Empire. The image of Arthur bore a suspicious resemblance to Henry himself, but who better to be a model of what the great warrior king looked like?

The events that cemented Arthur's medieval reputation as a secular national hero, and established Edward I's right to overlordship of Britain, took place in 1278 in Glastonbury and Westminster Abbeys. One of the great state occasions took place at Easter when, fresh from his conquest of North Wales, Edward I and Queen Eleanor arrived at Glastonbury Abbey. Edward was a man of calculated gestures. On his way south he had visited Worcester Cathedral where he prayed at the shrine of St Wulfstan, the important Anglo-Saxon saint, and now at Glastonbury he was paying homage to the traditions of Wales. A Glastonbury monk, Adam of Domerham, wrote an eyewitness account of the visit, during which the king and queen took part in the ostentatious exhumation of the bones of Arthur and Guinevere. These were subsequently placed in a shrine before the high altar. The shrine stood to the east of, and therefore could be seen to have precedence over, the shrines to Saints Patrick, Benignus and Indracht, but Arthur was always ranked below the Anglo-Saxon kings at Glastonbury. The ceremony by which they were taken to the shrine resembled the translation of a saint's bones. Edward wrapped Arthur's bones in a cloth, Eleanor wrapped Guinevere's bones, in each case marked with their royal seals. The remains were placed in a chest and taken to their new resting place. The skulls and knee bones were kept back, to be used for the devotion of pilgrims. The tomb was described in the sixteenth century by John Leland. He said it was a black marble tomb, adorned with an effigy of the king and guarded by lions at each corner. Edward's actions reminded Wales, as if it needed reminding again, that Arthur was dead and that he was the once but not future king. His bones lay in an English monastery under the seal of the English king, the division of the land into two nations was unhistorical, perhaps even unnatural, and the heir to Arthur's kingdom was not a Welsh prince but Edward himself.

Edward was deliberately anglicising this British hero, and took a step further in the marginalisation of Welsh culture. It took place in 1284, after the death of the last Welsh prince of Wales, Llywelyn ap Gruffudd, and the execution of his brother Dafydd. Edward's eldest son, Alphonso, presented Llywelyn's crown (or what they thought was his crown, handed down from Arthur himself) at the shrine of Edward the Confessor in Westminster Abbey, although first it had to be gilded to make it worthy of the occasion. Edward's manipulation of the heritage of King Arthur was intended to further erase his Welsh identity, but it also enacted Welsh submission to the crown of England. Equally, it was a signal of his intention towards the Scots. Arthur was the ruler of all the Britons, an ambition that Edward had every intention of fulfilling for himself. Edward removed the Stone of Scone to Westminster in 1296, and confiscated the Scottish crown in 1299, both of which were similar symbolic acts intended to subordinate Scotland to the English king, as Arthur's memorial and Llywelyn's crown asserted Edward's rightful overlordship of Wales. All were presented at the shrine of the Confessor, the patron of the English royal bloodline after whom Edward himself had been named.

At Glastonbury Abbey Edward I had created a national memorial. The first king to pay homage to it was his grandson, Edward III. Edward inherited the throne in 1327 at the age of fourteen, but the country was ruled by his mother Isabella and her lover, Roger Mortimer. Three years later Edward deposed them in an audacious coup, a triumph for which his subjects hailed the new king as 'Arthur *redivivus*'. In the first year of his rule proper, aged only eighteen, his itinerary took him through Somerset in December 1331, where he visited one of the Cadbury's on the way to Glastonbury Abbey with his queen, Philippa. This is potentially significant because a tradition that South Cadbury was Camelot was recorded by John Leland in the sixteenth century but could have been considered as such as early as the 1330s. The two days spent at Glastonbury signalled his wish to be more like his grandfather than his father, especially in his desire to unite the nation of Britain under his rule.

Edward enjoyed tournaments and chivalry and styled himself as a knight errant and military commander. In 1344, at a tournament at Windsor, he announced his intention to re-establish the Round Table with 300 knights, although he subsequently abandoned the plans for reasons that are not entirely clear. In 1348, after his victory at Crécy, he created the more modest Order of the Garter, secular counterpart of the college of priests that he had established at the newly built chapel in Windsor Castle, dedicated to St George. Windsor now became the new Camelot where the knights celebrated their patronal festival on 23 April. In medieval romance, Arthur's Round Table drew from the company of the Holy Grail and, ultimately, the table of the Last Supper. Edward's attention was therefore directed back to Glastonbury and another of its emerging traditions, that of Joseph of Arimathea.

4

Joseph and the Holy Grail

By the early thirteenth century Glastonbury Abbey seemed to have a secure vision of its past, based on its association with Celtic and Anglo-Saxon saints and kings. While the abbey church was slowly being rebuilt there was little apparent need to enlist a new saint to its cause. But this was the period in which the legend of Joseph of Arimathea's adventures in the west flourished, which would descend almost fully formed upon Glastonbury Abbey by the 1240s. For Joseph's link to Glastonbury to emerge, several unconnected cultures had first to come together. These were the Biblical writings about Joseph, the legend of the Holy Grail, the French *roman*, Arthurian legends and the cult of relics brought back from the Holy Land by Crusaders. The result was a distinctly medieval Joseph, but one in which the Biblical Joseph was still recognisable.

Joseph of Arimathea appears briefly in each of the four Gospels, although not as the blood relative of Christ that many centuries later he would be assumed to be. He was, nevertheless, a follower of Jesus. Joseph is described in Matthew as a rich man from Arimathea, a town about 30 miles from Jerusalem. Mark and Luke describe him as a *decurio*, a member of the Jewish council, but not one of those who plotted Jesus' downfall. His role after the death of Jesus was crucial because it was Joseph who asked Pilate for the body of Christ, who then took him down from the cross, wrapped him in linen and, according to custom, laid him in an unused tomb in the cemetery. The account of Christ's burial given in John's Gospel introduces an important accomplice, his friend Nicodemus. Nicodemus is mentioned elsewhere in the Gospel of John, where he is described as a Pharisee who sought out Jesus and his teachings.[1]

Joseph's brief appearance after the crucifixion ensured that he was mentioned in many early Christian writings. St Ambrose (339–97) was bishop of Milan when the city was the administrative centre of the western Roman Empire, and is one of the Four Doctors of the Roman church. He pointed out that, unlike the other apostles, Joseph did not desert Christ in his hour of need and acted through a sense of justice in his burial of Christ. Ambrose even compared the unused tomb with the immaculate womb of the Blessed Virgin. St John Chrysostom (347–407), Patriarch of Constantinople, was the first to write that Joseph was one of the seventy-two apostles appointed by Jesus in the Gospel of Luke, from which a tradition arose that the apostles travelled across Europe preaching the word of God.[2]

However, it was to be chiefly through writings attributed to Nicodemus that Joseph would become known and revered in later centuries. More than 400 manuscripts of the Latin *Gospel of Nicodemus* have survived and it was trans- lated into many European languages. The work was not written until the fourth century, and is largely a reworking of an older text known as *Acts of Pilate*. It is one of the apocryphal gospels, which is a misleading term because in this context 'apocryphal' is just the word applied to the disparate group of early writings about Jesus that were disputed or were considered less authoritative than the New Testament. The *Gospel of Nicodemus* was never part of the New Testament canon, but it was taken seriously by medieval Christians—Richard II had a Bible made in which it was placed between the Gospel of John and the Acts of the Apostles. The most well-known episode in the *Gospel of Nicodemus* in medieval times did not feature Joseph, but spoke of Christ's descent into hell (or Hades) after his crucifixion. He broke down its gates and led a procession of the righteous, with Adam at its head, from the depths of hell to be baptised. This episode, known as the Harrowing of Hell, was familiar in medieval Christendom and was depicted in stone and on parchment, was performed in mystery plays and was incorporated into the Easter liturgy.

In the *Gospel of Nicodemus* the story of Joseph is much more dramatic than in the Gospels. He is introduced as an innocent member of the Jewish council that plotted Jesus' downfall, and who subsequently asked Pilate for his body so that he could give him a dignified burial. When they found out what he had done the other Jews turned on Joseph and on others who had spoken up for Jesus in front of Pilate, including Nicodemus. Joseph was unrepentant about the burial. 'I have placed it in my new tomb, having wrapped it in clean linen, and I rolled a stone before the door of the cave.' He even admonished the members of the council: 'And you have not done well with the righteous one, for you did not repent of having crucified him, but also pierced him with a spear'. Joseph was seized and imprisoned 'in a building without a window', with guards stationed at the door'.[3]

After the Sabbath the rulers of the synagogue and the priests met to discuss Joseph's fate, but when they opened the sealed door of his prison they found that Joseph had vanished. Simultaneously, the guards keeping watch at the tomb of Jesus arrived, talking about an earthquake and the appearance of an angel who rolled away the stone at the tomb. Questioned about how Jesus could have vanished, the guards suggested that, however Jesus left the tomb, so did Joseph escape his prison: 'give us Joseph and we will give you Jesus' they said. Jesus, it was later reported, had been with his disciples, from where he ascended to heaven. Joseph, meanwhile, was found in his home town of Arimathea. No one dared seize him now, but he was persuaded to meet with the council at the house of Nicodemus, where he recounted the events of his incarceration.

During his imprisonment, Jesus appeared to him bathed in light, then anointed and kissed him. Joseph could hardly believe his eyes, and he questioned Jesus.

> Show me the place where I laid you. And he took me and showed me the place where I laid him. And the linen cloth lay there, and the cloth that was upon his face. Then I recognised that it was Jesus. And he took me by the hand and placed me in the middle of my house, with doors shut, and led me to my bed and said to me: Peace be with you![4]

This encounter with Jesus ensured that Christians wanted to know what became of Joseph of Arimathea and, just as important, where he was buried. Joseph of Arimathea was the subject of competing claims across medieval Christendom, a reminder that the literature did not always support, and often flatly contradicted, the claims made for Joseph at Glastonbury. In an age before the printing press, however, the Glastonbury monks were understandably unaware of the earlier and, to them, obscure literature and traditions of eastern Christendom. Apocryphal literature emerged mainly from Byzantium and so it was around the eastern Mediterranean that the earliest traditions of Joseph developed. It was claimed that Joseph of Arimathea's body was preserved in the royal chapel of Jerusalem. A Syrian-Nestorian *Chronicle* of the seventh century had argued that Joseph's sarcophagus had been found near the Holy Sepulchre in Jerusalem, and the early-thirteenth century *Chronicle of Sens* says that in the early ninth century the Patriarch of Jerusalem fled the city when he was attacked by Pagans, carrying with him the body of Joseph and other precious relics. He took them to a monastery at Moyenmoutier in the Vosges mountains, which was pillaged by Hungarians *c.* 917.

The content of eastern literature filtered through to the west and was eventually to be felt at Glastonbury. In the eighth century a manuscript attributed to Joseph claimed that Christ had sent Joseph and St Philip on an apostolic mission to Lydda (in Palestine), where a site was chosen for a church to be consecrated to the Blessed Virgin.[5] A thirteenth-century Italian composition known as the *Transitus Mariae* (the Assumption of Mary) depicted Joseph as one of the chosen disciples and guardian of the Virgin until her assumption into heaven. Both of these manuscripts, five centuries apart, emphasised the association of Joseph of Arimathea with the Virgin Mary, as would also be the case at Glastonbury, where Joseph was said to have dedicated his founding chapel to Our Lady. For what became Roman Catholic orthodoxy we can look at the much later *Acta Sanctorum*, the encyclopedia of saints that was initiated by the Jesuits and was published in several volumes beginning in 1643. In it Joseph is credited with missionary journeys west to Spain and France with St James, and to France with Veronica, Lazarus, Mary Magdalene and others in AD 48.

The second and third elements that coalesced in the creation of the medieval Joseph legend were the Grail and Arthurian traditions. The origin of the Holy Grail, variously a chalice, plate or cauldron, has been debated, without ever achieving a critical consensus. An obvious place to start looking would be Celtic oral traditions. One promising source is the poem *Preiddeu Annwn*, or the *Spoils of Annwn*, attributed to the sixth-century poet Taliesin. Arthur leads a raid on Annwn, the Isle of the Dead, from where he obtains a magic cauldron. This is similar to the magic cauldron in 'Branwen daughter of Llyr', the second branch of the *Mabinogi*, which features a magic cauldron that has the power to restore the dead. This was not a characteristic of the Holy Grail, however. Many elements of the Grail legend are alien to the Celtic tradition and must therefore derive from another source. As we will see, the Grail is carried in procession and it was imperative that the seeker questioned it. The chief knights of the Grail quest, like Sir Perceval, do not come from native Arthurian tradition. It has been argued persuasively that the Grail legend has an eastern origin, perhaps brought to the west by Sarmatian and Alanic settlers from ancient Scythia, who settled in the west during the Roman empire. Sarmatians were recruited into the army and served as auxiliaries on Hadrian's Wall; Alans settled in enclaves in Gaul and the Iberian peninsula. From the Alans may derive the character of Alain li Gros, who we will meet, and perhaps also Alanus à Lot, better known as Lancelot.[6]

The Grail legend was not exclusive to northern Europe. It has been argued that the German *Parzifal*, with its Grail Castle in the Pyrenees, was influenced directly from southern Gaul. The Cathars of southern France descended from settlers from the Middle East in the ninth century and lived in a semi-independent state ruled by the Count of Toulouse. Their distinct form of Christianity, which challenged the worldly power of the Roman Catholic church, may have incorporated Grail legends. We will never know for sure. The Albigensian Crusade was launched against these perceived heretics in 1208 and the Cathars endured bloody persecution.

The Grail enters the literature of northern Europe not in the Celtic territories but in France, in a verse romance written in the 1180s, but left unfinished, by Chrétien de Troyes. *Perceval*, or *The Story of the Grail*, marks a new kind of literature, the *roman*, which is still the word for novel in French. Chrétien writes about the peacetime pursuits of chivalry and tournaments rather than prowess in war, as would have happened in an earlier time, but set in the court of king Arthur at a distant but undefined past. They are magical tales of adventure written at a time when the life of a knight was, in reality, a good deal more prosaic.

In Chrétien's handling of it the Grail is mysterious and magical, but is not Christian. When Perceval first saw the Grail, it was accompanied by 'so brilliant a light ... that the candles lost their brightness like the stars or the moon when the sun rises'. We are told that the Grail is manufactured of pure gold and encrusted with jewels, but it does not seem to have been a chalice, more likely a dish or a platter, since it is a vessel from which food could be served to its keeper, the Fisher King. The Grail is never really explained and its mystery was open to interpretation. Chrétien was at pains to stress that it was not a product of his imagination. In his dedicatory prologue he speaks of a book given to him by his patron, Count Philip of Flanders, which he claimed was the source of his story. It was common for writers to attribute their material to some unidentified earlier source, giving the impression that because the story had previously been written down it must have greater veracity.

Crucial elements that would appear in later stories are here: the Fisher King as guardian of the Grail; a procession of young girls bearing various objects, including the Grail and the bleeding lance used by a Roman soldier to pierce the crucified body of Christ; the need to question the Fisher King and the consequences of initial failure. As described above, Chrétien's work was not finished. In succeeding decades this story was continued by at least four other authors, or continuators. And where Chrétien writes of the Grail, it was not a giant leap for later authors to describe it as the Holy Grail.

Robert de Boron was the first author to combine the story of the Grail with the *Gospel of Nicodemus* and other apocryphal writing. Robert and Chrétien were writing at the time of, or in the immediate aftermath of, the Third and Fourth Crusades (1187–1992 and 1202–1204). At this time all manner of relics were brought back from the Holy Land, many of which were thought to have been associated with Christ's Passion, like pieces of the cross, nails and crown of thorns. Perhaps the most dramatic of the discoveries made at this time was the Holy Lance, the spear that pierced Christ's side, the fifth of his Five Wounds, mentioned in John's Gospel and by Nicodemus, where the soldier who wielded it is named as Longinus. Use of the spear can be seen either as the final act of cruelty or as an act of mercy that put an end to Christ's suffering. That Chrétien incorporated a bleeding lance into his *Perceval* suggests that he was well aware of this miraculous recent discovery. Even if only in the imagination, Robert de Boron's reinvention of the Holy Grail as the cup of the Last Supper is therefore simply one more item from Christ's Passion that found its way to northern Europe at the end of the twelfth century. And the widespread interest in holy relics may help to account for the popularity of the story.

It is possible that Robert had some personal experience of the Orient. His patron, Gautier de Montbéliard, joined the Fourth Crusade in 1202 and, while in the Holy Land, married Burgundia, daughter of the king of Jerusalem and Cyprus. Gautier was regent of Cyprus for five years until his brother-in-law came of age in 1210. If Robert also visited Cyprus he could have profited from its mix of cultures east and west. He could have learned, for example, of the Byzantine cult of Joseph, the legend of his founding the church at Lydda, and the collection of his relics by the king of Jerusalem.[7]

Robert de Boron was also influenced by the cult of the Holy Blood that thrived in Flanders and Normandy at the end of the twelfth century. Several religious institutions claimed to possess relics of the holy blood that was collected at the time of Christ's deposition and burial, which found its way to northern Europe in incredible journeys. One such relic was discovered at Mantua in 804 and was said to have been taken there by Nicodemus. For a while it was lost, but after it was rediscovered in 1048 part was given to Count Baldwin V of Flanders, from whose family it passed to the abbey of Weingarten, where it was kept at the end of the twelfth century. Another relic was at the abbey of Fécamp in Normandy. In 1120 the bishop of Dol in Brittany referred to the abbey as 'guardian of the blood of Lord Jesus, buried by Nicodemus, as the blessed John bears witness, collected from his limbs'.[8] According to the legend, Nicodemus had carefully collected the clotted blood from Christ's wounds, which was later inherited by his nephew Isaac. Isaac heard a voice from heaven that told him to seal the relic in lead, put it in the trunk of a fig tree, then cast the trunk into the sea. The tree was washed ashore in Normandy, in a field known as *ficus campus* (field of the fig tree) and a monastery was founded in the place where it was recovered. In 1171 its abbot, Henri de Sully, announced the rediscovery of the relics, put them on public display, and Fécamp became a principal centre of pilgrimage in northern France during the rebuilding of the abbey in the final quarter of the twelfth century. (Henri de Sully was the nephew of Henry of Blois, abbot of Glastonbury 1126–70, and was later elected Archbishop of Bourges; he should not be confused with his contemporary namesake who was Abbot of Glastonbury.)

As we will see, Robert de Boron's awareness of the Holy Blood relics is obvious but his version of the Grail story is quite different from Chrétien's in other ways too. The Grail is linked specifically with the Last Supper. In the preamble Robert is careful to stress his orthodox Christianity, in case any readers should think his story blasphemous. Robert's prose *Joseph of Arimathea* combines Joseph from the *Gospel of Nicodemus* with the Grail legend that Chrétien had written about, to produce a Christian version of what now became the Holy Grail, which was incorporated into Arthurian legend in the two subsequent works that constitute Robert's trilogy, *Merlin* and *Perceval*.

Robert even explains why more is not written about Joseph of Arimathea in the Gospels. The apostles apparently either knew nothing beyond the fact that Joseph was imprisoned, or did not know who he was and wrote only about their own doings and experiences. Robert did not claim that his story was original, far from it. Like Chrétien, he established its credentials by referring to an earlier, unnamed source. This may have been true, since Robert was not the only author to write of Joseph of Arimathea at the beginning of the thirteenth century. Hélinand was a monk at the Cistercian monastery of Froidmont near Beauvais. He wrote his *Chronicon*, a chronicle of world history, in the second decade of the thirteenth century, in which Britain, Joseph and the Holy Grail are mentioned in the entry for 718.

> At this time in Britain a certain miraculous vision of the Decurion St Joseph who took down our Lord's body from the cross was shown to a certain hermit by an angel, and of the dish or paropsis from which our Lord supped with his disciples. The hermit wrote down a description of this which is called the story of the Grail.[9]

Did Robert copy Hélinand, Hélinand copy Robert, or did they draw upon the same source or sources?

In Robert's story, Joseph of Arimathea was a soldier under Pilate, governor of Judea, and secretly became a follower of Jesus. Judas betrayed Jesus at the house of Simon the Leper, and was arrested by the band of Jews who hated and feared him. One of them also took away the vessel that Jesus had drunk from at Simon's house. Pilate washed his hands of the affair, although he did take in hand the vessel that had been used at the disciples' last supper.

Joseph was grief-stricken at the death of Jesus. He asked Pilate if he could be granted the body of Christ as a reward for his service to the governor. Pilate agreed to the strange request, and also gave him the vessel that had been in his safekeeping. With the help of his friend Nicodemus, Joseph took down the body of Christ, but then a strange thing happened. As he washed the body he noticed that the wounds continued to bleed and, remembering the cup, collected the drops of blood in it. This event is not found in Nicodemus but was not Robert's invention either, since it is illustrated, along with the figure of Longinus holding a spear, in twelfth-century manuscript illuminations showing Christ being taken from the cross. Its ultimate origin seems to be the apocryphal *Narratio Josephi de Arimathea*, but with one crucial difference. The apocryphal account has Joseph state: 'I climbed the Holy Golgotha, where the Lord's cross stood, and I collected in ... the large shroud the precious blood that had flowed from his holy side'.[10] This shroud was later known as the Holy Mandylion, or Edessa icon, and was one of the most famous relics of eastern Christendom. It was an image of Christ's body imprinted in cloth which, in the tenth century, was noticed to contain drops of blood from the Five Wounds. The cloth was slowly understood to have been Jesus' burial cloth and to contain the real presence of Christ. The association of Joseph with the burial cloth, and its presence in Edessa, may be the ultimate derivation of Joseph's link with Britain, since Edessa was the kingdom of Lucius, whose citadel of Britium was mistaken for Britain. In 944 the icon was transferred to Constantinople but legends of it presumably persisted. Edessa was captured in 1097 in the First Crusade and was under Christian rule until it fell to the Turks in 1144. Perhaps Robert had heard of the Holy Mandylion and substituted it for a cup in the Grail story.

Let us return to Robert's story. The Jews imprisoned Jesus for his part in the burial of Jesus. In his prison Christ appeared to Joseph, told him about the table of the Last Supper and foretold that 'several tables will be established in my service', which predicts the table of the Grail company and the Round Table of Arthur. He brought with him the vessel that Joseph had hidden safely in his house. Jesus charged Joseph with being its keeper, and stressed that there should never be more than three keepers of it. It contained the blood of Christ which had the power of the Father, Son and Holy Spirit.

> And all who see the vessel and remain in its presence will have lasting joy and fulfilment for their souls. And all who take these words to heart will be more gracious and admired both in this world and in the eyes of Our Lord, and will never be victims of injustice or deprived of their rights.[11]

The cup of the Last Supper held the blood of the crucified Christ and had now become the Holy Grail.

But the Holy Grail bore other mysteries that Robert was not willing to reveal:–

> Then Jesus spoke other words to Joseph which I dare not tell you—nor could I, even if I wanted to, if I did not have the high book in which they are written: and that is the creed of the great mystery of the Grail. And I beg all those who hear this tale to ask me no more about it at this point, in God's name.[12]

So the mysteries of the Holy Grail emanated from Jesus Christ himself.

Joseph was eventually freed from his dungeon, where he had been abandoned and left to die. His ordeal paralleled the forty days and forty nights that Jesus spent in the desert, and also the experience of those saints who had sought out the Biblical desert to test themselves. His holiness was very recognisable to a contemporary readership. Joseph emerged from incarceration as a figure of considerable spiritual authority who converted all those around him.

Robert's story now moves beyond the apocryphal literature. The Holy Grail becomes the channel through which Joseph communicates with the Holy Spirit, asking its advice on spiritual matters and matters of moral conduct. It was from this source that Joseph was instructed to set up the Grail table, around which he and his followers would sit. It was to be a remembrance of the table at the Last Supper, and there was to be an empty space beside Joseph that would signify the place vacated by Judas. Joseph's brother-in-law Bron was told to go out and catch fish for the table. The Grail was set up by Joseph's place but was covered by the edge of the tablecloth. Around the table sat the virtuous among Joseph's disciples, except for the place that could not be filled. Those that were admitted to the company of the Grail entered a state of grace, a kind of euphoria which stayed with them for they met daily. When one of the outsiders begged to be allowed to join, claiming to lead a life free of sin, he enquired about the vessel 'of which we know nothing, for it has never been presented to us'. Warned that 'it will allow no sinner in its presence' the outsider, named Moyse, continued to insist that he was worthy to be admitted to the company of Grail, and was in the end admitted. But there was only one seat, next to Joseph of Arimathea himself, and as soon as he sat down he was swallowed up and vanished.

The story now shifts to the family of Joseph's sister Enigeus and her husband Bron. They had twelve sons. The Holy Spirit had ordained that they should marry but that the last to marry should become the chief of the brothers. His name was Alain li Gros. A great destiny awaited him, because it was he who lead would his brothers and their families into unspecified 'strange lands', recounting the life and death of Jesus Christ wherever he went. From Alain would eventually be born a male child to whom the Grail would ultimately pass. Meanwhile one of the Grail company, Petrus, was to go out into the world as God's messenger, and it was foretold that he would travel west, to the *vaus d'Avaron*, where he was to await the son of Alain. Alain leading his party out of Jerusalem had an obvious parallel with Moses leading his people to the Promised Land and his wanderings also bring to mind the peripatetic Celtic missionaries. Alain is a cross between these, and a figure with which contemporary readers could have identified. With these revelations from the Holy Spirit the work of Joseph was almost done. He was to pass the Grail to Bron, who was to be the second keeper of the Grail and who, because he caught fish for the table at the first assembly of the Grail company, would be known as the Fisher King. He too departed on his travels. Joseph, meanwhile, ended his days in the land of his birth.

The interpretation of *vaus d'Avaron* is uncertain. To interpret it as the Glastonbury Avalon is wishful thinking, since the district around Glastonbury was anything but a vale. The Glastonbury monks had referred to it as *insula Avallonia*, or isle of Avalon, which was a more accurate topographical description. There is an Avallon in Burgundy, not far from the home of Robert de Boron, and perhaps it was that place that Robert had in mind.

There are many loose ends in Robert's story, some of which are clarified in the later works, *Merlin* and *Perceval*. Whereas Joseph had been the medium through which the divine message was delivered, that role passed to Merlin as the scene shifted to Britain. Merlin, the magician advisor to Utherpendragon, announces that 'our Lord omnipotent has given me knowledge of things to come'. He told Utherpendragon about the table of the Last Supper and its empty seat, and he told him of the Grail table with its empty seat. Merlin advised the king 'to establish a third table in the name of the Trinity, which these three tables will signify'. He had it made at Carduel in Wales. At Pentecost, Merlin selected fifty of the worthiest men to sit around it, careful to leave one empty seat. His table had the same effect as Joseph's. Those who sat around it had never felt more contented, and 'some of us have never seen each other before, yet now we love one other as sons love their fathers'. Then Merlin declared that the empty seat can only be taken by the son of Alain li Gros, but that he had not yet taken a wife, although he was living in the island of Britain. And the prophecy will not be fulfilled in the time of Utherpendragon, but in the reign of the king that succeeds him.

And so when Arthur is proclaimed king, Merlin requests a private meeting with him and his two most trusted knights, Sir Kay and Sir Gawain, at which he informed Arthur that his destiny had been decided two centuries before his birth, and there were things he must do to fulfil it. Arthur learned about the three tables and about Alain li Gros, whom he was destined never to meet. He also learned of the Fisher King, who was gravely ill, living in Ireland, but who could not die until one of the knights of the Round Table had performed enough feats of chivalry and arms to become the most renowned knight in the world. Only then can he enter the court of the Fisher King to learn the secret of the Grail. At the end of the second of the trilogy of Arthur and the Grail the mood has shifted from religion and has become part of the world of chivalry, romance and knightly adventures.

Alain li Gros had a son, Perceval. When his father died Perceval left home to join the court of King Arthur, where he became a knight. Neither he nor Arthur knew his destiny or identity. Arthur, meanwhile, had remembered Merlin's strange words and had re-established the Round Table, at which twelve of the finest knights were invited to sit, leaving one seat empty. They assemble at Pentecost where a tournament was established. Perceval defeated all-comers, including Lancelot of the Lake, and was invited to join the Round Table. But there was only one spare place and only reluctantly did Arthur allow him to sit there. Perceval:–

> sat in the empty seat. And the moment he did so the stone split beneath him, uttering such an anguished groan that it seemed to all those present that the earth itself was crumbling into an abyss. And with the earth's groan came so great a darkness that for a league and more no man could see his neighbour.[13]

Then the Holy Spirit spoke. Arthur had disobeyed the command of Merlin, 'and it will cost [Perceval] and all the knights of the Round Table the greatest suffering in the world'. Were it not for the goodness of his father and grandfather Perceval would have been cast into oblivion like Moyse at the table of Joseph. 'Our Lord sends you word that the vessel which He gave Joseph in prison is here in this land, and is called the Grail.' But its keeper, the Fisher King, had fallen into a great sickness and would never be healed until one of the knights seated at the Round Table had performed enough feats of arms and goodness and prowess. Some of the knights vowed instantly not to rest until they had tracked down the house of the rich Fisher King. Gawain, Erec, Saigremor and Perceval were given leave to go. And so began the quest for the Holy Grail.

Perceval rides out into the forest and, at first, his adventures go well, as he defeats many knights and sends them to the court of Arthur to declare themselves the prisoner of Perceval of Wales. He meets the brother of Alain, his uncle, who lives as an old hermit and who tells Perceval that it is God's will that the Grail should be passed to him when he has proved himself worthy. He has luck. An old fisherman directs him to the castle of the Fisher King which, when he finally meets his grandfather, realises that it was the fisherman he had met on the river. But at the first test Perceval fails. A procession of servants passes the Fisher King and Perceval while they are eating, bearing the Holy Grail and the bleeding lance. But Perceval is curiously tongue-tied and fails to ask the Fisher King the purpose of the Grail (it is obvious that the Fisher King is used to such disappointment). And so the quest fails, he wakes up the following morning and there is no Fisher King and no Grail.

Perceval's next seven years were spent searching for the castle of the Fisher King, away from the court of Arthur. It resembles Christ's sojourn in the desert and Joseph's term of imprisonment, the necessary rite of passage to prepare him for his destiny. It is Merlin who unexpectedly appears and directs him to the house of the Fisher King, where at last destiny is fulfilled. The Holy Spirit spoke to the Fisher King: 'Our Lord bids you entrust to this man's keeping the sacred words that He taught Joseph when he gave him the Grail in prison'. But these words remain a secret as the author insists that 'I cannot—and must not—tell you'. So the Fisher King died and Perceval watched him ascend to heaven, greeted by David with his harp and a host of angels with censers. It is also the last we see of Percival. As Merlin informed Arthur, 'he has taken his leave of chivalry, and wishes to live henceforth in the grace of his Creator'.

Other contemporaries of Robert were also writing about the Holy Grail. These included the continuators of Chrétien's unfinished *Perceval*, and a separate work, entitled *Perlesvaus*, in which Joseph is portrayed as a missionary to Britain. Whether these works were influenced by Robert or linked the Grail and Joseph independently is unknown. *Perlesvaus* was written for Jean de Lisle, castellan of Bruges, at the request of the lord of Cambrin. Jean de Lisle fought in Crusade between 1203 and 1206, and in 1222, and so some direct influence from the east may be contained within the work.

The *Prose Lancelot*, otherwise known as the *Quest of the Holy Grail*, *Vulgate Cycle*, or *Lancelot-Grail*, was also written in the early thirteenth century. A prequel to the story of the Grail was subsequently added, known as the *History of the Holy Grail*, or *Estoire del Saint Graal*, written at some time between 1215 and 1230. It focuses on the long adventures of Joseph and his followers, chief among whom was his son Josephus, and their eventual arrival in Britain. Joseph's wanderings with the Grail resemble the Old Testament wanderings of the Jewish people looking for the Promised Land. In the *Estoire* the Promised Land is Britain and the Grail is kept in an Ark. And it is this work that is most crucial for the subsequent history of Joseph and Glastonbury.

Josephus reaches Britain with 150 of his disciples, who he leads across the English Channel walking on one of his garments, like Moses leading the faithful across the Red Sea. Some of the British rulers, like duke Ganor, accept Christianity, while others, like Crudel in North Wales, resist. Crudel imprisons Josephus, but is subsequently defeated. In the city of Camelot, its ruler king Agrestes at first converts but then turns apostate. Twelve of Josephus' followers are executed by a cross that Josephus had erected. Another cross was burned by Agrestes. His punishment for this blasphemy was a divinely inflicted madness, which kills him. The bloody cross at the place of execution of the martyrs turned black, and it remained so until the reign of Arthur. The cross later became a legend and an object of veneration in its own right. It found its way to St Paul's cathedral, where it was set up at the north door, a reminder that Glastonbury would not be the only institution to lay claim to the miracles of Joseph. The legend of it was recounted in the fifteenth century by John Hardyng and in a *Lyfe of Joseph of Armathia* printed in 1520.

In the *Estoire*, meanwhile, Camelot is won over to the Christian faith and Josephus founds the church of St Stephen the Martyr. There are many battles to come. Josephus makes a cross with his own blood on a white shield, used by one of his disciples, Mordrains, in battle. The shield is subsequently placed in the abbey to which Mordrains has retreated. The *Estoire* ends with the death of Josephus and the succession of Alain as keeper of the Grail.

In this relatively rapid outpouring of Grail stories in the early thirteenth century Joseph of Arimathea emerged as a major figure in the conversion of the British to Christianity, but none of it was the work of Glastonbury monks. There are significant references to Glastonbury in the *Perlesvaus* manuscript. It is the place where the head of Arthur's murdered son is buried, and the Lady Chapel is the place where Guinevere is buried. The author appears to have been aware of the discoveries made at Glastonbury in 1191. The colophon of the text claims that:–

> the Latin text from which this story was set down in the vernacular was taken from the Isle of Avalon, from a holy religious house which stands at the edge of the Lands of Adventure; there lie King Arthur and the queen, by the testimony of the worthy religious men who dwell there.[14]

Glastonbury seems an unlikely source for an early text of the Grail story, because Joseph's link with Glastonbury was not made until the middle of the thirteenth century. Likewise, although the most likely source for Robert de Boron's story was probably exactly what he said it was—an older manuscript—it probably did not come from Glastonbury either. It is much more likely that the Grail legends influenced Glastonbury than the other way round. The worst charge that can be levelled at the Glastonbury monks, therefore, is that they treated the French romances as history rather than fiction. But those were hardly fixed categories in the middle ages, when early romancers such as Chrétien and Robert, as well as British historians like Geoffrey of Monmouth, all claimed to have based their works on older books, and all of them claimed to be telling the truth. The crucial text was that of the *Estoire* because it linked Joseph with Camelot and Avalon, which by now was synonymous with Glastonbury.

The Grail legend could not be transposed directly to the Glastonbury story. What it did hint at was the identity of an early founder, and that is what Glastonbury needed to find out. William of Malmesbury's original text seems always to have been considered far too conservative in its interpretations. The *Chronicle* of Freculf, written *c.* 830, had mentioned St Philip's visit to Gaul, and so the monks had previously wondered whether the *vetusta ecclesia* had been built by his disciples, to be discovered later by Phagan and Deruvian. William of Malmesbury was unconvinced, but many of the monks must have favoured it, as it was included in the Charter of St Patrick, written in the early thirteenth century. But as soon as Joseph became a candidate he and his disciples appeared to make much more sense and seemed to answer the riddle of the *vetusta ecclesia*.

To take account of this new knowledge, marginal additions were soon made to William of Malmesbury's manuscript history *De Antiquitate Glastonie Ecclesie*. In 1247 a new transcription of it was made, which incidentally constitutes the oldest surviving copy of William of Malmesbury's work on Glastonbury, in which the scribe inserted the legend of Joseph at the beginning. The Glastonbury link was reiterated by Adam of Domerham, the Glastonbury monk who witnessed Edward I's visit in 1278, and who was active in the second half of the thirteenth century in keeping the abbey's history up to date. His *Historia de rebus gestis Glastoniensibus* had the avowed intention of increasing the prosperity of the abbey in a period when its independence was again threatened by the bishop.

There was nothing exceptional about the revision of Glastonbury history. Thirteenth-century elaboration of the Glastonbury myths followed a pattern repeated at other religious houses that were anxious to press claims for very early foundations. For example, a chronicle of the monastery at Abingdon, produced about 1130, had attributed its origin to the West Saxon king Cissa, but by the late thirteenth century the story had been pushed back to the time of the mission sent to England at the request of Lucius. The monastery's founder was said to have been an Irish monk Abennus, who lived through the persecutions of the Emperor Diocletian, and who founded a successful religious community that was inherited by the English. Bede recorded the foundation of Ely Cathedral in 660 by Etheldreda, but by the twelfth century its foundation had been re-interpreted: Etheldreda merely rebuilt an older church founded by Augustine during his mission of 597, who established the church there because there were already holy men living there. The monastery at Ely had become the seat of a bishop in 1109 and the need of the monks to establish their independence of episcopal control became urgent. For once, development of myths at Glastonbury seems simply to have followed the external stimulus of secular literature, rather than answering to an internal need. The abbey made comparatively little of its association with Joseph at first, but it was an association that would steadily increase in importance as the middle ages progressed.

5

First Among Christian Nations

It was primarily to King Arthur, not Joseph of Arimathea, that Glastonbury owed its special status in the thirteenth and fourteenth centuries. Not until the early fifteenth century would Joseph finally eclipse the king of the Britons. The reason is largely political. Arthur was needed to help establish the English kings' right to rule over Britain before Joseph was recruited to press the claim for England's precedence over the other Christian nations.

Momentum built up gradually behind the cult of Joseph. As kings were mixed in their enthusiasm for Glastonbury's legends, so its abbots varied in their enthusiasm for Joseph at an abbey that never had to worry about a deficit of cults. Little interest was shown by Adam of Sodbury (1323–34), who entertained Edward III in 1331. During the abbacy of John of Breynton (1334–42) the Great Cartulary of Glastonbury Abbey was compiled, itemising its landholdings and how they came into the possession of the monastery. It seems that it was Breynton who commissioned a monk, known as John Sheen or John of Glastonbury, to write a new history of the abbey, known as the *Cronica sive Antiquitates Glastoniensis Ecclesie*, or *Chronicle of Glastonbury Abbey*. As to its purpose, the most likely interpretation is that it was written initially to counter a claim that the monks of Glastonbury were mistakenly remembering the wrong Patrick and that they should have remembered an abbot of Glastonbury and not the apostle of the Irish. But the abbey had other reasons for re-emphasising its ancient foundation, in particular its long running dispute with the bishops of Bath and Wells over episcopal jurisdiction, the right to appoint its own abbot and the right to retain the land that was given to the abbey.

Walter of Monnington became abbot in 1342 and it was during his tenure that Edward III had envisaged creating a new Round Table, a direct descendant of the Grail table. It was probably this that prompted a renewed interest in Joseph. And John's recently completed *Chronicle* might explain Edward III's interest in the genealogy of Arthur and finding Joseph's grave. In 1345 the king issued a royal writ to John Blome of London to search for the burial of Joseph at Glastonbury, on the basis that the location of his grave was the subject of a prophecy, probably the one quoted by John of Glastonbury. Later in the century a chronicler from Boston in Lincolnshire, known only by his initial 'R', claimed that the body was discovered in 1367, but evidence from Glastonbury itself suggests that this was not the case. Walter of Monnington did not pursue any active interest himself in Joseph. That changed with the election in 1375 of his successor, John Chinnock. In 1382 Chinnock restored the chapel of St Michael on Glastonbury Tor and adorned the altar with a triptych showing the Deposition from the Cross, with Joseph of Arimathea prominent. In 1382 he restored a chapel in the cemetery of the abbey and dedicated it to St Michael and St Joseph.

John of Glastonbury had plenty of new material on which to draw that would provide an updated account to replace William of Malmesbury's history, which had been tinkered with in the thirteenth century. He acknowledged his debt to his predecessors, William of Malmesbury and Adam of Domerham, and could draw on the recent Great Cartulary, and on secular literature, especially the Grail romances. In consequence, John's *Chronicle* gave a clear and definitive version of the Joseph legend at medieval Glastonbury.

John of Glastonbury included a 'Treatise of Joseph of Arimathea', essentially a retelling from the *Gospel of Nicodemus* and Robert de Boron, and then took the story forward that St Philip sent Joseph and his son Josephes to Britain with a party of disciples. Their adventures in Britain and founding of the church at Glastonbury are adapted from the *Estoire del Saint Graal*. The wattle church (the *vetusta ecclesia* of William of Malmesbury) they founded was then discovered with great joy by Phagan and Deruvian in 166. According to John, Pope Eleutherius also granted thirty years' indulgence for all Christians who visited the *vetusta ecclesia* and the church of St Michael on Glastonbury Tor, the first time that the latter church was drawn into the early history of Glastonbury. John also provided a genealogy that showed how Arthur was descended from Helains, a nephew of Joseph nine generations back.

All this was a synthesis of established stories. A crucial new source is brought into the legend of Joseph by the prophecies of a bard named Melkin. Melkin was not an invention of John of Glastonbury. John Leland, when he visited Glastonbury in the 1540s, discovered other literature attributed to the same man. Other sixteenth century historians referred to him, including William Camden, John Pits and John Capgrave. It has been argued that his name was a confusion of Maelgwyn of Gwynedd, a Welsh king and noted poet who died in 547. Leland understood him to have been a Welshman who trained as a bard and who flourished in the period before Merlin, whenever that was.

Melkin's prophecy concerning Joseph seems Delphic in its inscrutability, probably because it became mixed up with the story of Rainald, of Marksbury in

Somerset. Rainald was a crusader, perhaps joining the Ninth Crusade of 1270. He was captured by a Sultan who allowed his release only once he had arranged for the Sultan to be sent a handful of soil from the Glastonbury Abbey cemetery. Rainald's story is told by John in order to establish the international reputation of the 'island between two mountains where the noble Decurion Joseph of Arimathea rested'. On receiving a glove full of Glastonbury soil the Sultan is made to exclaim: 'Those who live there do not know what virtue there is in that earth; anyone, however great a sinner among a thousand men, if he is buried there, will hardly suffer the pains of hell'.[1]

The crucial part of the 'book of Melkin' was that:–

> Joseph of Arimathea found eternal slumber in a marble tomb, and he lies on a divided line next to the oratory's southern corner where the wickerwork is constructed above the mighty and venerable Maiden and where the aforesaid thirteen spheres rest. Joseph has with him in the sarcophagus two white and silver vessels, full of blood and sweat of the prophet Jesus. Once his sarcophagus is discovered, it will be visible, whole and undecayed, and open to the whole world. From then on those who dwell in that noble island will lack neither water nor the dew of heaven.[2]

In this passage something of Rainald's Arabian exploits seems to have infiltrated the language of Melkin's prophecies. It explains some otherwise odd phrases, such as reference to thirteen spheres (probably the twelve zodiac signs plus the sun), an obvious Islamic reference to the 'prophet Jesus' and a promise that the watery Somerset Levels will never lack water. The 'mighty and venerable maiden' was probably referring to an image of the Virgin Mary.

In short, Melkin said that when he came to Britain Joseph brought two cruets containing the blood and sweat of Christ, which were buried with him near the *vetusta ecclesia*. As the Church disapproved of the Grail legend as a heterodox fiction, its transmutation into two cruets was both wise and timely. Such relics actually existed. As related by Robert Grosseteste, bishop of Lincoln, Joseph was supposed to have collected the blood of Christ when he took him down from the cross and buried him. These relics were passed from father to son until they came into the possession of the Patriarch of Jerusalem. The Patriarch sent two ampoules containing the holy relics to Henry III in 1247. Perhaps it was this occasion that suggested Melkin's two cruets. It certainly sounded credible and gave the monks plausible evidence with which to promote his cult at Glastonbury.

Evidence of an early foundation was much more than a matter of local prestige. John of Glastonbury was one of the several monastic historians tasked with establishing the primacy his own religious house against the claims of rival churches. Even to a contemporary reader, it was obvious that not all of these histories could have been right. John Flete's history of Westminster Abbey claimed its foundation in 184, while Thomas Rudborne's history of St Swithun's priory in Winchester claimed that it had been founded by Lucius and consecrated by Phagan and Deruvian in 164. Rudborne placed Glastonbury's foundation during the reign of King Ine and was dismissive of its earlier and Arthurian pretensions. York Minster also claimed foundation by Phagan and Deruvian and the church of St Peter-upon-Cornhill in London claimed to have been founded by Lucius in 179. Most of these histories were based on earlier written accounts and on charters, whereas John's *Chronicle of Glastonbury Abbey* included more legends than the others, although as we have seen few of these originated in Glastonbury itself.

Other countries traced their origins back to the Apostles of Christ and by doing so claimed precedence as Christian nations over those nations that learned the Christian faith, as it were, not second hand but third hand. Perhaps the most illustrious of apostolic origins concerned St James the Great, one of the disciples who witnessed the Transfiguration of Christ. According to manuscripts of the seventh and ninth centuries he preached in Iberia in AD 40, during which time he saw a vision of the Virgin Mary and returned to Judea, where he was martyred by King Herod Agrippa I in AD 44, an event recorded in the New Testament *Acts of the Apostles*.[3] His friends are said to have carried his body across the sea to western Iberia, where he was buried at Compostela. In a slightly different version, although James was beheaded, his body was taken up and made whole again by angels who sailed to the western Iberian coast where a rock closed around the body, which was then moved to Compostela. The shrine at Santiago de Compostela was one of the three principal pilgrimage cults in medieval Christendom, along with the Holy Land and Rome. But it did not acquire this status without assiduous cultivation, for example by Bishop Diego Gelmirez who commissioned the *Historia Compostellana* in the twelfth century. The cult of St James made him Spain's national saint (and a warrior saint in the guise of James the Moorslayer). James became the patron saint of pilgrims and the emblem of the Santiago pilgrimage, the scallop shell, became the universal symbol of the medieval pilgrim.

France made strong claims too. Several apostles were said to have preached in France, including Martha, Mary Magdalene, Lazarus and St Philip, but its preferred national saint was Dionysus the Areopagite, also known as Pseudo-Dionysus but better known in France as St Denis (the Pseudo is not to imply pretentious fakery, but to distinguish him from the Greek God of the same name). Dionysus was converted at the Athenian law court, or Areopagus, after hearing St Paul preach. But the abbey of St Denis, near Paris, was founded where a different Denis had built a church on an island in the Seine and was martyred *c.* 250. The conflation of these two individuals, and with a third namesake, the influential neo-Platonist writer of the fifth century, began in the ninth century, initiated by Hilduin, abbot of St Denis. It has an obvious parallel with the alleged confusion of Patricks at Glastonbury.

Scotland also made claims for the high prestige of its Christian origins. Until the mid twelfth century the cathedral of St Andrews was thought to have been founded in the eighth century. But this tradition was re-worked from about 1165, coincident with a confrontation with England's Henry II over the independence of Scotland and its church. The origin of St Andrews was now placed as far back as the fourth century, when relics of St Andrew were brought to Scotland. St Andrew was one of the first apostles and was brother of Peter. Legend had it that he was martyred in AD 60 at Patras in Greece. His remains were said to have been removed to Constantinople in 357 at the behest of the Emperor Constantius, but after the city was sacked in 1204 they were taken to the monastery of St Andrew at Amalfi in Italy. In the mid twelfth century Scottish claims to the relics of St Andrew were adapted to synchronise with his removal to Constantinople. Two days before the relics were transferred, Regulus (or Rule), the abbot of Patras, was visited by an angel who charged him to take three fingers of the right hand, the bone of the forearm hanging down from the shoulder, one tooth and a knee cap, then conceal them. Some years later the same angel instructed Regulus to take them to the north-west end of the Earth where, with a company of holy men and virgins, he was to found a church. It was prophesied that 'the whole west … will be graced forever by the wonders which shall be worked by his relics' and that the place 'chosen by God, shall be an Apostolic See forever … and it shall likewise be the staunch and steadfast anchor of the kingdom wherein it is situated'.[4] That place on the coast of Fife was, of course, St Andrews, which was therefore founded long before the pagan English were converted by Augustine in 597. It also reminded the English that St Andrews deserved to take precedence over the archdiocese of York, which had imperial ambitions in Scotland.

St Andrew's relics were used to argue that the Scots were among the first to receive the faith, and that Scotland should have privileges and prerogatives consonant with a nation whose saint was the brother of Peter. In 1299, the period when Edward I wanted to colonise Scotland, Pope Boniface VIII wrote a letter to the English king saying that he supported Scottish independence because Scotland had been converted by the relics of the blessed apostle Andrew. Reference to St Andrew was also made in a letter written in 1320 on behalf of the Scottish nobility to Pope John XXII, popularly known as the Declaration of Arbroath. It claimed Scotland's right to independence and refuted claims that the English king was their overlord. Scotland's precedence over England as a Christian nation was part of their argument:–

The high quality and deserts of these people, were they not otherwise manifest, gain glory enough from this: that the King of kings and Lord of lords, our Lord Jesus Christ, after his Passion and Resurrection, called them [the Scots], even though settled in the uttermost parts of the earth, almost the first to His most holy faith. Nor would he have them confirmed in that faith by merely anyone but by the first of his Apostles—by calling, though second or third rank—the most gentle St Andrew, the Blessed Peter's brother, and desired him to keep them under his protection as their patron forever.

At the time England had no recognisable strong claim to apostolic conversion and in the inter-state politics of the day it needed one.

The status of national churches was high on the ecclesiastical agenda in the period of the Great Schism, beginning also a long period in which spiritual matters were at the forefront of secular politics. In 1378 an Italian, Urban VI, was elected pope, but the French cardinals withdrew their support for him and elected a French rival, Clement VII. This was the beginning of the Great Schism, the era of two popes, one in Rome, the other in Avignon. England, Italy and the Germanic countries supported Pope Urban VI in Rome, while France and the Celtic countries supported his rival in Avignon. This did not mean that the authority of Rome was accepted wholesale by any of the parties that supported Urban VI, far from it. The church was seen increasingly in nationalist terms and the right of the pope to interfere in the governance of churches on foreign soil was increasingly resented.

The sense of a national church naturally drew in secular rulers who had their own reasons for cultivating it. Throughout the fourteenth century the English Parliament had sought greater control over the administration of the church in England, at the same time as it acquired a greater sense of nationhood. Alien priories—religious houses that owed allegiance to a mother house in France—were suppressed during the Hundred Years' War. The church began to propagate the notion of the king as a 'soldier of Christ' and British saints like Chad, Winifred, St John of Beverly and David were promoted with new feast days. Another, unplanned manifestation of this tendency was Lollardy, the loose movement that followed John Wyclif, who challenged the authority of church institutions and championed instead the inner religious life. Legends that promoted the independence of the national church, that demonstrated the apostolic conversion of Britain without being mediated by Rome, and the descent from the apostles of the heroic British king Arthur, were all useful in challenging the international ecclesiastical hierarchy. That would be the contribution of Glastonbury to international politics. The legend of Arthur was also useful in confounding attempts to secure independence from England of the Welsh church, by lobbying to ensure that the pope did not elevate the diocese of St David's to an archdiocese.

The most successful attempt to heal the divisions in the Catholic church, to reconcile the desire for a unified church in an international atmosphere of emerging nations, was known as the conciliar movement. It tried to organise the church into a council of five voting nations—Italy, Germany, Spain, France and England. None of them were nations in the form we understand them today, although England and France were the closest to becoming them. The movement wanted decentralisation and a greater role for nations, promoting a concept of church and nation as a single entity that had strong appeal among the English.

The conciliar movement had to conduct its business in an atmosphere of considerable national tensions. The challenge to the pope's authority was felt as a loss of status by Italians. Relations between France and England were soured by the Hundred Years' War and especially by the battle of Agincourt in 1415. France continually argued that England was too small a nation to represent a fifth of Christendom. England's counter claim that it was as rich and populous as France, Spain, Germany and Italy fooled nobody, and yet England seemed to be too large to consign to the margins. There were four councils in the early fifteenth century during which the status of Christian nations was at issue: Pisa in 1409, Constance in 1414, Pavia-Siena in 1424 and Basle in 1434. Each of them was attended by an English delegation that included the abbot of Glastonbury and the bishop of Bath and Wells.

At the Council of Pisa in 1409 the English delegation argued that national rule should prevail over Rome, and that western Christendom was a union of nations. England was equal with France, Spain, Italy and Germany. The English envoy, Bishop Robert Hallum of Salisbury, argued that England's national rights had been denied because it was under the rule of the papacy. To stake his claim he invoked the legend of Joseph of Arimathea and sought to bring forward the date of conversion earlier than the accepted date of AD 63, largely to counter the French claims that they had been converted first through Saints Mary Magdalene, Martha and Lazarus. England should not play second fiddle to Rome; it had claims to apostolic conversion even more ancient.

The second of the great councils convened at the southern German town of Constance (Konstanz) in October 1414 and continued until 1417. It was summoned on the initiative of Sigismund, king of the Romans, and was to be the most successful meeting of the conciliar movement. One pope resigned, the other was deposed, and a new pope, Martin V, was elected. Nevertheless, simmering national tensions, rather than cooperation, mark the exchanges between English and French delegations. The two nations evidently found it difficult to treat each other as equal partners. Cardinal Guillaume Fillastre recorded the exchanges between the French and English delegations. Cardinal Pierre D'Ailly, the advocate of the king of France, claimed that 'it is manifest that the kingdom of England, particularly as regards its ecclesiastical status ... forms but a thirtieth part of Christendom and the Church, not even a fourth of the kingdom of France' and if so then France should have six or seven times the voting power of England. The French also noted the refusal of Wales and Scotland to accept the authority of the king of England. Also to be taken into account was 'the excellence of the kingdom of France and the length of time since it received the faith of Christ, from which it has never deviated, as compared with the kingdom of England'.[5] Only at the end of its written submission had the French delegation boasted of the antiquity of the French church, but it was this that rankled most with the English, perhaps because antiquity was the one and only issue in which the English were confident of their case.

England's riposte was the work of Thomas Polton, later to be elected Bishop of Worcester. Polton had held a number of livings in Somerset parishes from the early 1390s and probably had first-hand knowledge of Glastonbury traditions. He argued that the English nation should include all those nations that were obedient to the king of England, principally Wales, Scotland and the Irish kingdoms, and pointed out that St Helen had given birth to Constantine, the first Christian Emperor of Rome, in the city of York. The trump card, however, was the rival claims concerning Joseph of Arimathea and Dionysus the Areopagite:–

> if they would consider the time when the kingdom of England first received the faith of Christ and when the kingdom of France did; and how Christ's faith has persisted continuously in England up till now, despite the fact that for periods a great wave of unbelieving savages stormed into the kingdom in a partial attempt to eradicate the Christian faith there, they would not have written as they did. For immediately after Christ's Passion Joseph of Arimathea, a noble Decurion, who took Christ down from the cross, came to England with twelve companions to a vineyard to be cultivated early for the Lord, and converted the people to the faith. The king gave them twelve hides of land, and assigned the diocese of Bath as the livelihood. They are buried in the abbey of Glastonbury ... according to written testimony, and the abbey is known to have been endowed from early times with those twelve hides. But France received the faith of Christ at the time of St Denis and through his ministry.[6]

The status of Joseph, an apostle of Christ himself, was compared favourably against that of Dionysus the Areopagite, who was only a follower of St Paul and had not known Christ personally. But there was one fatal flaw in the English argument. According to the 'written testimony' that Polton cited, Joseph was with the apostle Philip in France before journeying to England, and so France self-evidently received the faith before England.

In spite of their bickering, Constance was a success. A council of five nations was established that could resolve important issues and unite the church. England, although the smallest, enjoyed equal status with the other four major components of European Christendom. But its position remained precarious. The status of England was questioned at the council of Siena in 1424 by Spain, Scotland and France, when the bishop of Lincoln, Richard Fleming, again invoked Joseph. At the council of Basle in 1434 the authenticity of England's claims came under even closer scrutiny from the Castilian ambassador, Alphonso Garcia de Sancta Maria, who was Dean of the churches of Segovia and Compostela. Until now the Glastonbury legends had evolved locally and the works were read by those who were inclined to be sympathetic to them, and so they had not been rigorously tested. At Basle the authority of one written account was challenged by the authority of another. According to the *Golden Legend* compiled by the Italian chronicler Jacobus de Voraigne (1230–98) Joseph was freed from Jerusalem in AD 70 and therefore could not have founded a church at Glastonbury as early as was claimed. Secondly, even if he did reach Britain, Joseph converted only one corner of England—the remainder was pagan for centuries to come and had to be converted by Augustine's papal mission. This put Joseph below the status of the apostle St James. The English were ready with counter arguments. James was slaughtered by Herod at Jerusalem and the notion that his body was carried as far as Spain stretched credulity too far. The *Golden Legend* was dismissed as a pious fiction and it was pointed out that no apostle of Christ, not Joseph nor James nor even Denis, had ever converted a nation single-handed.

The English delegation could have resolved the matter decisively if only the monks of Glastonbury could discover the graves of Joseph and his fellow missionaries. Cynical historians have not been slow to point out that Arthur's grave was found in 1191, just when it was needed, and that the discovery of the burial was to all intents and purposes staged. As a publicity coup, the discovery of Joseph would have far outstripped the discovery of Arthur, and yet a search for the remains of Joseph of Arimathea by the monks of Glastonbury, supposedly masters of forgery and propaganda, was not successful.

It seems likely that Henry V requested a search for Joseph's grave at Glastonbury. In 1421 the new abbot, Nicholas Frome, wrote to the king to update him on excavations made at Glastonbury in 1419 under John Chinnock, who of course was a strong advocate of the Joseph legend. In part of the abbey cemetery three graves were found at the considerable depth of 14 feet, which is more plausible than it sounds. Arthur's grave had also been found at a great depth not, as was then supposed, to protect it from pagan Saxons, but because the ground had been raised during Dunstan's abbacy in the tenth century. Two of the graves contained the remains of individuals but in the third grave were the relics of twelve individuals. The reader of the abbot's letter is left to put two and two together. Might the twelve be the original missionaries sent to Britain in AD 63, and might the individuals be Phagan and Deruvian who came here a century later, as related by Gildas and Bede, and named by Geoffrey of Monmouth? Within one of the abbey's chapels:–

under the southern corner of the altar another coffin was found with the bones of a decayed man. This coffin was adorned most excellently beyond the others, with linen cloth inside all over. And because it excelled all the others in delicacy of scent and eminence of place it was enclosed in another large coffin until clearer notice of it will be able to be had in the future.[7]

Again, no conclusion is drawn. That is left to the reader, with the obvious implication that it was Joseph, but that there was more to discover about the remains than had hitherto been carried out.

The arguments put forward at Constance would have made the timing of Joseph's discovery perfect, and yet the abbot never pressed a claim. There could be several reasons for this. His letter may have been designed to prepare the ground for a major revelation that could be timed to coincide with a royal visitation. If this was intended, the scheme died with the death of Henry V in 1422. Nicholas Frome may have lacked his predecessor's enthusiasm for the project, and he may have been unconvinced by the results of the excavations. The monks were probably under considerable pressure to locate the grave and so Frome may have chosen his words carefully so as not to disappoint the king and fall out of favour. Or perhaps the abbot was disappointed and did not want to break the bad news to the king, using suggestive language that kept alive the possibility of finding Joseph's grave.

The trickiest aspect was that the excavated remains would have to be reconciled with the prophecy of Melkin, as related in John's *Chronicle*. The perfect nature of the body and the presence of two cruets are an essential part of Melkin's prophecy. Excavators would need to verify it in order to make a convincing case that the body of Joseph had been discovered, and yet they did not produce a perfect body and there were no cruets. Perhaps the monks were just baffled by what they found. The discovery of the multiple grave is intriguing, and could not be vouchsafed after the event. Apparently the bones of the twelve corpses 'were so ingeniously and so finely arranged within the casket that after their extraction, indeed, nobody there knew how to arrange them again in the aforesaid casket'.[8]

Glastonbury Abbey would never claim that it had found the grave of Joseph, and within a decade the urgency of the project had passed. The conciliar approach was rejected by the time of Basle and the issue became a largely academic one. But the continual reference to Joseph at Glastonbury by senior English churchmen testifies that Joseph had become an integral component of England's national interest, and he had far outstripped the local status of an English monastery and its pilgrim trade.

In fact the monks at Glastonbury did have theories about the grave of Joseph. What we know of them emerges at second-hand after the Reformation, by those who had been associated with the abbey before its dissolution in 1539. According to William Good (1527–86), who served as an acolyte at Glastonbury Abbey just before it was dissolved, and who was later a Jesuit priest in Italy, there had been plenty of incentive to find it:–

> The monks never knew for certain the place of this saint's burial, or pointed it out. They said the body was hidden most carefully, either there [at Glastonbury], or on a hill near Montacute, which they called Hamden Hill [i.e. Ham Hill], and that when his body should be found, the whole world should wend their way thither on account of the number and wondrous nature of the miracles worked there.[9]

The autobiography of another Jesuit, William Weston (c. 1550–1615), describes episodes as a missionary working in England from 1584 until his arrest in 1586. It includes a meeting with a man living near Glastonbury who had served at the abbey in the years before the dissolution. When the agents of Henry VIII arrived at Glastonbury to seize its relics, the man managed to retrieve a richly adorned crucifix and a nail that was said to have come from the Crucifixion and to have been brought to England by Joseph of Arimathea himself. Although the nail was eventually confiscated by the Anglican bishop of Salisbury, the man kept the reliquary that contained it, in the form of a cross and a box. He continued to make pilgrimage to a 'high mountain' where Joseph 'had fixed the seat of his abode' and where:–

> ancient foundations and confused ruins are still extant to be seen. To this place he told me that he was accustomed sometimes to ascend, out of a motive of religion and devotion, not on his feet, but on his knees, carrying with him the cross and the case of the nail as a safeguard against "attacks of spirits, for I have heard there wailings and groans and the mournful voices of people in grief" so that he thought it was some entrance and passage to the pains of Purgatory.[10]

He also kept a lamp burning in that part of his house that looked towards the hill. This was not Glastonbury Tor or Ham Hill (the Hamden Hill in William Good's above quote), but Montacute Hill, 14 miles south of Glastonbury.

The ruined medieval chapel of St Michael remained on the hill in the seventeenth century when it was still visited by recusants. By that time a slightly different story had come into circulation: 'in this chapel was found one of those nayles which fastened Our Saviour to the crosse, which a gentleman (Mr H) not farr of kept sometime and after sold for a greate sume of money to be transported beyond the seas'. Catholics visited it because 'they believe that ... the body of Aremathea ... was here interred'.[11] There was a tradition that Joseph was buried on this hill within sight of Glastonbury Tor. This could have been another reason why the abbey was reluctant to claim that they had found the bones of Joseph at Glastonbury. And they might not want the bones to be discovered at Montacute, a long way south of the abbey, which would divert pilgrims to a rival location and reduce the prestige of the abbey.

The emergence of Montacute into the story is intriguing because a holy cross was found there at the end of Canute's reign, in about 1035. Attention was said to have been drawn there by the persistent visions of a blacksmith working in Montacute village. The landowner, Tovi the Proud, ordered an excavation there which yielded a large and a small cross, a bell and a book known as the *Liber Niger*. The smaller cross was taken to the local church. The larger cross was put on a cart but the twelve oxen yoked to it were unable to pull it away. Only when Tovi mentioned his land at Waltham in Essex were the oxen able to move. It was taken immediately to Waltham where a church dedicated to the Holy Cross was founded. It was venerated by, among other people, Harold Godwinson, and 'the Holy Cross' was the English battle cry at Hastings. The Glastonbury monks would have known about the legend because Henry of Blois had been a dean of Waltham before he was elected abbot of Glastonbury in 1126. Trained as a Cluniac, Henry might even previously have been at Montacute Priory, which was founded in the first decade of the twelfth century. James Carley has pointed out that the account of digging at Montacute in 1035 bears a suspicious resemblance to the accounts of excavations for Arthur at Glastonbury in 1191, although that may be just an example of a formulaic description. Perhaps the monks suspected that the real resting place of Joseph of Arimathea was not Glastonbury but Montacute, and that the Holy Cross discovered there in 1035 was associated with it.

As Joseph's story emerged in religious literature so it flourished in secular literature. Grail legends were popular in medieval romances, derived mainly from French texts rather than Joseph's cult at Glastonbury. An English alliterative poem *Joseph of Arimathie*, appeared in about 1350. It was based on the earlier French romances and therefore did not mention Glastonbury. In the final quarter of the fourteenth century the verse romance *Titus and Vespasian, or the Destruction of Jerusalem* was written. It draws on Robert de Boron's story of Joseph's imprisonment in Jerusalem until freed by Titus, but does not take the story to Britain, let alone Glastonbury. By the fifteenth century Joseph's connection to Glastonbury was harder to ignore. Herry Lovelich's *History of the Holy Grail* (c. 1450) is derived from French romance, including the deeds of Joseph's fictional son Josephes. Lovelich tweaked some of the earlier legends in the *Estoire*, for example that the body of Josephes was taken to an English monastery, whereas in previous accounts the body of Josephes was taken to a Scottish monastery, where its presence ended a terrible famine. Instead, and invoking the prophecies of Melkin, Lovelich has the body of Joseph at Glastonbury Abbey. By far the most popular work of the period was Thomas Malory's *Le Morte d'Arthur*, written about 1469–70 and successfully printed and published by William Caxton in 1485. Joseph's activities in England are documented although his connection with Glastonbury is not made specific. Glastonbury is where Lancelot takes the body of Guinevere to be buried.

Until well into the sixteenth century Geoffrey of Monmouth's *History of the Kings of Britain* remained the most authoritative account of Britain's history. Geoffrey had not mentioned Joseph or Glastonbury, but John Hardyng's verse *Chronicle*, the latest version of which was completed in 1465, merges the Grail legends with Geoffrey's history of kings, romance with chronicle, and adapts it to his main theme: the right of England to rule over Scotland. Unlike many medieval authors, Hardyng's star waned in subsequent centuries and the most modern edition of his work was published as long ago as 1812. Over his life Hardyng had presented sixteen documents to Henry V, Henry VI and Edward IV, purporting to show that Scottish kings had declared themselves vassals of Edward the Confessor. These have been widely condemned as crude forgeries which, coupled with the perceived 'doggerel stupidity' of his verse, are the reasons why Hardyng's *Chronicle* has never been taken seriously. But to his contemporaries and near contemporaries he was a more credible source. A printed version was published in 1543 and it was read by Holinshed and Spenser among others. He is therefore an important channel through which the Joseph legend emerged as popular history. Arthur's Round Table, for example, is credited in an early version as an exact copy of the table made by Joseph for the Grail knights, and in a later version is one and the same table. In Hardyng's version the Holy Grail has receded in importance, but other ingredients in the story, including the early church and other Glastonbury foundation myths such as the granting of the twelve hides, are prominent.

Hardyng had his theories on the origin of the English flag. When Joseph converted the British king Arviragus (who was great grandfather to king Lucius in the earlier origin myths, showing how the date of conversion had been put back in history) he gave him a silver shield on which he painted a cross in his own blood, a detail taken from the *Estoire del Saint Graal*. It was a neat retrospective story of the flag of St George:–

The Aremes were used in all Britayne
For comoun signe eche man' to knowe his nacioun
Fro hys enemyse Which nowe we call certayne
Seynt Georges armes

but the red cross is much older, a symbol of Britain's religious legacy and Christian pre-eminence:–

Which Armes here were hade after Crist passioun,
Full long afore seynt George was generate.[12]

Herry Lovelich also had Josephes preparing a battle shield with a cross of red cloth on a white background. It meant that the nation's flag was a native British invention even though its patron saint was a foreigner. The Cappadocian St George was a protector of soldiers and had become patron saint of England. Edward III had promoted his cult as he wanted association with a warrior saint. In 1415, in the aftermath of Agincourt, the feast of St George was declared a major festival by Henry V and all were expected to pray that the saint be the protector of the nation. Hardyng wanted to defend against the notion that St George is just a modern appropriation by showing that the red cross had antique authenticity in Glastonbury. In his *Chronicle* Galahad finds Joseph's shield in Glastonbury and takes it to the Holy Land where he establishes the Order of the Holy Grail. The cross is the emblem of this order and, when Percival brings home the heart of Galahad to be buried at Glastonbury, it is buried with the shield in Joseph's sepulchre.

Joseph of Arimathea had become a figure of popular history and romance, but he was not widely invoked as a saint. There have been few churches in England dedicated to him, largely because the patronage of most churches had been set-tled by the fifteenth century. He appears seldom if at all in medieval applied art such as stained glass or wall painting. The main reason for this is proba-bly that he had not appeared in early hagiographic collections such as Aelfric's tenth-century *Lives of Saints*, Mirk's fourteenth-century book of sermons, the *Festial*, or John of Tynemouth's fourteenth-century compendium of the saints of England, Scotland, Ireland and Wales, the *Santilogium Angliae Walliae Scotiae et Hiberniae*, or its revised version of the mid fifteenth century. A life of Joseph, the *De Sancto Joseph ab Armathia*, did appear in the *Nova Legenda Angliae* printed by Wynkyn de Worde in 1516, but this was only two decades before the Reformation.

Popular devotion to Joseph and other Glastonbury saints was expressed by pilgrimage. The town became busy with the traffic of pilgrims, not unlike the seekers of spirituality that come to the town today, and facilities were needed to accommodate at least the more affluent of them. To that end the George and Pilgrim Inn on High Street was built about 1450 by Abbot John Selwood and is one of the finest surviving pre-Reformation inns in Britain. The town was said to have ninety-five taverns in this period, a number that can only have included ordinary houses whose occupants let out rooms, although other pilgrim centres such as St Albans were well known for their proliferation of inns. Other facilities sprang up on the main pilgrimage routes. At Chapel Plaster near the Somerset-Wiltshire border, is a fifteenth-century chapel and hospital thought to have served Glastonbury pilgrims.

Glastonbury seems to have drawn most of its pilgrims from the south-west of England. At least, it is this local aspect that is best attested by contemporary documentary evidence. In wills the testators often asked for pilgrimages to be made in their memory to compensate for their own negligence during their lifetime. In 1532 James Hadley bequeathed offerings to be made at many Somerset churches, including Cleeve Abbey, the tiny coastal church of Culbone, and 3*d* to 'St Jophe', almost certainly referring to Joseph at Glastonbury. Another Somerset will, that of Sir Richard Place, vicar of Kingston near Taunton, stipulated for a pilgrim to offer 3*s* 4*d* to St Joseph, and lesser sums at other churches in Somerset, Dorset and Devon.

In the early fifteenth century the abbey produced for the edification of pilgrims the *Magna Tabula*, a large manuscript of six leaves mounted on wooden tablets and hung from a pillar. The most remarkable thing about the *Magna Tabula* is its survival—the leaves are now in the Bodleian Library. Only one other example, from York Minster, has survived but *tabulae* were common in the fifteenth century as a sort of guide book for pilgrims, in a form that was too large and heavy to be mislaid or stolen. Durham, Lincoln, Lichfield and Ripon cathedrals all had them, as did many monastic pilgrimage centres such as Bury St Edmunds. These tablets were especially favoured by churches that wanted to establish their ancient foundation, draw attention to indulgences, the relics held there, and to miracles that had occurred there. The Glastonbury tablets are just text, in verse or prose form, and therefore indicate a degree of literacy among pilgrims. These pilgrims were often literate people themselves, perhaps because they were priests. Alternatively, parties of pilgrims could have been accompanied by a literate chaplain, or the abbey itself might have offered guide services to visitors.

The tablets recounted the well-known legends of Joseph, Arthur and Dunstan, taken from William of Malmesbury and John of Glastonbury. They quoted from the *Gospel of Nicodemus*, named some of Joseph's companions, such as Nascien and Celidoine, noting the latter's marriage and acquisition of the kingdom of North Wales, inviting Welsh pilgrims into the Grail tradition. They informed visitors of all the saints that had been associated with Glastonbury, who came from all corners of Britain. Due weight was given to the Charter of St Patrick, to draw in the Irish pilgrims.

The cult of Joseph at Glastonbury was still being developed in the early sixteenth century. Joseph had a coat of arms created for him, a white shield with drops of blood around a central green knotted cross, flanked on either side by a golden ampoule. Encomiums extolled Joseph as the apostle of Britain and Glastonbury as its holiest ground. Glastonbury Abbey had no relics of Joseph, but in the early sixteenth century Abbot Richard Bere had a crypt built below the Lady Chapel (thus destroying any archaeological evidence for the *vetusta ecclesia* in the process), dedicated to him and where a shrine was set up. Some perspective is gained as to the relative status of Joseph at Glastonbury, however, when we remember that the major building project of this period was the chapel dedicated to King Edgar attached to the east end of the abbey church.

Richard Bere was appointed abbot in 1494 and served until 1525. He was a scholar and friend of Erasmus, a leading figure in the humanist movement, which makes him an unlikely standard bearer for the relatively conservative project of promoting the cult of saints. But the practical business of keeping the abbey finances in good order and secure in the long term, despite being one of the richest abbeys in England, may have encouraged a business-like approach to its pilgrims. There were also political factors to consider. Perkin Warbeck's rebellion in the West Country against Henry VII in 1497 implicated many, and was dealt with by the imposition of punitive taxes on Glastonbury property. The abbey had not supported the rebellion, but it had provided succour to the rebels in need. It is just possible that promotion of national cults of Joseph and King Edgar helped Glastonbury restore its prestige with the Crown. In the long run Henry VIII, who acceded to the throne in 1509, was to be no lover of Glastonbury or any other monastery. Joseph achieved his due place in Glastonbury Abbey just before the institution that promoted him was destroyed.

6

Protestants and Pilgrims

In November 1539 Richard Whiting, abbot of Glastonbury, was dragged on a hurdle to the summit of Glastonbury Tor, along with the abbey treasurer John Thorne and a young monk called Roger James. They were hanged there on Somerset's own Calvary, in which three gallows on the hill had all-too obvious biblical associations. The hanging was a carefully orchestrated public humiliation for an abbot, by now an old man in his late seventies, who dared to defy the will of the king. Henry VIII had personally approved the appointment of Whiting, but the king was guilty of a profligate lifestyle that the monasteries were now expected to pay for. In the three years that it had taken for the government to close down the monasteries of England and Wales, disband their communities and seize their assets, no other abbot had been treated as a common criminal. His severed head was placed on the abbey gateway as if he had been a traitor, and his quartered body was displayed at Wells, Bath, Bridgwater and Ilchester. It was an emphatic demonstration that the power of the monastery was finished.

The suppression of monasteries had begun in 1536 and by the spring of 1539 Glastonbury was the last abbey in Somerset to resist closure, while for the king's commissioners it was the greatest prize of them all. Henry VIII was well aware of the wealth of Glastonbury Abbey—only in 1522 the abbot had been able to loan £1,000 to the king to cover his expenses in France. Finally its monks were pensioned off, its estates were seized by the Crown and the church and cloisters stood empty. By rights its redundant legends and traditions should have died with it, as they did at other suppressed monasteries.

The Reformation of the 1540s was also a devastating attack on the religious culture that had nurtured and sustained the Glastonbury legends. Superstitious practices were condemned and swept away from the official church. Priests now spoke in English rather than Latin; the Bible was available for everyone to read, no longer a mysterious body of sacred knowledge communicated by the priesthood. Inside the parish churches of Glastonbury and elsewhere altars were stripped of their colourful vestments, candles were extinguished, statues were removed and images were painted over. Many of the latter were depictions of saints, who lost their status as intercessors between God and mortals in a brave new world that rejected the notion of purgatory. Logic would suggest a waning interest in Joseph of Arimathea, but the reverse was to be the case, if only eventually. Somerset parishes complied with new government laws and appear to have been more disposed to Protestantism than in some other parts of the country, but the religious instincts of many people remained traditional without being Catholic in a doctrinaire sense.

Amid the religious upheavals of the period the dispersal of Glastonbury's holiest relics appeared to attract little comment. Ironically, the one tomb that was remembered was one that never was—that of Joseph of Arimathea. In 1635 Sir William Brereton encountered 'a fair, capacious tomb, wherein they say Joseph of Arimathea was interred'.[1] Perhaps that tradition had grown up because there were no longer any monks to correct it. Shrines were evidently destroyed and the bones of saints destroyed or confiscated. Another casualty of the abbey's demise was the cult of kings. The graves and monuments to the Saxon kings Edmund I, Edmund Ironside and Edgar, were all lost. So were the memorial and relics of Arthur and Guinevere. Perhaps the monument to Arthur had long since served its political purpose. In any case Arthur was now arguably best memorialised not in the form of objects or even images, but in the word: Sir Thomas Malory's *Le Morte d'Arthur* had been published by William Caxton in 1485 and was to become the medium through which the Arthurian past was experienced. It is a fitting metaphor for the cultural shift of the Reformation period: the image and object gave way to the word, and the word in English at that.

In the immediate post-dissolution years the cult of Glastonbury lived on in the form of two miraculous trees, which now assumed a much higher profile than they had previously enjoyed. A walnut tree in the grounds of the abbey and a thorn tree at the foot of Wearyall Hill, just south of the town, enjoyed a more or less equal status in the century after the abbey was closed. Neither of them was associated directly with Joseph of Arimathea. They are first mentioned in an anonymous verse *Lyfe of Joseph of Aramthia* in 1520, although for how long before then they had been revered is unknown. There were apparently three hawthorns growing on Wearyall Hill that blossomed at Christmas:–

The Hawthornes also, that growth in Werall
Do burge and bere grene leaves at Christmas
As fresh as other yn May.[2]

On the eve of the suppression of monasteries, commissioners were appointed by the government to audit the property and financial assets of religious houses.

Somerset monasteries were visited by Dr Richard Layton. He sent from Bristol
two flowers from the thorn that were said to have blossomed on Christmas Eve.
It might be proof that the abbey was promoting the cult of the holy thorn, but
there is good reason to be sceptical. Visitors were instructed to report evidence
of monkish superstition and pious racketeering, and wherever they looked for
it they inevitably found it. Layton was good at his job. For example, he sent
from Bath Abbey other examples of what he deemed to be phoney relics, like
the chains of St Peter and the combs of women saints, all of which were used by
women for superstitious purposes. The thorn tree was useful ammunition with
which to attack the monastery.

As the thorn was a winter tree, the walnut tree growing by the Lady Chapel
was a summer tree. It was said never to have sprouted before St Barnabus Day
(11 June). These two trees acquired something of a national reputation—what
we know of the trees in the early post-Reformation years is learned from people
who came from far afield. William Camden, whose *Britannia* was published in
1586, was anxious to avoid appearing credulous, but the trees were impossible
to ignore: 'I shall be reckon'd among those in our age who are taken with every
fable, should I speak anything of the *Wallnut tree* ... or the *Hawthorn-tree* which
buds on Christmas-day as if it were in May; and yet (if one may be trusted) these
things are affirmed by several credible persons'.[3] The thorn was also mentioned
in John Gerard's *Herball* of 1597, which was a work of natural history. The
thorn was so well known by the late seventeenth century that Sir Charles Sedley
could use it to flatter a mature lady by comparison with it:–

> Cornelia's charms inspire my lays,
>   Who, fair in nature's scorn,
> Blooms in the winter of her days,
>   Like Glastonbury Thorn.[4]

The fame of Glastonbury's trees was spread across all social classes, and across
the religious divide separating diehard Catholics and establishment Protestants.
James Montagu was bishop of Bath and Wells from 1608 to 1616 and combined his position with the role of royal chaplain. One Christmas he organised
at Wells a 'panegyricall entertainment' for Anne of Denmark, the crypto-Catholic
queen of James I. Four characters represented saints Peter, Paul, Andrew (patron
saint of the cathedral church) and Joseph. He had the character of Joseph of
Arimathea declare to the queen: 'I am the herald of these saints Peter, Paul, and
Andrew, sent hither by them full fifteene hundred and fortie yeares agoe, to bring
the waters of life into this isle of britayne'. In a new twist to legends concerning
the grave of Joseph he then declares: 'I rested from my labours, and my body

lay buried in a grave of honour, hoping yerely that since I had that honour to intombe that blessed body, no body would have done themselves that dishonour, as to have violated my sepulchre'. So Joseph deserved to rest in peace, unviolated by seekers after relics and liberated from the prophecies of Melkin. Then he gave to the queen two branches, one from the thorn, one from the walnut tree:–

> I have nothing left mee, but these boughs; the one a Branch of that Thorne, that in memory of my blessed Maister ever buddeth on the day that he was borne. The other in memory of his martyrs, which [on] the longest day begins to live. [St Barnabus day was sometimes regarded as the longest day].[5]

This is the first known occasion when Joseph and the thorn are directly linked, but the thorn had no special status above the walnut tree.

Whether or not visitors to these trees should be called pilgrims or just curious sightseers, came they did. By the 1630s the walnut tree was in a sorry state, however, victim of the enthusiasts who broke off branches as souvenirs or carved their names on its trunk. In cultural terms this was a very medieval practice and reminiscent of pilgrims who chipped off bits of shrines to be used as talismans. According to Richard Broughton in 1633 the tree 'keepeth the same miraculous course every yeare in florishing', but 'when I sawe it of late yeares' the branches were 'too small, younge and tender' to fruit and bear nuts. Two decades later Elias Ashmole, in his *Theatrum Chemicum Brittanicum* (1652), could only write of the walnut tree that 'anciently grew in Glastenbury Church-yard'. Henceforth the walnut tree disappears from the Glastonbury mythology.

The thorn suffered the same kind of attention and was hacked and scratched to within an inch of its life, as recorded in the travels of Sir William Brereton in 1635:–

> hereof I took a special view, brought away many branches and leaves, and left the first letters of my name thereupon record; the tree and bark is much decayed (as I conceive) by this practice of those that visit it; many of the boughs and branches are much broken off, and it is much blemished hereby, as being very naked; none almost resort thither without making bold with a branch'.[6]

In 1635, having lost many twigs and branches to souvenir hunters, it looked 'as if it would not flourish in Summer, much lesse sprout forth on that nipping day in Winter'. But it did continue to flourish. By the mid seventeenth century people gathered by it at Christmas Eve and kept a candlelight vigil until the tree blossomed.

The thorn aroused strong feelings for and against, and in the mid seventeenth century became a symbol of a divided religion. Richard Broughton was writing in the 1630s, the decade when the Archbishop of Canterbury, William Laud, was moving the Church of England back in the direction of Catholicism. There were grounds for optimism among the recusant priests like himself who were exiled in Europe. So the annual blossoming of the thorn could be taken as a vindication of Laud and Charles I. Broughton went further and implied that the survival of the tree was proof of the uncorrupted truth of Catholicism. When he saw it the trunk was:–

> so cut and mangled rounde about in the barke by engraving the letters of peoples names resorting thither ... how the sap and nutriment should be diffused from the roote, to the bowes and branches thereof, which also be so maimed and broken of by the corners thither, to carry them away for shew ... a marvaile it is, how it can continue any vegetation or growing at all.[7]

And yet, despite growing on a hillside otherwise naked of trees (as hawthorns have a tendency to do), 'the armes and bowes are spred and dilated in a circular manner as farre, or father than other trees freed from such impediments'.

Godfrey Goodman, who had been deposed as bishop of Gloucester during the Civil War, interpreted the thorn as a recent manifestation, a sign of God's anger at the dissolution of the monasteries. Writing in *The Two Great Mysteries of Christian Religion* (1653) he argued that 'it may well be that this white-thorn did then spring, and began to blossom upon Christmas day, to give a Testimony to Religion, that it might flourish in Persecution, as the Thorn did blossom in the coldest time of Winter'.[8] So the thorn was a symbol of religious defiance, springing up when the monasteries were pulled down. A good reason, then, for it to be a target among hardline Puritans.

The first known attempt to cut down the thorn tree occurred at the end of the sixteenth century. It failed, and Richard Broughton was able to explain why. The tree branched naturally into two main trunks, of which:–

> a prophane Protestant endeavouring to cut downe the greatest, and likely both, if God had not miraculously prevented his wicked designement, was extraordinarily punished by cutting his legge, and one of the chips he hewed of, flying up to his head put out one of his eyes, was enforced to desist.

He failed to detach it entirely from the main trunk, and so it refused to die:–

> having cut downe the greater Trunke only, except a little of the barke on one side, this body of the tree so separated from the roote, and lying upon the grounde 30 years together, still continued the miraculous flourishing ... and

after being taken quite away, and cast into a ditch farre of from this place, it likewise flourished and budded as used before.[9]

The tree, then, was a dispenser of divine justice and could be seen as a metaphor for defiant Catholicism, which the destructive years of the Reformation could never kill off. Retribution would always therefore befall the desecrators. James Howell, in a royalist allegory *Dodona's Grove* (1645), made much of the retributive punishment experienced by the 'prophane Protestant'.

A further attempt to be rid of the tree was made during the Commonwealth. John Eachard had heralded the miracle of the flowering thorn as a vindication of Christmas, in a pamphlet entitled *Good Newes for all Christian Soldiers* in 1644. For hardline Protestants, Yuletide was simply another frivolous, ungodly and superstitious anathema, and the thorn's association with it made it vulnerable. The *Weekly Post*, a Royalist newsbook, reported in its post-Christmas issue in 1654 that a 'Canaanite' had attempted to cut down the tree but the axe had rebounded and sliced through his leg, which was turning gangrenous. Other evidence suggests that the axe had done its intended job. The Anglican minister at Rayne in Essex, Edward Symmons, writing in a pamphlet *A Vindication of King Charles* in 1648, pointed the finger at 'Militia men' who cut it into pieces 'that it might no longer Preach unto men, the Birth day of their Saviour'.[10] According to William Annand, writing in 1670, the tree had been grubbed up by the roots and burned to ashes by zealots because it was guilty of the old superstition. All that was left now were descendants from the original tree, to which attention was subsequently redirected.

The history of the holy thorn provides a good case study of the disenchantment of the natural world, of how the supernatural became natural, how superstitious ignorance was replaced by rational study. The Glastonbury thorn belonged to a world which was and continued to be regarded in supernatural terms. This state of affairs was not, of course, a creation of Protestantism, but was a cultural legacy built up over many centuries. And the dismantling of it has been a long process too. The comments by William Camden, writing as early as 1586, remind us that for a long time there had been people sceptical of supernatural agency.

In the Bible supernatural events associated with trees signal the presence of the divine, a means by which a message is delivered. God announced his presence to Moses through the medium of a burning bush. Later, to settle a dispute over which of the tribes of Israel should assume the priesthood, God told Moses to bring a staff from each of the twelve tribes and communicated his judgment when Aaron's staff blossomed, flowered and produced almonds by the following day.[11] The winter-blossoming thorn was therefore understood to be a sign. The problem was in how to interpret it.

In many religions plants and trees either embody supernatural powers or they host them. Pliny the Elder documented the veneration of trees in the pagan ancient world, where individual trees like the famous oak of Dodona dedicated to Zeus, were associated with particular Gods. Tacitus wrote of the hallowed groves of the Germanic tribes, which were a gateway to the underworld of spirits. Ireland provides evidence too, in the story of 'Finn and the man in the tree', where Finn encounters a man up a tree, with a blackbird on his right shoulder and a bronze vessel in his left hand, in which a trout was swimming. It was the presiding deity of the tree. Strange deities still dwelt in trees in the Christian era. St Wulfstan famously rid a walnut tree at Longney in Gloucestershire of the devil who was residing in it. The point here is not to reveal the pagan origin of Christian beliefs, but to highlight that seeing the divine in the natural world has been a universal reflex.

Belief in the supernatural properties of plants and trees remained widespread in the Protestant centuries. The role of plants as charms is implicit in otherwise innocent uses of them during the ritual year, from holly and ivy at Christmas, willow branches on Palm Sunday, May blossoms on May Day and box and bays at funerals. People hung mistletoe over their doors to protect against witchcraft. Some of these beliefs were less innocent. Mandrake roots were credited with powerful magical and aphrodisiacal properties. The roots occasionally grew into the rough shape of a human figure, shrieked when they were pulled from the ground, and supposedly grew under gallows from the seeds of hanged men. Unscrupulous counterfeiters were known to carve human shapes from the roots of other plants like bryony, and sell them to women who wore them around their necks to help them conceive.

Individual trees were still venerated in the seventeenth century. Perhaps the most famous example is a secular one, the Boscobel oak, the tree in which Charles II was said to have hidden after his ignominious defeat at the Battle of Worcester in 1651. Enthusiasts cut branches from that tree too. And it was no different to the visitors who chipped pieces off the stones at Stonehenge as souvenirs. Anglican bishops such as James Montagu, mentioned above, mined their rich Catholic heritage when they needed to, but modified it so that they remained within the bounds of a Protestant world view. The cuttings of the walnut and thorn were presented to the Queen merely as mementoes; he did not suggest they had any magical or talismanic powers, even if he did speak of Glastonbury as 'the goodlyest Monastery that ever eye in any Island did behold'.

Trees with magical properties have also been documented after the Reformation. In 1561 a tree at St Donats in Glamorgan blew down and a crucifix was discerned in the grain of its trunk. The pagan and animistic tones of such events were anathema to Puritans, who sometimes took action to destroy them. For example, a tree overhanging a spring at St Endellion in Cornwall was destroyed in Elizabethan times. Catholic and Puritan embody opposing views of the natural world. The Catholic and traditional view was that God revealed himself in certain special places like trees and springs, or places where saints had performed miracles; the Puritan view was that all places were equal, that God was everywhere, and therefore they rejected any place that seemed to be acquiring cult status. The latter was religious and rational, but was not really a scientific view.

The Reformation did not destroy cultural and religious traditions, but it did engender a subtle shift in the view of nature. It is possible to view the thorn and walnut tree as substitutes for the venerated relics that were confiscated when Glastonbury Abbey was closed down in 1539. They were living things that embodied a divine message, but had no other miraculous power or virtue. That these trees received widespread attention outside of the locality was due primarily to the reputation that Glastonbury had built up as a place of sanctity. It is culturally Catholic, or at least a relic of 'traditional religion' in the historian Eamon Duffy's phrase, although it was not inimical to Protestants. It has also been pointed out that emphasis on the sanctity of natural places was a classic counter-Reformation strategy, which had particular relevance to Catholics in England and Wales who could no longer worship in church. Instead they often chose special natural places. In Ireland, at the height of the Protestant repression, Catholics held masses at special mass bushes, usually hawthorns. The Glastonbury thorn, then, became an unspoken rallying point for Catholics, which is why writers such as Richard Broughton devoted so much attention to it.

But was its winter flowering really divinely determined? A debate began in the seventeenth century about whether the flowering of the thorn at Christmas was an act of nature or an act of God. Disdain for 'vulgar superstition' had been current in Elizabethan England, but in the next two centuries it was to intensify as rational knowledge and an attitude of scepticism increased. In the seventeenth century there were still plenty of people in Glastonbury prepared to vouchsafe the claims that the thorn blossomed on Christmas day, although all of these accounts have come down to us second-hand. Sir William Brereton was told in 1635 by a local minister that the thorn blossomed only for the twelve days of Christmas, and conversations with other local people seemed to confirm that status, as well as confirming that grafts of the original tree were found elsewhere in the town. Brereton did not challenge these eyewitness accounts. Once the original tree had been destroyed c. 1650 its properties could be vouchsafed only by oral testimony, and it seems that, the further this tree receded into the past, the more memories of it sharpened. Evidence about the tree was collected in a wider search for the spiritual presence in nature by the erstwhile vicar of St

Mary, Kidderminster, Richard Baxter (1615–91). One of his correspondents was Samuel Winney, vicar of St John in Glastonbury, but by 1659 he had to make enquiries among the older generation in the town.

> One ancient man tells me, that he hath gone on the Eve to it, and he hath found it like another dead thorn, without any blossom, or likelihood to have a sudden forwardness to it ... and he hath gone on Christmas-day, and found the blossoms as though it was the midst of May.[12]

An old woman told him that when she was living at the house of Sir Thomas Hughes in Wells in the first quarter of the seventeenth century, two men were sent to Glastonbury to verify the story about the thorn.

> On the Eve, towards night, they found it as another thorn, only the breaking out of the beginning of buds; and staying in Glastonbury all night, to observe, as near as might be, the time when they began to sprout forth into a perfect blossom, they have gone again toward the turn of the night, and have found the perfect blossom about two or three of the clock, so that at morning they have returned to their master with them.[13]

Descendants of the original tree were said to have retained its miraculous qualities. Another of Baxter's correspondents, John Chetwind, a pastor at Wells, noted that a thorn grafted from the original tree would 'bud and blossom near about that time, but not upon the day'. William Thomas, rector of Ubley, considered that this could be just because 'the soil is not so suitable to it'. However, Thomas struck a note of caution to those who had forgotten that Christmas was authenticated by the Bible, not the thorn.

> Christmass-day is not to gain its estimation from such a providence, but from scripture, from reason. ... The thorn might so blossom (by Providence) as a just hardening of the wilfully superstitious (a great part of whose religion is to put a crown upon Christmass-day, caring little for Christ), or as a trial of the truly conscientious, to see whether they will build their religion upon a famous thorn.[14]

Baxter may have believed in supernatural events but his correspondents show collectively a burgeoning scientific approach into the 'providential rarity' of the thorn. Thomas Fuller, writing in his *Church History of Great Britain* (1655), also acknowledged that the thorn was an 'annual Miracle' but found it hard to interpret because there was no obvious natural explanation. Protestants could accommodate these kinds of unexplained phenomena: 'God sometimes puts forth such questions and riddles in nature, on purpose to pose the pride of men conceited of their skill in such matters'. But such riddles often invite the notion that the devil is at work. 'The devil, to dandle the infant faith of fond people, works these petty feats and petty wonders, having farther intents to invite them to superstition, and mould them to saint worship thereby'.[15] Thomas Fuller saw no reason to associate the thorn with any supernatural agent. He knew of an oak in the New Forest that put out leaves at the same time, and it was always interpreted as a natural phenomenon. There were other winter-flowering thorns too. In the seventeenth century there was one at Parham in Suffolk, which attracted crowds on Christmas day, while the seventeenth-century antiquary John Aubrey knew of winter-flowering blackthorns on the road from Worcester to Droitwich, and naturally winter-flowering thorns on Romney Marsh in Kent.[16]

Field naturalists began their quest to identify and classify plants in the sixteenth century. Early classifications based, for instance, on medical properties, were superseded by more structured classifications by naturalists such as John Ray, before the Linnaean system became established in the eighteenth century. Most of these early naturalists were apothecaries and physicians, who enjoyed a close relationship with plants because they have medicinal properties. The positive medicinal effects of plants were at one time regarded as supernatural, and like all encounters with the supernatural, the medicine had to be prepared in the right way just like a religious ritual. Early naturalists therefore needed to separate the science from the superstition. Herbalists relied on local knowledge and customs, even into the eighteenth century, but their translation of traditional virtues into scientific properties was a social as well as a scientific process. A noted example is the old woman practising as a folk herbalist in Shropshire in the late eighteenth century who alerted Dr William Withering to the efficacy of using digitalis to treat heart disease. Erasmus Darwin subsequently published a scientific paper on it, after which he and Withering fell out, competing, apparently without irony, for the kudos of having discovered it.[17]

A necessary part of developing classifications based on natural history was that naturalists needed to emancipate themselves from fabulous tales. The Glastonbury thorn, like the mandrake root described above, was in this category. As early as 1608 Sir Hugh Platt reckoned that if the thorn blossomed on Christmas day it must have been the result of some 'philosophical medicine' applied to the root. Thomas Browne pointed out in his *Pseudodoxia Epidemica* (1646) that there were many 'precocious trees' and therefore that the holy thorn was not as special as people had assumed, noting that 'strange effects, are naturally taken for Miracles by weaker heads'.[18] Robert Plot, writing in 1676, suggested that the thorn may have been transplanted from a warmer climate and continued to flower at its traditional time of year, despite having been moved to a colder climate. In Staffordshire he discovered a pear tree that also blossomed at Christmas, but to Plot it was a problem of nature and not a supernatural event.

Philip Miller, in his *Gardener's Dictionary* which first appeared in 1731, knew of several grafts from the original tree that grew in gardens at Glastonbury 'as a curiosity'. Although they often flowered in winter and also in May they did not otherwise differ from the common hawthorn. Whether they blossomed on Christmas day or slightly later had nothing to do with the work of God, but depended on the mildness of the weather: 'the fabulous story of its budding on Christmas-day ... is now with good reason disbelieved'. By the time William Withering published *his Botanical Arrangement of British Plants* in 1787 the thorn had been thoroughly demystified, and was just a variety of the *cratoegus*, or hawthorn.

The cult of Joseph of Arimathea was not yet linked to the Glastonbury thorn, but its standing experienced a downward curve similar to that of the thorn in the century and half that followed the Reformation. For a while, Joseph would prove useful as an ally for scholars in Protestant rivalry with the church in Rome, just as he had done in the time of the conciliar movement in the fifteenth century. Thereafter Joseph declined in parallel with the holy thorn in the intellectual culture of the seventeenth century, one of the myths that society could comfortably leave behind.

The Reformation had not been kind to saints with their feast days, shrines and relics, but the Biblical saints fared much better than local saints. Joseph was mentioned in the Bible, even if only as a marginal figure, but memory of him was kept alive because his establishment of Christianity at Glastonbury had become part of the national story. William Camden, for example, did not doubt that Joseph had founded a church at Glastonbury, which saw 'the rise and fountain of all Religion in England'.[19] Joseph was also mentioned in Edmund Spenser's *The Faerie Queene* among the list of British kings:–

> ... good Lucius,
> That first received Christianity,
> The sacred pledge of Christ's Evangely.
> Yet true it is, that long before that day
> Hither came Joseph of Arimathy,
> Who brought with him the holy grayle, they say,
> And preacht the truth; but since it greatly did decay.[20]

Spenser learned his ancient history from medieval authors, notably Geoffrey of Monmouth, and probably learned of Joseph through the popularity of John Hardyng. The origin of Christianity in England remained a live issue now that the Church of England was in direct opposition to Rome. And yet the intellectual climate had changed since the time of the Great Schism when nations squared up behind their national saints. The humanist movement of late medieval Europe, Renaissance scholarship and the printing press had all contributed to an increase in knowledge. Some of the hoarier ancient myths were now exposed, affecting the Holy See of Rome as much as the remainder of Christendom. Scholars of the sixteenth and seventeenth centuries were much better informed than in the time of William of Malmesbury and even John of Glastonbury, and applied much closer scrutiny to early literature. But it would be a while before they could shed their prejudices against Rome.

Scholarship of the immediate post-Reformation period was more about politics than intellectual rigour. In the sixteenth century the establishment treated the Joseph legend as orthodox, which allowed the Church of England to claim apostolic purity, and to argue that Augustine's well-documented mission to England in 597 corrupted the English church with papist superstitions. Matthew Parker, archbishop of Canterbury from 1559 to 1575, was a strong exponent of the notion of the English episcopacy derived from Joseph, who arrived in Britain in AD 63. Richard Davies, bishop of St Davids and author of the preface to the Welsh translation of the New Testament, published in 1567, also stressed British religious independence, pointing out that the Anglo-Saxons had imported paganism and had then succumbed to Augustine's mission.

Catholics developed rival foundation arguments. In 1565 Thomas Stapleton published in Antwerp an English translation of Bede's *The history of the church of Englande*. The work mentioned neither Joseph nor Glastonbury. Stapleton and other Catholics argued that Augustine's mission was the third effort to convert the English. The second was the mission sent by Pope Eleutherius. Joseph of Arimathea was only one of the candidates for establishing Christianity in Britain, as there was a competing possibility that St Peter was the first to cross the English Channel. Other Catholic authors followed suit. Robert Parsons (1546–1610), from Nether Stowey in the Quantock Hills of Somerset, had been trained as an Anglican priest but became a Jesuit priest in Rome in 1575. In his *A Treatise of Three Conversions* (1603) he argued that England was subject to Rome because St Peter was the first to evangelise in Britain and Rome was the church of St Peter. That Rome was the mother church of Britain was reinforced when pope Eleutherius sent the first missionaries to England and converted King Lucius, and was reinforced again when Augustine was sent to England by Pope Gregory in 597. Perhaps Joseph lost some of his credibility among Catholics because he was championed by Protestants, leading them to seek a much more important founding figurehead. Compared to Peter and Paul, Joseph was a lesser saint.

Predictably, Parsons' arguments were dismissed as 'dreames and fancies' and 'conjectures' by Matthew Sutcliffe in his riposte, *Subversion of Robert Parsons* (1606). Testimonies that Peter was in Britain were deemed especially flimsy. The point was also made by Francis Goodwin (1562–1633), Bishop of Hereford. He argued that Parsons' claims were based on the work of the tenth-century Byzantine hagiographer Simon Metaphrastes, who was a 'notable lyer ... of notorious untruthes'. In an appendix to his *Catalogue of the Bishops of England* (1615) Goodwin championed the claims of Joseph of Arimathea and St Paul. Joseph came first: 'For Joseph of Arimathea, the testimonies of his coming here, and his actions here, they are so many, so cleere and pregnant'.[21] Goodwin cited the grant of twelve hides of land to the monks of Glastonbury, and described the inscription on a brass plate that was fixed to the wall of St Joseph's chapel and that, along with the *Magna Tabula*, had survived the Reformation. The continuity of the Anglican church was therefore traced back to the time of Joseph and was a vindication of England's independence from Rome. The relationship between Eleutherius and Lucius was one of brothers rather than the vicar and lieutenant relationship suggested by Parsons.

These early claims came under more rigorous scrutiny in the seventeenth century. The biggest problem for the Arimathean tradition was that it was not mentioned by any of the early authors, notably the Venerable Bede and before him Gildas, had become well known in the sixteenth century by publication of his work by Polydore Vergil. James Ussher, in his *Britannicarum Ecclesiarum Antiquitates* (1639) carefully examined the claims for Joseph as the founder of Christianity in Britain and detected monastic embellishment. In the same year Sir Henry Spelman published *Concilia, Decreta, leges, Constitutiones*, which discusses the early origins of the British church and the claims that apostles such as Peter, Paul and James visited Britain, as well as Joseph. Spelman (1562–1641), however, was a critic of the Joseph legends. In the introductory *Apparatus* to his study of Christian origins in Britain he looked closely at the evidence for Joseph of Arimathea that was then available. In particular he illustrated the brass tablet used by Goodwin to advance his case for Joseph and found that it was a late-medieval work, and therefore was not more authoritative than the early authors. This caused him to reject the Arimathean tradition and place the origin of Christianity in 185 with the arrival of Phagan and Deruvian.[22]

Both Ussher and Spelman were popular in the seventeenth century and spawned other polemical literature. Thomas Jones, actively anti-Catholic, published *Of the Heart and its Right Sovereign* (1678). It strongly reiterated the Anglican point of view that Joseph had come to Britain although, perhaps mindful of recent scholarship, he shed the story of some of its more fabulous episodes. As proof he cited extant manuscripts and charters, and the fact that it was tested at the great councils such as Constance but was not discredited. Analysis of later popish interventions concluded that Lucius was used as the pope's 'vicar' in Britain, and that Augustine had conspired with pagan Saxon kings to eradicate the true religion in Britain that had been planted by Joseph. The Reformation, therefore, was the means by which the British reclaimed their independence and restored the true religion.

Catholic versions continued to find adherents too, for example in converts such as the Benedictine monk Serenus Cressy and the Jesuit Matthew Alford (1587–1652). Cressy (1605–74) was born Hugh de Cressy in Yorkshire, had been an Anglican priest, but later converted to Catholicism and took his monastic vow. His *The church history of Brittany* (i.e. Britain) was published in 1668. Both Cressy and Alford used Glastonbury Abbey's Charter of St Patrick to suggest that Joseph, inspired by the Archangel Gabriel, founded a church at Glastonbury dedicated to the Virgin Mary.

The most destructive critique of the Arimathean tradition was provided by an Anglican, Edward Stillingfleet (1635–99), who became bishop of Worcester in 1689. He was instinctively sceptical about Joseph's connection with Britain, although he was quite prepared to accept Glastonbury as the Isle of Avalon and the burial place of Arthur. His *Origines Britannicae* was published in 1685. Gildas had not mentioned Joseph (and Gildas was said to have ended his days at Glastonbury). Nor had Nennius or William of Malmesbury, who had access to the earliest writings. Glastonbury had genuine ancient traditions, but 'the fabulous mixtures which monks thought to adorn it with' were exposed as 'dreams and visions'.[23] He pointed out that the Charter of St Patrick purported to have been written in 425, but that was before that system of dates was adopted, and so was clearly a forgery. King Ine's charter which declared that the original church was dedicated to St Mary was also exposed as a forgery. That Ine founded a church was not in dispute, but the abbey's claims that Joseph, St Patrick and St David had been associated with it were rejected. Stillingfleet nevertheless argued for an apostolic conversion of the British. He was minded to investigate the remark made by Gildas that Christianity was founded in Britain while Tiberius was Emperor of Rome (i.e. before AD 37). Stillingfleet made a case for St Paul as the apostolic founder of Christianity in Britain. He cited Theodoret, Bishop of Cyrrhus in Syria in the fifth century, to claim that St Paul was released from prison in Rome, who then travelled to Spain and across the ocean to Britain.

The case against Joseph of Arimathea was compellingly made by Jeremy Collier. In his *Ecclesiastical History of Great Britain* (1708) he systematically crushed all the evidence in favour of him and the false assumptions that lay behind his cult. Benedictines were notorious for forging charters, the motive for which was to establish an abbey's claims to its estates, which could not otherwise be properly verified and would therefore be open to challenge. As historical sources, therefore, they could not be relied upon. None of the early Glastonbury historians even mentioned Joseph's name. Other aspects of the Joseph legend smacked of later invention: churches were not dedicated to saints in the first century and so the dedication of the first church at Glastonbury to the Virgin was unconvincing; first-century apostolic Christians did not engage in monastic retreat like Joseph and his followers were said to have done; evidence of early Christian authors such as Eusebius, writing in the early fourth century, indicated that Philip proselytised in the East rather than in the West, and so could not have sent Joseph across the sea from Gaul; the 'hide', so important in establishing the original grant of land to Joseph's disciples, was a Saxon land measure, not a British one which it would have to be to date from the first century; there was no such British king as Arviragus in 63, when Britain was part of the Roman Empire; if there was an important British leader called Arviragus he would surely have been mentioned in *Agricola*, the account of his father-in-law's governorship of Britain at this time written by Tacitus. After such a sustained assault Collier could only conclude that 'the Records for the Glassenbury tradition won't bear a thorough Examination, they look untowardly when put to the test'.[24]

The decline of Joseph's reputation at the expense of St Paul was summed up by another bishop of St Davids, Thomas Burgess (1756–1837). Traditions concerning Joseph (and also of various other candidates St Peter, Simon Zelotes and James) 'are either destitute of evidence, or are full of difficulties and contradictions, which cannot be said of the western travels of St Paul'. St Paul had preached the Gospel in Britain and thus 'the Church of Britain was fully established before the Church of Rome' because the first bishop of Rome was appointed jointly by Paul and Peter.[25]

Much had changed in the century and a half since the closure of Glastonbury Abbey. The burgeoning discipline of natural history had concluded that the blossoming of the holy thorn was a natural phenomenon. Glastonbury, meanwhile, was losing some its lustre as the fount of British Christianity, by scholars who rejected the idea that Joseph could ever have visited Britain. In the end, however, Joseph had lost out, not to rational history, but to a rival myth of St Paul. Even so, the destructive critiques of Stillingfleet and Collier should have been the end of the story, but not in a society where only a minority of people had access to books.

7

Vulgar Errors

By the beginning of the eighteenth century Joseph had been cut down metaphorically, while the thorn had been cut down literally. The thorn had at least fared better than the walnut tree, because by the time it had been felled descendants of the original tree had been propagated elsewhere in the town and, as we will see, further afield. Its propensity to multiply ought to have diminished its reputation as a singular curiosity, but in fact the Glastonbury thorns were habitually spoken of as a single entity. Mental adjustment to the original myth seems to have been instinctive. Joseph, meanwhile, was lucky to survive at all, but the high minds that had dismissed him underestimated the adaptability of the Glastonbury legends. Joseph and the thorn thrived by joining forces.

Cuttings from the Glastonbury thorn were propagated locally, nationally and internationally as early as the seventeenth century. Andrew Paschal reported in 1684 that a nursery in Glastonbury was selling young thorns for a crown each. There was plenty of opportunity for fraud here, but such trees were not always necessarily venerated as cult objects. When John Taylor, the Thames water poet, visited Glastonbury in 1649 he encountered a graft of the original thorn planted by a local vintner. 'I saw the sayd branch, and it was ten foote high, greene, and flourishing; I did take a dead sprigged from it, wherewith I made two or three tobacco stoppers'.[1] This is probably the same tree that Lieutenant Hammond from Norwich saw in 1635, then only 'a young Bud and off spring of [the original thorn] planted in a Taverne Garden'.[2] There was a tree in the garden of a currier in the High Street, one at the White Hart Inn and one in the garden of William Strode—this is possibly the 'farm house in the vicinity of the abbey' that was built in 1714 using stone from the abbot's house. One of them was probably the 'Holly Thorn growing on a chimney' that Celia Fiennes saw in 1698. She also noticed winter-flowering thorns growing in several gardens in the town, as did the Reverend Richard Warner in the early nineteenth century. Descendants were also planted in the grounds of the abbey and the churchyard of St John which have become foci of the legend in modern times. There were many examples cited elsewhere in Somerset, some documented as late as the nineteenth century, at Bath, Chaffcombe, Dillington Park, Ilminster, Nimmer, West Buckland and Whitestaunton, and at the aptly-named Thorncombe Thorn in neighbouring Dorset.

Glastonbury thorns found their way to several parts of the country, sometimes with a very precise story attached to them. In the nineteenth century a thorn at Appleton in Cheshire was said to have been grafted from the Glastonbury thorn and brought there in 1125 by Adam de Dutton, a returning crusader. Other claims belong to the sixteenth, seventeenth and eighteenth centuries. Bernard Gilpin, rector of Houghton in Tyne and Wear, was said to have transplanted a cutting to his parish from Glastonbury in the sixteenth century. In the seventeenth century Robert Plot cited a thorn in the home of Lord Norreys in Rycote in Oxfordshire, which was said to have been grafted from the Glastonbury thorn. He also noted another, much older winter-flowering thorn that was in his time dying, and must have come from Glastonbury at a much earlier time, if indeed that was its source. According to John Aubrey, in the 1630s 'Mr Anthony Hinton ... did inoculate ... a bud of Glastonbury Thorne, on a thorn at his farmhouse in Wilton [Wiltshire], which blossoms at Christmas as the other did. My mother has had branches off them for a flower-pott several Christmasses, which I have seen'.[3] Quainton in Buckinghamshire attracted Yuletide crowds to see its thorn blossom at Christmas in the eighteenth century. Lancelot Lake took a cutting and planted it in the grounds of his house at Edgworth in Middlesex, where it apparently grew into a full-sized, healthy tree. John Jackson encountered one at Patchway near Bristol, on his pilgrimage to Glastonbury in 1755. In more recent times claims have been made for a thorn at Shenley, now part of Milton Keynes, and in the 1940s Brian Waters encountered one on the bank of the River Severn at Oldbury.

Richard Broughton reported that in 1633 there was already an international market for these 'miraculous remembrances' through the port of Bristol. The branches became sought after as if they were saints' relics. By the twentieth century foreign interest was dominated by America. In the late 1920s the writer H. V. Morton met a workman at Glastonbury Abbey who told him, 'you'd be surprised at the number of slips we send away. One is going to a big church they are building in New York. We sent one to America not long ago [in 1924] for the tomb of President Wilson'. A specimen was given to the New York Botanical Garden in 1940.[4]

Traditional belief in the properties of the thorn was alive and well in the eighteenth century, as visitors to Glastonbury testified. Even those who repudiated the reverence for such miraculous trees nevertheless found them objects of intellectual curiosity. William Stukeley saw the tree in 1723, but remained sceptical. That 'it so strictly observed Christmas day to an hour, nay a minute as they here assert', he did not believe. He could sense 'the dregs of monkery', but it was still a story worth telling.[5]

It was Richard Broughton who first made a direct link between Joseph and the tree. Joseph and two of his companions had come 'tyred and wearie neare unto the situation of that Towne, to an Hill allmost a mile distant from thence, called ... Wearyall'. They prayed, seeking directions, and the will of God was that they should settle in the adjoining place, Glastonbury. Subsequently, 'in the very place where S. Joseph and two others of his holy company first rested their weary bodies ... there sprung up, and still growth a miraculous Thorn Tree'.[6]

By the mid seventeenth century, then, the thorn was gradually becoming the holy thorn, and its sanctity was being ascribed to Joseph. Robert Plot understood it that the thorn was planted by Joseph of Arimathea in remembrance of Christ's birth. Word on the streets of Glastonbury had another story, which was told to Thomas Wyllie and his son Robert Wyllie, two Scottish Presbyterian ministers who visited Glastonbury in 1689:–

> Joseph coming a shoare stook a hathorn staff he had it seems in his hand, into the ground saying we ar weary all, and thence the hill has its name, but what is wonderful is, that the staff growing up into a tree blossom'd every year thereafter precisely on Christmas morning and was growing there at the reformation.[7]

By Glastonbury standards 'weary all' is a lame explanation for one of its fundamental myths.

It was from a Glastonbury innkeeper that Charles Eyston learned of the same, and published the first account of it in 1715. The town's proprietors were beginning to realise the commercial potential of the town's legends. The innkeeper plied tourists with fabulous stories, even introducing a new tree to replace the lost walnut in the abbey grounds, the 'oak of Avalon'. Eyston was told by the innkeeper, who also rented part of the abbey grounds:–

> that St Joseph of Arimathea landed not far from the Town, at a Place, where there was an Oak planted in memory of his landing, called *the Oak of Avalon*: That he and his companions marched thence to a Hill, near a Mile on the south side of the Town, and there being weary rested themselves, which gave the Hill the name *Weary all Hill*: That St Joseph stuck on the Hill his Staff, being a dry Hawthorn Stick, which grew and constantly budded and blow'd upon Christmas Day.[8]

Eyston was less credulous than the Wyllies, but did not want to reject the story completely. 'Whether it sprung from St Joseph of Arimathea's dry Staff, stuck by him on the Ground, when he rested there, I cannot find; but, beyond all dispute, it sprung up miraculously'.[9] The innkeeper seems to have been especially talkative, and the story soon gained currency. Although William Stukeley seems to have been unaware of it during his visit to Glastonbury in 1723, Daniel Defoe knew the story of Joseph and the staff when he came to Glastonbury in 1724: 'when he fixed his staff in the ground, which was on Christmas day, it immediately took root, budded, put forth white-thorn leaves, and the next day, was in full bloom, white as a sheet', since when the 'plant is preserved, and blows every Christmas day'. Defoe was taken 'to a gentleman's garden in the town, where it was preserved, and I brought a piece of it away in my hat, but took it upon their honour, that it really does blow ... on Christmas day'.[10] For Defoe, it seems, the thorn was a curiosity. He wanted to see it and have a piece of it regardless of whether the claims made of it were true.

We know where the story of the flowering staff came from. A story told of St Benignus by the medieval hagiographers was simply transposed to Joseph. Benignus was a disciple of St Patrick and in 462 he came to Somerset. He crossed marshes and forests until he reached an island, which he decided was a suitable place to establish a hermitage. Here he fixed his staff in the ground, where it put forth shoots and branches. A roof boss in the church of St Benedict in Glastonbury shows the saint holding a branch rather than a book. Far from being a unique event, it is one of the generic miracles that appeared in medieval hagiographies. Etheldreda, abbess of Ely in the seventh century, fled from her husband in Northumbria and on her journey to Ely, she stopped to rest, planted her staff in the ground, whereupon it grew into an ash tree that sheltered her. Two other saints with local connections possessed sprouting staffs. At Congresbury St Congar's staff grew into a yew tree. Congar was a popular saint and his feast day was celebrated across Somerset in the middle ages, so the story of a flowering staff may also have been familiar from that source. One of the attributes of St Aldhelm, bishop of Sherborne at the end of the seventh century, is of a staff sprouting ash leaves—one of his sermons was apparently so long that his staff became a tree again. Association of the thorn with Joseph had the effect of turning the tree into a holy relic, of the kind that had been discarded at the Reformation. The holy thorn was a place where the past had a physical presence, a concept which seemed just as important as it had been in the middle ages.

A critical test for the descendants of the original thorn came when Britain switched from the Julian to the Gregorian calendar in 1752–53, when eleven days in the calendar were lost. Would the trees flower on Christmas day new-style or old-style? Various reports of events at the 'Glastonbury thorn' appeared in the London and provincial press. According to the London *Evening Post*:–

a vast concourse of people attended the noted thorn on Christmas-day new-style; but, to their great disappointment, there was no appearance of its blowing, which made them watch it narrowly the 5th of January, the Christmas-day old style, when it blowed as usual'.[11]

The same report claimed that in Quainton, Buckinghamshire, 2,000 people witnessed the failure of the thorn to blossom on new Christmas day and so the parish celebrated old Christmas day instead. Other sources disputed these stories. The vicar of Glastonbury had claimed that the thorn flowered closer to the new-style Christmas, as had the thorn at Parham in Suffolk. The *Gloucester Journal* confidently declared that 'the Glastonbury Thorn is in as Full Blossom This Day, the 25th of December, *New Stile*, as it was ever known to be the 25th December, *Old Stile*', and predicted that the old calendar would thus quickly be forgotten.[12]

Calendar change went deeper than the issue of thorn trees, however. There was a popular feeling that the festival had a right relationship with the natural year. The enlightened could claim that the old saints' days were a relic of popery and, as we saw above, the authority of the church rested on the Bible, based on faith and reason, and not on natural phenomena. Protestant rituals were in any case only commemorations, not re-enactments, the most obvious example of which is the contrast between Protestant Eucharist and Catholic mass, with its belief in transubstantiation. The calendar was a civil, not a scriptural matter. But resistance to calendar change was a defence of traditional culture and religion and shows how slowly the old religious ways faded. It also revived memories of other attempts to erode popular culture, such as the prohibition of Christmas and maypoles during the Commonwealth.

Calendar change was also read in terms of urban sophistication against, in Marx's phrase, 'the idiocy of rural life'. Chapbook writers who supported the old calendar were well aware that they were mocked in some quarters, which seems to have strengthened their resolve.

A famous Tree sprung from the Staff,
Though modern Fools are apt to laugh,
Yet at Christ's Birth were Blossoms fair,
Which to this Day remaineth there.[13]

One of the mockers was Horace Walpole, writing under the pseudonym Adam Fitz-Adam in the periodical *The World*. He declared satirically that the thorn is the 'most protestant plant in the universe'. The Gregorian calendar was, after all, introduced by Pope Gregory in 1582 to replace the calendar of Julius Caesar who, whatever his shortcomings, could never be accused of being Catholic. And was it not arrogant and blasphemous for astronomers, mathematicians and parliamentarians to contradict the authority of a tree in Somerset? 'Had I been consulted ... instead of turning the calendar topsy-turvy by fantastic calculations, I should have proposed to regulate the year by the infallible Somersetshire thorn', whatever the minor inconveniences.

> If the course of the sun varies, astronomers may find some way to adjust that: but it is preposterous, not to say presumptuous, to be celebrating Christmas-day, when the Glastonbury thorn, which certainly must know times and seasons better than an almanack-maker, declares it to be heresy'.[14]

To what extent the people of Glastonbury revered the thorn is difficult to tell. Newspaper accounts of the 1752 Christmas rarely distinguish townsfolk from visitors. A correspondent from Glastonbury reported in the *Ipswich Journal* that a great many people visited Glastonbury to see the thorn blossom on Christmas day. It was 'a Thorn the Inhabitants of this Place are utter Strangers to', but 'as these religious or curious people always spend some Money in the Town, they may depend upon always being welcome'.[15] Already the townsfolk had acquired a reputation for cynical commercial exploitation (with obvious echoes of Glastonbury Abbey), but it seems true that the myth of the Glastonbury thorn was by now sustained by people living outside of the town. Samuel Saunders wrote of the tree in his guide book to Glastonbury of 1781. By now the original tree was deemed to have been 'so much esteemed by the papists ... and being deemed a Romish relique, was ordered to be destroyed when the abbey was demolished'.[16] Local memory of the abbey's dissolution and of the Civil Wars had evidently been lost, and so a new myth was created to explain the past.

In the 1750s the debate about the Glastonbury thorn shifted to, of all places, the East Riding of Yorkshire. It demonstrates the nationwide reach of a tree that was no longer just a local curiosity. In a sense the Glastonbury of the mind, the one that belongs to the nation at the expense of those who live there, is already apparent by this time. A few weeks after the thorn had apparently vindicated the calendar refuseniks a chapbook entitled *The Wonderful Works of God* appeared in Hull extolling its virtues. The author certainly saw calendar change and the Glastonbury thorn as a national issue:–

> there was a great many Gentleman and Ladies from all Parts of England to see [that] beautiful Thorn where Joseph of Arimathea pitched his Staff, within two Miles of Glastonbury, to the great surprise of the Spectators, to see it bud, blossom, and fade, at the Hour of twelve, on Old Christmas Day.[17]

Sceptical of this account, a Mr Sherwood of Warter, near Pocklington in the East Riding, made enquiries with the vicar of Glastonbury, the Reverend Richard Prat, and was told that it blossomed before new Christmas day, and thus well before old Christmas. This was an attempt to replace rumours amplified by distance with the facts on the ground. Prat was not a neutral observer, however. He had little time for the 'ridiculously stupid and egregiously false' claims made for the winter flowering of 1752–53. Moreover, he also pointed out that since the original tree had been destroyed in the Civil Wars, modern pilgrims gathered at a mere descendant of the ancient tree, a fact that seemed to have been forgotten by the faithful.

The *York Courant* noted disapprovingly that *The Wonderful Works of God* had greatly increased popular belief in the legend in the north of England. Large parts of the text are shared with another successful chapbook, *The Holy Disciple, or The History of Joseph of Arimathea*, which could be an early draft of the former, or perhaps the work of a plagiarising later author. Versions of it were printed in the eighteenth century in London and provincial cities such as Newcastle-upon-Tyne, Glasgow, Derby, Bristol and Bath. A Welsh translation was published in Shrewsbury in 1760. Association with the thorn gave a fresh impetus to Joseph legends in these chapbooks. In *The Wonderful Works of God*, Joseph was said to have converted 5,000 souls in one day at nearby Wells, whereas *The Holy Disciple* credits 18,000 souls on the same occasion, the higher figure perhaps representing no more than the author's unbounded enthusiasm for the subject. The life of Joseph was now presented in much more detail, and a different man emerged from the Joseph who appears in the *Gospel of Nicodemus* and the Grail legends. The myth of Joseph was continuing to develop. In this new version, Joseph's religious devotion had begun in his teens when he lived for four years in the desert with a hermit known as Malachi. He repeated the voluntary exile for six months after he buried Christ, and then joined St Peter as one of the seventy-two disciples before travelling to Britain. Joseph was ten years older than Christ, lived to eighty-six years of age, and at his death his coffin was borne to his grave in Glastonbury Abbey by six native kings, who now embraced Christ at the expense of worshipping the sun, moon and stars.

One Yorkshireman who was inspired enough to make his own pilgrimage to Glastonbury to verify the story of the thorn was John Jackson. In November 1755 he set out from his home at Woodkirk near Wakefield, and wrote a diary of his travels. Needless to say, his diary entries adhered strictly to the Julian calendar. Jackson was known locally as Old Trash, was a well-known character, enjoying what would now be styled a portfolio career: stone-cutter, surveyor, mechanic, schoolmaster and clock-mender are indicated in his diary, and he was also a man of learning whose interest in topography and antiquities has been described as 'informed by a prophetic sense of the spiritual destiny of Britain'.[18] It is quite possible that William Blake read Jackson's journal, a subject to which we will return later.

Subsisting on charity, which seems to have been readily offered throughout his sojourn, his travels took him through the northern industrial towns to the pre-industrial south-west. Among his acts of worship he visited an offshoot of the Glastonbury thorn in the garden of William Barclat in Patchway near Bristol. On new Christmas day he was at Wells, from where he made his way to Glastonbury. He attended church led by the Reverend Prat, and did the sights—abbey, Tor and Wearyall Hill. At the latter he met a young man who told him where the original thorn grew, but it was more than fifty years since it had been seen there. The owner had apparently grubbed up the roots to stop the curious coming to see it, but subsequently 'nothing prosper'd but all he had went to ruin and he died a begar'. He visited the well-known specimen of hawthorn in 'Esquire Stroud's great Farmhouse', where he was very hospitably received:–

> ye Mistris sent an old man with me into ye garden, and he bid me climb into it, and I did and got two or three of its twigs and came away and went into the house and thanked gentlewoman and she gave me Bread and Cheess and Small Beer.[19]

He had intended to return to the farmhouse on old Christmas day but his landlady at the Seven Stars directed him to two trees in the town. In the morning he obtained a twig 'partly in bud and hardly in blossom' from a tree as thick as a man's waist in a garden in Nilot Street. Around noon he obtained another twig, from a garden at the north-west corner of the abbey grounds, in 'unopened blossom'. 'I enquired whether ye thorn did ever bud or blossom on ye New Christmas Day, and they angrily answered me nay nor never will'. As long as the Reverend Prat was in charge there were no services at the two Glastonbury churches to mark old Christmas day, but the bells of St John's were apparently rung for most of it.[20]

For a time after 1752 different calendars co-existed and evolved according to their specific context, such as religion, agriculture, festivities, law and government, nation and parish. Observance of thorns at old Christmas was to continue, and not just at Glastonbury. Knowledge of these Yuletide gatherings has usually become known to us because of disturbances reported in the press. Examples include gatherings near Crewkerne in Somerset in 1878, at Kingstone Grange in Herefordshire, and Sutton Poyntz in Dorset in 1844. In 1889 it was reported that a hundred people had visited a descendant of the Glastonbury thorn at West Buckland in west Somerset. On the day following old Christmas Day in 1878 the Reverend Francis Kilvert went to see the holy thorn at a small farmhouse in his Herefordshire parish of Bredwardine. The tree was said to have been grafted from a long-felled holy thorn at Tibberton (there are villages of that name in both Gloucestershire and Worcestershire). The farmer's:–

> kind daughter gave me a bit of a spray of the Holy Thorn which was gathered from the tree at midnight, old Christmas Eve. She set great store by the spray and always gathered and kept a bit each year. The blossoms were not fully out and the leaves were scarcely unfolded but the daughter of the house assured me that the little white bud clusters would soon come out into full blow if put in soft water.[21]

Reminiscing on old Christmas Eve with one of his parishioners, Kilvert learned of a related tradition. One of his parishioners was said to have reported that 'on old Christmas Eve ... at twelve o'clock the oxen that were standing knelt down upon their knees and those that were lying down rose up on their knees and there stayed kneeling and moaning, the tears running down their faces'.[22] This same tradition was current in the West Country. In Devon, at twelve o'clock at night on old Christmas Eve, oxen in their stalls were 'always found on their knees, as in an attitude of devotion'.[23] Ruth Tongue uncovered a similar story in Somerset in the twentieth century that conflated the traditions of oxen and thorn. A pilgrim was said to have returned from Glastonbury with a single thorn, which he planted at his home in Ilminster. He prayed by it everyday and a thorn tree grew unusually rapidly. He told his neighbours that the tree would blossom on Christmas day, but in the event it did not. Near midnight on old Christmas Eve, however, parishioners were awoken by a great commotion and found that the beasts from the neighbouring farms had come in from the fields and farm-yards and formed an orderly procession. The people followed them to the thorn, which was now in white blossom. The beasts all kneeled in the presence of the tree, by which means the people knew that the tree was truly a holy thorn. Ruth Tongue also met an old man in Taunton in 1948 who told her of a similar event in the 1880s.

Another factor came into the mix in 1751 with the discovery of healing water at Glastonbury. The eighteenth century was the age of the spa and Glastonbury was one of numerous towns that tried to reinvent itself with baths and pump rooms. The problem for Glastonbury was that the discovery of the waters was not verified scientifically and had religious overtones, and Roman Catholic ones at that. It came in a dream to Matthew Chancellor, a fifty-eight year old asthma sufferer from nearby North Wootton, who was told to drink the water on seven consecutive Sundays to effect a cure. The water had special properties: 'Where this water descends from, is holy Ground, where a vast number of Saints and Martyrs have been buried'. Chancellor seems to have been well-acquainted with Glastonbury's heritage, and he seems to have read his Bible too. His dream recalls the story of Naaman, advised to wash seven times in the Jordan to cure his leprosy.[24]

The reputation of the waters was quickly established. In that same year the Reverend J. Davies of Plympton reported that it cured scrofula, rheumatism, broken bones, asthma and consumption. Another, anonymous, account was written by an 'Inhabitant of Bath', which at that time was the capital of spa culture and could have seen Glastonbury as a potential rival. The author scoffed at the supposed miraculous virtues of the water, but endorsed an impressive inventory of successful cures. Most patients came from the region, i.e. Somerset, Dorset and Bristol, were in trade rather than being in the gentry class, and received cures for various ailments, including white leprosy, 'bloody cancer in the left hand' and smallpox.

An attempt to develop the town as a spa was only briefly successful. There were baths and a coffee house near the centre of the town, a pump room was built, and plans were made to bottle the water. (The coffee house boasted in its garden the oldest and largest graft of the original thorn, one that John Jackson visited in 1755.) But compared with the elegant streets and Assembly Room of Bath, Glastonbury was a rough country town and visitors complained that there was nothing to do and no one to meet there.

The Glastonbury waters were an amalgamation of six mineral springs on the north side of the Tor, which flowed across the abbey site to the Chaingate, where the baths were constructed. The waters could be taken at the Chaingate or at the springs themselves. Chancellor drank from a well in the abbey, what is known now as St Joseph's well, but it was at this time that the Blood Well, better known now as the Chalice Well, became part of the Glastonbury story. The iron deposit where the water rises gives the water there a reddish-brown colour. Here an immersion bath survives, and another tank is possibly a sedimentation tank associated with bottling of the water. What is most intriguing about the spring, at this stage of our story, is its suggestive name. This was not, as once believed, a creation of the nineteenth century when it was owned by the Roman Catholic church. Part of the present-day Chalice Hill was known as 'ground called Challice' in 1716, and the same term is found in rate-books of the 1730s. It could well have been a surname. There is no evidence, however, that it recalled the legend of Joseph of Arimathea arriving with his two cruets, or chalices. None of the authors who helped develop the Glastonbury legends in the seventeenth century, some of whom were Catholics, mention Chalice Well, whereas the thorn was mentioned by every author.

The importance of the miracle cure of the Glastonbury waters to our story is that, with the holy thorn, it is another example of popular culture with folk-Catholic overtones. Both belong to a phenomenon for which the historian E. P. Thompson coined the term 'Jacobite theatre', which is not the most intelligible of phrases to a non-technical readership, but encompasses popular acts of defiance against the established order in the mid eighteenth century, named after the supporters of the Catholic pretenders who invaded England in 1715 and 1745. Ironically Somerset was one of the stronger Protestant counties during and after the Reformation, but it is a reminder that Glastonbury was a symbol appropriated across a wide swathe of England. The Glastonbury waters were sought by people who were still impressed by claims for miracle cures, and whose culture was felt to be under siege from a rational, educated elite.

We can see in the eighteenth century a widening gap between the beliefs and self-image of polite culture in relation to vernacular or popular culture. It is a rift between the educated classes and the 'vulgar errors' of the people. The class divide is implicit in the condescending tone of the *Gentleman's Magazine* for 1753:–

> The stories of this thorn are so absurd, as scarce to need confutation. But as it has been adduced as a supernatural evidence for the old stile, and several ridiculous falsities grafted on it; this authentic account of the matter may be necessary to undeceive the weak and superstitious, and therefore we hope our readers will excuse our mentioning it.[25]

By now Glastonbury was a national phenomenon, its mythology disseminated in rumour and in cheap but accessible literature, acquiring a status that it has never since thrown off. But the eighteenth century was also the age of the Druid revival among antiquaries, and with it came the rise of outsiders with self-contained visions of the past. We will meet such people again in the early part of the twentieth century, but the prototype is perhaps John Wood, the talented Bath architect, who saw the West Country as the centre of the Druid civilisation, which he attempted to recreate in his ambitious architecture for the city of Bath, notably the Royal Circus. In Wood's account Joseph came to Britain with his disciples and established himself 'in the very heart of all the Druidical Works' like Stonehenge and Stanton Drew stone circles. Looking afresh at Glastonbury from a new perspective, in this case of the pre-Christian Druids, opened up new lines of thought quite different from issues posed by the abbey and the thorn tree. It would prove fertile ground in the following centuries, taking Glastonbury mythology to unexpected new places.

8

The Fall and Rise of Glastonbury Abbey

Very soon after the Dissolution, Glastonbury Abbey was dismembered. Roof lead, glass, perhaps the richest architectural mouldings, and its fixtures and furnishings (to say nothing of the relics that had not found their way into the official inventory of the abbey's wealth) disappeared. Among these disappearances was the tomb of Arthur and Guinevere, as well as shrines to other Anglo-Saxon kings, but there is no evidence that their loss was much lamented. There may have been popular support for the closure of the abbey, although how people thought about the dismantling of its vast edifice is difficult to judge. By the early seventeenth century there were few people alive who could have remembered the abbey as a functioning institution. It began to take on a different life as a historical monument. It is significant, however, that the buildings were not completely demolished and the ground was not built over. Once the people who inhabited it are removed any building acquires a sense of mystery. Ruins have in-built pathos, a life of their own as objects of nostalgia, of dreams about the past. At Glastonbury they could have been seen as evidence of Protestant triumph over Catholic error, but most contemporary accounts have a more wistful air. The ruins of Glastonbury Abbey haunted the town for centuries, a broken place at its heart, a powerful symbol of a lost world.

Glastonbury was only one ruined abbey in a country peppered with abandoned monasteries and there was little consensus in Protestant England that such buildings should be erased from memory. They shared with draughty old castles the dimension of time and the universal law that all the vanities of human endeavour will eventually crumble to dust. In the seventeenth century antiquaries began to lament the haste with which monasteries had been despoiled and ruined. In 1655 William Dugdale published the first volume of his *Monasticon Anglicanum*, aimed at providing a record of abbey ruins so that the memory of them would not be lost.

By this time the ruins of Glastonbury Abbey had already become a spectacle which left visitors feeling that they were in the presence of former greatness.

The place aroused mixed feelings. Glastonbury Abbey was Roman Catholic, but it was also English Catholic, a symbol of old England and, in the case of Glastonbury, the last resting place of kings. Far from providing an object lesson in triumph over ignorance and superstition, its crumbling ruins could be read as victims of a crime perpetrated across the nation. 'Glastonbury: The Threasory of the Carcasses of so famous, and so many rare Persons ... How lamentable is thy case now?' opined Dr John Dee. 'How hath Hypocrisie and Pride, wrought thy Desolation?'[1] Another early voice lamenting the abbey's demise was Michael Drayton, in his poem *Poly-Olbion* (1613), a lengthy rhapsody on the beauties and glories of Britain by an author for whom history had long been a favourite theme. On the subject of Glastonbury he was melancholy, knew exactly what had been lost and who was to blame:

> When not great Arthur's tomb, nor holy Joseph's grave,
> From sacrilege had power their sacred bones to save;
> He, who that God in Man to his sepulchre brought,
> Or he which for the Faith twelve holy battles fought—
> What? Did so many kings do honour to that place,
> For Avarice at last so vilely to deface?[2]

Even to Protestants like Sir William Brereton, who visited Glastonbury in 1635, the abbey ruins were impressive: 'I have never met with so large a sumptuous, spacious cloister neither in England, Fraunce, nor in the king of Spayne's dominions'.[3] Lieutenant Hammond, visiting Glastonbury from Norwich in 1635, was struck by 'a rich and rare architecture' even though it was 'almost quite demolished'. The only structure that remained roofed was the Abbot's Kitchen. The Lady Chapel retained its 'spacious, rich and stately' character, with its '2 Towers with stairs', i.e. the angle turrets.[4]

It became a place of superstition. The ruins were said to have yielded for Dr John Dee and Sir Edward Kelly the Elixir needed to make the Philosopher's Stone and which was 'incredibly Rich in vertue'. But its abandoned cloisters came eventually to harbour malign spirits, perhaps the just desert for a town that had abandoned and plundered a sacred place. The devil moved in. If a stone was thrown into the empty crypt below the Lady Chapel 'it gives a great echo, and the country people says it's the Devil set there on a tun of money, which makes that noise lest they should take it away from him'.[5] Memories seem to have given way to rumour, but perhaps they were also played up for visitors. The ruins had an undeniable mystique. Lieutenant Hammond in 1635 and Celia Fiennes in 1698 both learned of a secret passage linking the abbey with the Tor. Whatever mystery the abbey ruins guarded, it was a 'lamentable spectacle to behold the ruines of so many religious Houses, and sacred structures, of so magnificent, and resplendant [*sic*] eminency ... rac'd and pull'd downe'.[6] By the eighteenth century antiquaries could be far more strident in their criticism of those to blame for the ruination of the abbeys. Francis Grose directed his fire at Henry VIII and his henchmen. Referring to the execution of Abbot Whiting and his two fellow monks, 'the shepherd being slain, the sheep were easily dispersed; nor were there many religious men found after the death of these 3 abbots [*sic*] to oppose the king's tyranny. Henry, therefore, like a conqueror, invaded, threw down, plundered, and demolished all'. Then the king, 'that he might rejoice in wickedness, and glory in his sin' expected his subjects to rejoice that the men who brought Christianity to Britain over a thousand years ago had finally been sent packing.[7]

The site was clearly badly treated after the Dissolution, even if only for short episodes. The redundant abbey buildings were leased to Edward Seymour, Duke of Somerset, who settled a colony of Dutch weavers in the grounds in 1550, as if to emphasise that this was now irredeemably a secular place. The Abbot's Kitchen was used as a Quaker meeting house from 1667. In 1685 the forces of the Duke of Monmouth camped in the abbey grounds in the duke's vain campaign to overthrow James II that unravelled at the Battle of Sedgemoor. Armies are no respecters of historic properties. A hundred years after they had left, Samuel Saunders was shown a sculpted image lately dug up from the abbey, but it had been 'de-faced by the wanton sport of some militia then quartered in the town'.[8]

By the end of the eighteenth century the buildings around the cloister had been reduced to a 'heap of Rubbish'. The abbey's tenant was happy to sell off stone for hardcore to build a new road to Wells in 1784 and again 1792–94. By this time the site of the abbey was owned by John Down, mayor of Glastonbury and a local brickmaker, who is said to have used gunpowder to help dislodge recalcitrant masonry. Not until it was purchased by John Fry Reeves in 1825 did it cease to be a quarry. This impression of relentless plundering is contradicted by other evidence, however. It is clear from written accounts and contemporary engravings that the destruction of the abbey took place mainly in the first hundred years after its closure, after which sales of stone were mostly in the form of masonry that had already fallen and was lying around the site.

Wenceslas Hollar provided illustrations of selected sites for Dugdale and his engravings of Glastonbury, encompassing the town, abbey and Tor, is the earliest known visual representation of the monastery, just over a century after it was dissolved. Hollar's view shows only part of the ruins, but the Lady Chapel, Abbot's Kitchen and the former Abbot's lodgings, are clearly shown. It also appears to show a section of the cloister walls still standing, but most of the abbey church had come down. A more detailed record of the abbey ruins was

Above: 1.
The profile of
Glastonbury
Tor is one of the
unmistakable sights
of England.

Right: 2. The
Tribunal at
Glastonbury, seen
here in a drawing
of 1832 by A.
W. N. Pugin, is a
fifteenth-century
house on the High
Street. (*Yale Center
for British Art, Paul
Mellon Fund*)

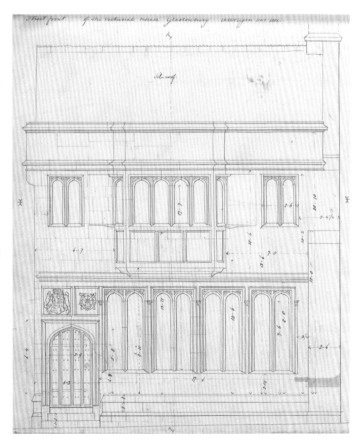

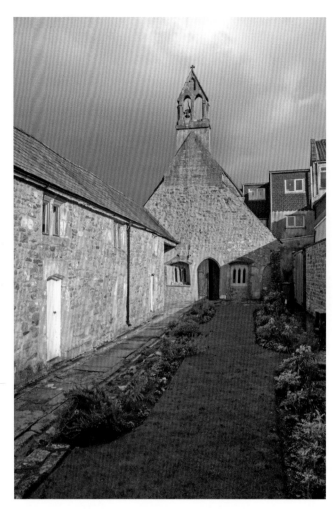

Left: 3. The medieval St Mary Magdalene hospital, concealed from view behind Magdalene Street, is one of the town's unobtrusive architectural treasures.

Below: 4. The fresco by Fleur Kelly in St Patrick's chapel in Glastonbury Abbey depicts some of the key characters in the abbey's history. On the left is St David, credited with reviving the abbey in the fifth century, then Phagan and Deruvian, sent by Pope Eleutherius in AD 166 to convert the British, St Dunstan, and finally Richard Whiting, hanged on the Tor in 1539.

5. The abbey barn, built *c.* 1361, is the most prominent surviving symbol of Glastonbury Abbey as a major landowner. It now houses the Somerset Rural Life Museum.

6. The fourteenth-century fish house at Meare, close to Meare Pool and other waterways, was used to store and salt fish from the abbey's estates, and is a reminder of the importance of fish in the medieval diet.

7. Glastonbury Tor, viewed across the River Brue from South Moor.

8. The church tower on the Tor is a looming presence all around Glastonbury. The tower is all that remains of the church built on the summit in the fourteenth century.

Above left: 9. St Dunstan, represented here in a window at Street parish church, made by Rachel de Montmorency in 1951. He holds a pair of tongs, which he traditionally used to hold the devil by the nose.

Above right: 10. St Gildas, depicted by Rachel de Montmorency in 1951. The parish church at Street, just by Glastonbury, was once dedicated to this British saint.

11. This fresco of St Patrick by Fleur Kelly shows the saint holding a Taw cross around which snakes are coiled (Patrick was a destroyer of snakes), with his Irish wolfhound by his side. In the distance is the Tor with chapel on the summit.

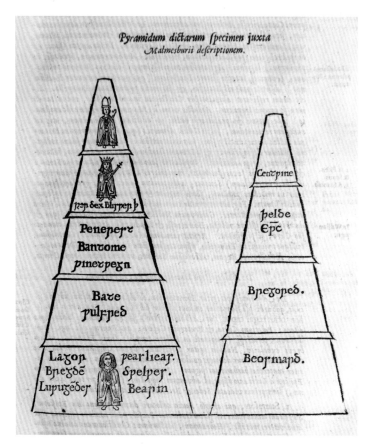

12. This visual recreation of the pyramids described by William of Malmesbury was made by Sir Henry Spelman in the seventeenth century. (*University of Birmingham, Special Collections*)

Icon primæ Ecclesiæ Regio permissu extructæ.

Above: 13. In the seventeenth century Sir Henry Spelman visualised the *vetusta ecclesia* as a kind of rustic Gothic log cabin. It may betray the tastes of his own time, but his attempt to recreate it shows that this long-lost building remained central to the story of early British Christianity. (*University of Birmingham, Special Collections*)

Right: 14. In 1586 William Camden published the only representation of the lead cross found with the grave of Arthur and Guinevere at Glastonbury in 1191. It reads 'HIC IACET SEPULTUS INCLITUS REX ARTURIUS IN INSULA AVALONIA' (Here lies buried the famous King Arthur in the Isle of Avalon).

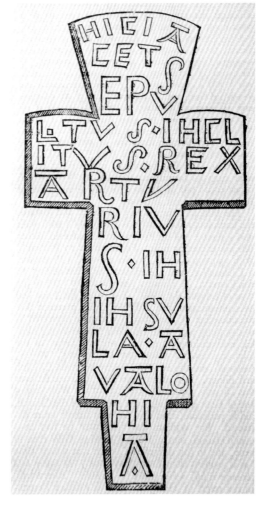

Above: 15. The Lady Chapel was begun immediately after the fire of 1184 and has the richest architectural detail of the abbey buildings. This reflects the symbolic importance of the site to the abbey's history.

Left: 16. The north doorway of the Lady Chapel.

Above: 17. The abbey ruins, as viewed from the east.

Right: 18. The place where Arthur's shrine was set up by Edward I in 1278 was found during excavations in the twentieth century.

19. Rachel de Montmorency's depiction of Joseph, made in 1950 for Street parish church, shows Joseph holding the linen cloth with which he wrapped the body of Jesus.

20. The story of Joseph of Arimathea is told in a stained glass window made in 1935 for St John's church in Glastonbury. Here Joseph protests about the condemnation of Jesus.

21. Joseph takes Jesus down from the cross and prepares to bury him. In this version he is attended by the weeping Mary and Mary Magdalene, but there is no Nicodemus.

22. In a stained-glass panel in St John's church, Joseph arrives at Glastonbury with his disciples, bearing the two cruets first mentioned in Melkin's prophecy.

Above left: 23. The stained glass figure of Joseph of Arimathea, made in 1935 for St John's church, shows him holding the two cruets.

Above right: 24. The figure of Arviragus appears in the window made in 1935 for St John's church in Glastonbury. Arviragus was the native king converted by Joseph when he landed in Britain.

25. The George and Pilgrim was built in the mid fifteenth century to cater for the influx of visitors to Glastonbury, and is one of the finest surviving pre-Reformation inns in Britain.

26. This small late medieval panel, part of a collection of old glass in one of the chancel windows in St John's church, shows the arms of Joseph. His cross is flanked by cruets containing the blood and sweat of Christ.

27. Joseph of Arimathea acquired his own Arms in the sixteenth century. A wooden cross, with two cruets and the blood and sweat of Jesus that they were supposed to contain.

28. Abbot Richard Whiting, who was hanged on Glastonbury Tor in 1539, is shown here in stained glass made by Rachel de Montmorency in 1950 for Street parish church.

29. Wenceslas Hollar's view of Glastonbury in the mid seventeenth century shows that the abbey ruins dominated the town. It is the first portrayal of Glastonbury to feature the Tor. (*University of Birmingham, Special Collections*)

30. One of the thorns descended from the tree on Wearyall Hill is in the abbey grounds, outside the chapel of St Patrick.

Above: 31. The thorn tree in the churchyard of St John, one of the descendants of the original tree on Wearyall Hill.

Left: 32. The brass tablet recounting Glastonbury's early history was one of the artefacts used to argue for its early foundation, but by the late seventeenth century it was revealed to be of late-medieval origin. (*University of Birmingham, Special Collections*)

33. The frontispiece of Jeremy Collier's *Ecclesiastical History of Great Britain* (1708) is a pictorial representation of England's conversion. In the foreground is Augustine converting Ethelbert of Kent; in the middle distance King Lucius sends two envoys to Rome, and in the far distance is the martyrdom of St Alban. Canterbury Cathedral is in the background. Glastonbury has been written out of the story. (*University of Birmingham, Special Collections*)

34. In the window made by A. J. Davies for St John's church in 1935, Joseph is seen arriving in Britain and is confronted by the native king Arviragus and his army. Joseph plants his staff on Wearyall Hill – the staff that would blossom into the Glastonbury Thorn.

35. A pump house was built on Magdalene Street, to the west of the abbey, in the hope of capitalising on the craze for healing water that was discovered at Glastonbury 1751.

WEST VIEW OF GLASTONBURY

36. In this view from the west in the early nineteenth century, Glastonbury is only a small town. Its medieval church towers, in the town and on the Tor, still dominated the skyline, but its social life was markedly provincial compared with Bath. (*University of Birmingham, Special Collections*)

37. The abbey ruins are dominated by the high piers of the former crossing tower.

38. In the century after the abbey's closure the crypt below the Lady Chapel was rumoured to harbour malign spirits. (*University of Birmingham, Special Collections*)

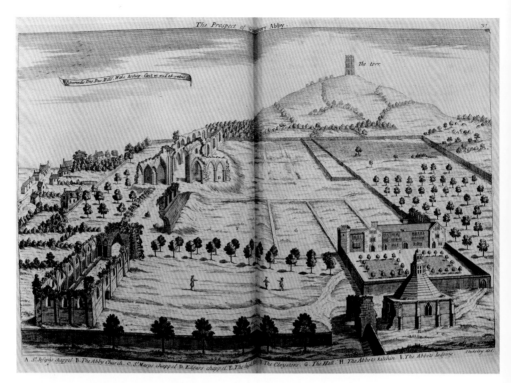

A. St Josephs chappel. B. The Abby Church. C. St Marys chappel. D. Edgars chappel. E. The hall. The Cloysters. G. The Hall. H. The Abbots kitchin. I. The Abbots lodging.

39. William Stukeley's view of the abbey ruins from the west in 1723 shows that very little of the standing fabric has fallen since his time. The Abbot's lodging on the right had already been taken down, so Stukeley relied on a drawing of it to compose his own picture. (*University of Birmingham, Special Collections*)

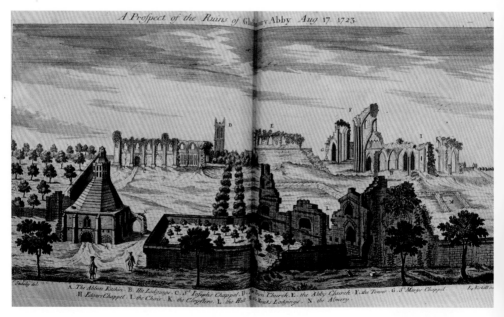

A Prospect of the Ruins of Glastonbury Abby Aug 17. 1723.

A. The Abbots Kitchin. B. His Lodginge. C. St Josephs Chappel. D. Con Church. E. the Abby Church. F. the Tower. G. St Marys Chappel. H. Edgars Chappel. I. the Choir. K. the Cloysters. L. the Hall. Monks Lodginge. N. the Almery.

40. William Stukeley's view of the Abbey ruins was drawn in 1723. It shows, in the foreground, the recently demolished Abbot's lodgings. (*University of Birmingham, Special Collections*)

41. Glastonbury Abbey was a picturesque ruin by the late eighteenth century, in spite of it still being exploited as a quarry. This 1795 view of the Abbot's kitchen is by Michael Angelo Rooker. (*Yale Center for British Art, Paul Mellon Collection*)

CONEY'S VIEW OF THE ABBEY (1817).

42. Glastonbury Abbey ruins in 1817, showing some architectural fragments in the foreground. In reality the place was probably far less neat and tidy.

43. The well found in the crypt below the Lady Chapel in the 1820s was quickly attributed to the cult of St Joseph at Glastonbury. (*University of Birmingham, Special Collections*)

VIEW OF RUINS, (FROM THE EAST.)

44. This view of the abbey ruins from the east was published in 1826. It shows how the foundations of the walls were in many cases no longer visible, making it difficult to ascertain the original plan of the building. (*University of Birmingham, Special Collections*)

45. William Blake's engraving 'Joseph among
the rocks of Albion' of *c.* 1773 is copied
from a work by Michelangelo, and makes no
reference to the British legend of Joseph.

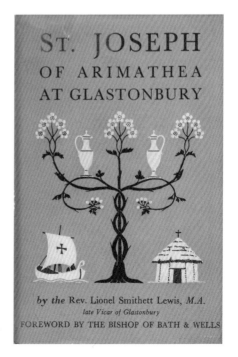

46. *St Joseph of Arimathea at Glastonbury*
was published in numerous editions from its
first printing in 1922 until the author's death
in 1953, and is still in print today.

Above: 47. The figure of Joseph of Arimathea on the wall of St Patrick's chapel at Glastonbury Abbey is by Fleur Kelly. Arriving by ship, Joseph holds the model of a church he was inspired by the Archangel Gabriel to build at Beckery near Glastonbury. His flowering staff is behind him.

Left: 48. The figure of Joseph of Arimathea in St Patrick's chapel in Glastonbury Abbey, by Wayne Ricketts of Bristol, marks the enduring success of Joseph's revival at Glastonbury, initiated by the Reverend L. S. Lewis.

Right: 49.
Rutland Boughton
(1887-1960) at
Glastonbury. (*Rutland
Boughton Trust*)

Below: 50. The
cast of *The Birth of
Arthur*, performed in
Glastonbury in 1915.
(*Rutland Boughton
Trust*)

51. Gwen Ffrangcon-Davies in the character of Igraine from *The Birth of Arthur*. (*Rutland Boughton Trust*)

GLASTONBURY FESTIVAL
August–September, 1925.

PROGRAMME

Price 2d.

Directors:
RUTLAND BOUGHTON, Chairman,
LAURENCE HOUSMAN,   CHRISTINA WALSHE,
PENELOPE SPENCER,   FREDERICK WOODHOUSE,

Secretary:
THOMAS W. WALLER, The Festival School, Glastonbury.

52. The programme for the 1925 Glastonbury Festival, designed by Boughton's collaborator and erstwhile lover, Christina Walshe. (*Rutland Boughton Trust*)

53. Alice Buckton at the Chalice Well in 1915, with a pupil, Miss Ellis. The cloak worn by Alice was given to her by Alfred Lord Tennyson. (*Chalice Well Trust*)

54. The Chalice Well, with the ornate wrought-iron cover designed in 1919 by Frederick Bligh Bond.

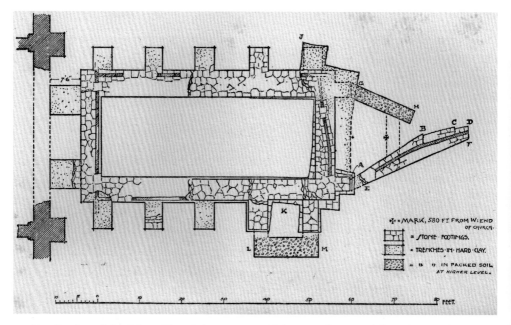

55. Bond's plan of the Edgar Chapel shows an apsidal east end, unusual for a late-Gothic building, but his interpretation was rejected by other archaeologists.

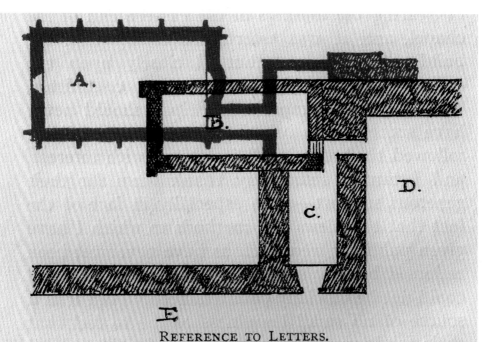

REFERENCE TO LETTERS.

A, Loretto Chapel as inferred from the script; *B*, Loretto Chapel as found; *C*, the cloister; *D*, the north transept; *E*, the north aisle of the nave.

56. Bond's plan of the Loretto chapel shows how the automatic scripts received in 1911 and 1916 erred slightly in determining the position of the chapel.

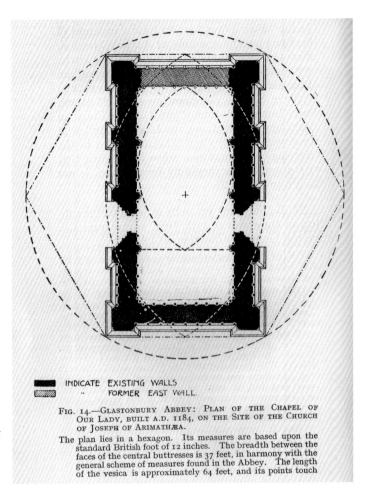

57. Bond's plan of the Lady Chapel fitted neatly into a regular hexagon, and he was able to draw the outline of two vesica shapes that he thought were significant.

INDICATE EXISTING WALLS
  "   FORMER EAST WALL.

FIG. 14.—GLASTONBURY ABBEY: PLAN OF THE CHAPEL OF
OUR LADY, BUILT A.D. 1184, ON THE SITE OF THE CHURCH
OF JOSEPH OF ARIMATHÆA.

The plan lies in a hexagon. Its measures are based upon the
standard British foot of 12 inches. The breadth between the
faces of the central buttresses is 37 feet, in harmony with the
general scheme of measures found in the Abbey. The length
of the vesica is approximately 64 feet, and its points touch

58. The glass bowl purchased on the Italian Riviera in 1885, which would later be sensationalised in the press as the Holy Grail. (*Chalice Well Trust*)

Above left: 59. Katharine Maltwood (1878-1961). Her Glastonbury Zodiac found little support in her own times but inspired a generation of thinkers in the 1960s.

Above right: 60. Dion Fortune (1890-1946), author of *Avalon of the Heart,* was one of the first people to alternate between metropolitan London and mystical Somerset.

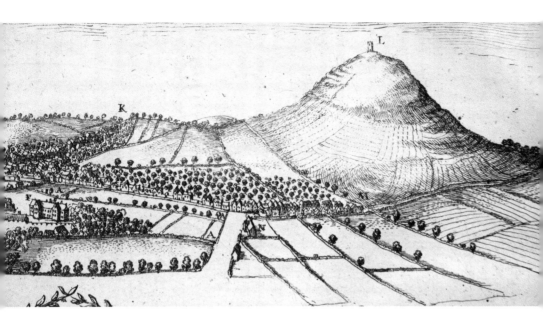

Above: 61. Wenceslas Hollar's view of Glastonbury in the mid seventeenth century shows that crops were grown on the lower slopes of the Tor, but it also clearly shows terraces near the summit. (*University of Birmingham, Special Collections*)

Right: 62. John Michell at Glastonbury Tor in the 1960s.

63. The terraces on the sides of Glastonbury Tor give the hill its distinct profile, but a consensus maintains that they are not natural. They have been interpreted as a processional way and as astronomical markers.

64. The Chalice Well garden, incorporating a pool designed in the form of the *vesica piscis* in 1979.

published in 1724 by William Stukeley, who had made two drawings the previous year. Samuel Gale, a correspondent of the antiquary Browne Willis, described the abbey ruins at about the same time and broadly corroborates Stukeley's record. Of the abbey church, the nave, transepts and crossing had largely been demolished. Of the chancel, 'both the walls and side Isles by the Choir remain, containing eight windows in each; and the wall at the east end for about three feet high, is yet seen above the Rubbish'. The interior of the Lady Chapel was 'curiously wrought and painted after the Gothick style'. Francis Grose noted in 1756 that 'the walls are painted with pictures of saints, as still easily seen', of the kind universal in all churches before the Reformation, but which survived in parish churches only under layers of whitewash.[9]

The appearance of the site in the 1720s is not unrecognisable from the ruins as they exist today. Stukeley's view clearly shows that the abbey had done most of its falling down before he arrived there. He showed that, although the roof had been taken down, the Lady Chapel walls stood nearly to their full height. The remainder of the abbey church was less well preserved, unroofed and with sections of its walls taken down completely. There is only a small section of the south wall of the nave, incorporating three windows, which is what survives today. The eastern piers of the crossing tower survive, with attached walls of the transepts and chancel, although the transept arches are not rendered very accurately by Stukeley. Some of the north chancel wall has come down since Stukeley's time but otherwise the chancel walls shown in his view remain standing today. The cloisters and conventual buildings, which were placed on the south side of the abbey church, a standard layout for a Benedictine monastery, had been almost entirely demolished by Stukeley's time. The exceptions were the Abbot's Kitchen and the Abbot's lodging. The latter was a Tudor mansion and was inhabited into the eighteenth century. It was demolished in about 1720 by Thomas Prew, who used some of the stone to build a new house in Magdalene Street. One view by Stukeley, made in 1723, shows it in ruins, but in another view he shows it in its former glory, but he had to rely on a drawing of it made by his friend Mr Strachey.

The most interesting aspect of Stukeley's drawings is that they show how the hierarchy of abbey buildings was respected. The secular ranges were the first to disappear, but the abbey church was reasonably well preserved, especially the more important east end of the church. The Lady Chapel was the most sacred and special of the abbey buildings and was correspondingly the least plundered.

One of the reasons that demolition of the buildings ceased may have been superstition. Although William Stukeley noticed that every other cottage in Glastonbury seemed to have been built or repaired using pieces of doorway, windows, bases, capitals and piers from the abbey, none were of recent date. The abbey grounds were an architectural salvage yard and yet the townspeople had apparently developed a fear of using abbey stone in case it brought bad luck, and if they did so it was used for outhouses like stables and cattle sheds rather than dwellings. That those who continued to desecrate the ruins would be punished is a typical example of Protestant belief in divine retribution, the kind that afflicted the man who cut the thorn tree. Abbey stone had recently been used to construct a new market house in the town, since when the town's commercial fortunes had apparently declined.

William Stukeley was one of the earliest voices to call for the preservation of Glastonbury Abbey ruins, 'if only to preserve old monuments for the benefit of our history'.[10] An engraving of the abbey was published in the mid eighteenth century by the topographical artists Samuel and Nathaniel Buck, a reliable indicator that Glastonbury was beginning to attract tourists as the age of travelling for pleasure was gathering pace. Stebbing Shaw, who visited Glastonbury in a tour of western England in the 1780s, was astonished that the inhabitants had failed to grasp the commercial potential of the abbey ruins:–

> It is a matter of some astonishment that the inhabitants should be so blind to their own interest to pull down for their own private use what would have made some recompense for the loss of those former revenues spent among them, by bringing to the town a great concourse of people to admire its mouldering fabric.[11]

Having been a centre of pilgrimage in a former religious age, Glastonbury was now urged to re-invent itself in its secular equivalent, as a tourist destination.

As soon as it ceased to be a quarry the antiquaries moved in. *The Avalonian Guide*, first published in 1810, already enlightened visitors on the subject of the town's history, and could direct travellers to other worthy spectacles in the locality, such as Wells Cathedral and Wookey Hole. It was published at the White Hart Inn, through which the abbey ruins could be entered. Already there were problems of conservation, however, and compromises had to be made. In 1807 ivy was cut from the walls of the Lady Chapel. 'The ivy considerably increased the venerable and interesting appearance of the ruin, but so injured it that it was obliged to be removed'.[12] Once the romantic gloss had been taken off, the focus shifted to the architectural character of the abbey, only fragments of which survived. Visitors at this time could see only the upstanding remains and so had to imagine for themselves the cloisters and the nave of the church. The Reverend Richard Warner of Bath published his *A History of the Abbey of Glaston* in 1826, which reported some of the earliest archaeological investigations at the abbey, specifically the clearance of the crypt below the Lady Chapel to expose the basin of a well, christened St Joseph's well.

Joseph of Arimathea lived on in local histories and guide books, although his story was now demoted to one of tradition, or the dubious status 'according to the monastick annalists'. Samuel Saunders in 1781 had defended the tradition saying that, even if it were untrue, it was still worth knowing about, for 'if totally false, must be allowed, if justice is done it, to have been as well told a story as most of the legendary tribe ... and, on the whole, as probable as any of its kind'.[13] The trouble was, antiquaries wanted facts and Joseph dwelt in the realm of tradition, an inferior brand of history. The study of Glastonbury Abbey in the nineteenth century was largely concerned with establishing just what it looked like when it was standing complete. The depredations of the sixteenth and seventeenth centuries had left many parts of the abbey complex hidden under the debris of demolition. The leading architectural historian of his day, Robert Willis, published his own interpretation in 1866 but it was never satisfactory and the issue of the ground plan would not be resolved until the twentieth century.

The study of Glastonbury Abbey went further than local or even monastic history. Glastonbury is in the west. It was colonised late by the Anglo-Saxons, who were converted to Christianity in a mission led by Augustine in 597. The implications of this are powerful and were well understood in Victorian Britain. Professor Edward Freeman, speaking to the Somerset Archaeological and Natural History Society in 1880, claimed that 'among all the greater churches of England, Glastonbury is the only one where we may be content to lay aside the name of England and fall back on the older name of Britain'.[14] It was a perfect symbol for British Christianity, begun by the Britons, honoured and enriched by their Anglo-Saxon conquerors, and later by their Norman overlords. Professor Freeman again: 'talk about the ancient British church, which is simply childish nonsense when it is talked at Canterbury or York or London, ceases to be childish nonsense when it is talked at Glastonbury'.[15] Canterbury was created by the English but in the mind of the Victorian antiquary Glastonbury trumped it as the church of the British past and present, the place that binds the memories of Briton (or Welsh if you prefer) and Englishman together. It has a place in the national imagination. The following quotation was made by Geoffrey Ashe in the 1960s but could have been made by any Englishman since the official union of England and Wales in 1536: 'At Glastonbury, for the first time, the English adopted a major Celtic institution and made it their own in a spirit of collaboration. Here, in a sense, the United Kingdom was born.'[16]

It was in literature, not in the study of its ruins, that Glastonbury, Joseph and especially Arthur thrived in the nineteenth century. The nineteenth century was in love with medieval architecture and with medieval romance. The rediscovery by Sir Walter Scott of Sir Thomas Malory's *Le Morte d'Arthur* initiated a new Arthurian cult. In this epic and discursive narrative the Victorians found a comprehensive source of lost stories, chivalry, mystic religion and a strong cast of characters, all written in language that was still intelligible to a modern readership. The geography of these Arthurian tales was now firmly fixed. In 'King Arthur's Tomb', part of *The Defence of Guenevere* (1858) by William Morris, Glastonbury is identified firmly as Avalon. Other writers concurred.

The writer most closely associated with the Arthurian craze was Alfred Lord Tennyson. Tennyson alluded to Joseph and Glastonbury in his 'The Holy Grail' (1869), one of the poems that make up *The Idylls of the King*. It confirms the status of the Glastonbury legend as part of the Grail mythology, although the poem as a whole is more concerned with a personal rather than spiritual challenge. The story is told by Sir Percivale, who had retired to a monastery and was in conversation with a monk, Ambrosius, who wanted to know about the knight's chivalrous past. Percivale introduced the Holy Grail as the cup of the Last Supper and both Percivale and the monk knew how it came to be in England.

> '... the good saint
> Arimathean Joseph, journeying brought
> To Glastonbury, where the winter thorn
> Blossoms at Christmas, mindful of our Lord.
> And there awhile it bode; and if a man
> Could touch or see it, he was heal'd at once,
> By faith, of all his ills. But then the times
> Grew to such evil that the holy cup
> Was caught away to Heaven, and disappear'd.'
>
> To whom the monk: 'From our old books I know
> That Joseph came of old to Glastonbury,
> And there the heathen Prince, Arviragus,
> Gave him an isle of marsh whereon to build;
> And there he built with wattles from the marsh
> A little lonely church in days of yore,
> For so they say, these books of ours, but seem
> Mute of this miracle, far as I have read.'[17]

Robert Hawker (1803–1875), vicar of Morwenstow in Cornwall, had earlier written his own version, *The Quest of the Sangraal* (1863), although he was inspired to take up the subject after reading some of Tennyson's earlier Arthurian poems. Hawker was of a mystical cast of mind and the story of the Grail was a perfect vehicle for his poetic talents. The story of the quest necessarily begins with Joseph at Glastonbury, because it was he who brought the Grail to England:–

He lived long centuries and prophesied.
A gilded pilgrim ever and anon,
Cross-staff in hand, and folded at his side,
The mystic marvel of the feast of blood!
Once, in old time, he stood in this dear land,
Enthrall'd—for lo! a sign! his grounded staff
Took root, and branch'd, and bloom'd like Aaron's rod:
Thence came the shrine, the cell; therefore he dwelt,
The vassal of the Vase, at Avalon![18]

The holy thorn was now firmly embedded as part of the Protestant cult of Joseph of Arimathea. Joseph was inextricably linked with Glastonbury, as was Arthur. In Aubrey de Vere's poem 'King Henry II at the tomb of King Arthur' the poet muses on the ephemeral nature of fame and glory. On hearing of the fame of Arthur, Henry sought out his grave at Glastonbury, where stood 'St Joseph's church of woven wood / On England's baptism day'. When the grave was found and Henry expected to meet his hero:–

Alas! What found they there?
No kingly brow, no shapely mould;
But dust where such things were.

Henry realised that there was only one immortal, everlasting king:

Then Henry lifted from his head
The conqueror's iron crown:
That crown upon that dust he laid,
And knelt in reverence down,
And raised both hands to Heaven, and said,
'Thou, God, art King alone!

'Lie there, my crown, since God decrees
'This head a couch as low,
'What am I better now than these
'Six hundred years ago?
'Henceforth all mortal pageantries
'I count an idle show.'[19]

We are back to the vanities of human ambition, fertile ground for the archaeologist's trowel.

Archaeology got under way at Glastonbury Abbey in the early twentieth century at an optimistic moment when the future of the site suddenly looked very
bright indeed. The Church of England acquired Glastonbury Abbey in 1908. The
owner, Stanley Austin, had decided to sell by auction, which was won by Ernest
Jardine (1859–1947), a wealthy industrialist from Nottingham, and former
Nottingham Forest footballer, with a bid of £30,000. He outbid an American
interest led by Mrs Isabel Inez Garrison, who had wanted to found a school
of chivalry at Glastonbury. Rumours were soon confirmed that in fact Jardine
was acting as a holding agent for the Church of England. Dr George Kennion,
Bishop of Bath and Wells, launched a public appeal to raise the purchase price,
subscribers to which included Edward VII and the Prince of Wales. In June 1909
the deeds were passed the Church in a ceremony attended by the Archbishop
of Canterbury and the Prince and Princess of Wales, the future George V and
Queen Mary. Jardine's motives were not entirely altruistic, but part and parcel
of his political ambitions. Securing the long-term future of the abbey raised his
stock as a public figure, which helped him cruise to victory in the East Somerset
constituency at the 1910 General Election. He held the seat for eight years and a
year later was created first Baronet of Nottingham.

Coincident with the Church of England's acquisition of Glastonbury Abbey,
a programme of excavations was begun under the auspices of the Somerset
Archaeological and Natural History Society, led by the Bristol architect, Frederick
Bligh Bond (1864–1946). He was an obvious choice, a distinguished antiquary
with expertise in church furniture, and architect to the diocese of Bath and Wells.
The purpose of these excavations was not initially to answer questions about
Arthur, Joseph or the origins of Glastonbury Abbey. The layout of the buildings
was still a matter of debate. For example it was suspected, but not known, that
the abbey had two western towers, in the manner of York Minster and other
thirteenth-century churches. At first the excavations went well. Bond confirmed
the existence of the western towers, discovered a chapel beyond the east end
of the high altar, known as the Edgar Chapel, and uncovered the cloisters and
chapter house. All this was presented, with clear and informative plans, in annual
reports to the Somerset Archaeological and Natural History Society. He uncovered the well in the crypt of the Lady Chapel, which was fed by a conduit, and
uncovered the chapel in the monk's graveyard that had been rebuilt in 1382 by
John Chinnock, and dedicated to Saints Michael and Joseph.

Excavation was halted during the First World War, but afterwards Bond soon
ran into trouble. It emerged that Bond's work had been guided by paranormal
communications. When these revelations were published in 1918 in a book, *The
Gate of Remembrance*, diocesan authorities and the local archaeological society were appalled. For some it was just the last straw, as Bond was already on

the wrong side of many people at Glastonbury. As early as 1913 he had raised eyebrows by arguing that the plan of the abbey was laid out to strict geometric principles. Bond was so absorbed in his excavations that he did nothing to clear the accumulating spoil heaps, for which he was responsible. The untidy condition of the place was beginning to attract negative comment. The Somerset Archaeological and Natural History Society committed 'heavy expenditure' to removal of a thousand loads of earth by 1913, lamenting that there were 2,000 more loads left on the site. Bond's single mindedness looked to many people like the self-importance of a man who thought Glastonbury was his personal property. He was also dogged by revelations about his private life. In his ex-wife's determination to get even with him, he was subjected to a sustained campaign of public vilification from which his reputation undoubtedly suffered. What was just as bad, he had made a powerful enemy in the form of William Caroe, the distinguished architect who had replaced Bond as the diocesan architect and was in charge of restoring the surviving architectural fabric of the abbey. The Society could have sacked Bond from his post as director of its excavations, but seemed to lack the courage to do so. Instead it appointed a co-director in 1921, knowing that Bond would find the new arrangement intolerable. Bond quit. Soon, responsibility for the excavations would be passed to the Society of Antiquaries and Bond would thereafter find himself permanently out in the cold.

Ironically, his work at Glastonbury had mainly been in the uncovering of later accretions to the abbey, specifically the Edgar and Loretto Chapels, and so his excavations had not damaged the archaeological potential of the early history of the site. He had made up for the poor quality of previous work at Glastonbury, and although there were criticisms of some of his work, particularly in establishing the plan of the Edgar Chapel, they were minor and could easily be rectified. Sadly, subsequent excavators at Glastonbury failed to do the subject justice either. With hindsight, Bond's contribution can be seen as a high point in the undistinguished record of archaeology at Glastonbury Abbey.

By the 1920s there was less money to invest in excavations, but two seasons were directed by Theodore Fyfe, before 1928 when the excavation was conducted by a trio led by Charles Peers (1868–1952). He was the government's Chief Inspector of Ancient Monuments until his retirement in 1933. From now on there would be professional oversight of archaeology at Glastonbury. Research interest now shifted to the pre-Norman phases of the abbey's archaeology. A snapshot of how archaeology was conducted in these years is provided by H. V. Morton, who stopped by during his motor-car nostalgia tour of England in the 1920s. Morton grumbled about the failure to re-roof and re-consecrate the Lady Chapel as a living church, and lamented the absence of someone to give him a guided tour. At least workmen were busy uncovering its past. Having just unearthed part of a human arm, 'a man in spectacles is examining it expertly while the red face of the labourer gazes up earnestly over the parados of the trench'.[20]

These were the early days of professional archaeology. The problem with the 1920s work was not with the red-faced labourers but with the bespectacled experts. A series of interim reports appeared with the promise that a more comprehensive study of the evidence would follow later, but it never happened. Inconsistencies and contradictions in these reports needed clarification, but it was not forthcoming.

Glastonbury Abbey was already open to the public when excavations started in 1908, and one of the key aims of the excavations was to make the site easier to comprehend. Bligh Bond had published in 1909 a popular guide to the abbey, priced 6d, which had proved very successful; another was published locally by George Mantle. However this was an area in which Charles Peers excelled, and his influence is still felt in the way in which the ruins are presented to the public. The timing of the purchase of Glastonbury Abbey in 1908 had been fortuitous. Five years later, in 1913, Parliament passed the Ancient Monuments Consolidation and Amendment Act, which gave it powers to take over nationally important monuments and to maintain them at the public's expense. Charles Peers was appointed to the position of Inspector of Ancient Monuments in order to implement this policy. Glastonbury would have been a strong candidate to be taken into state care had it not been acquired by the Church of England.

Peers wanted to make the ruins comprehensible to visitors. His policy therefore was to expose the foundations of the abbey walls so that visitors could see its layout. It was like a surveyor's plan, except that the ink was masonry and the paper was mown grass. Peers had been instrumental in the adoption of this rather clinical style of presentation at state-maintained ancient monuments in England and Wales, and ensured that it was applied to Glastonbury Abbey as well. The romantic atmosphere of the place was lost when the ivy was cleared from the walls, and even later buildings were removed and discarded. This whole conservation ethos has been criticised, sometimes harshly, but it tells us something about how ancient monuments were appreciated in the early twentieth century. The site had enjoyed nearly four centuries as a ruin, but for Peers its story had ended in 1539. Only in the latter part of the twentieth century did archaeologists and historians decide that the afterlife of the abbey was a worthwhile study in its own right.

The Church of England always intended that Glastonbury Abbey should be a place of pilgrimage and not just a piece of dead heritage or romantic ruin. As a place of Christian worship, Glastonbury Abbey had a role to play in reconciling Anglican and Catholic, for both of whom its ruins retained a spiritual power. After the beatification of Richard Whiting, John Thorne and Roger James in 1895 the Roman Catholic church organised a pilgrimage to Glastonbury. Two years later, to celebrate the 1,300th anniversary of Augustine's mission to England, the Archbishop of Canterbury led a pilgrimage to Glastonbury that included 130 Anglican bishops, thirty-two of them from the United States. More regular pilgrimages began after the Great War. In 1923 Anglo-Catholic pilgrims arrived by charabanc from Bristol and Salisbury and a procession of over 1,500 worshippers took place from the church of St John to the abbey, led by the vicar, Lionel Smithett Lewis. The Anglican West of England Pilgrimage Association has organised annual pilgrimages since 1926. There have been Roman Catholic pilgrimages since the 1930s and in 1961 the Orthodox church joined in. In the 1960s the Catholic Mass was again celebrated inside the abbey walls, and the crypt of the Lady Chapel was re-consecrated for multi-denominational use. Since 1985 Catholics and Anglicans have processed together in the spirit of Christian unity.

Among the Christians, Joseph of Arimathea was revived at Glastonbury in these years. We know this because the leading figure in the revival of Glastonbury as a pilgrimage centre was the Reverend Lewis, who we will meet again later. But the creation of an establishment archaeological view of Glastonbury's past had little room for its ancient myths or its more individual interpretations. As we will see, these remained bubbling under (and we have not yet finished with Frederick Bligh Bond) and found their own ways to prominence in spite of occasional official disapproval. Joseph and Arthur were never part of the archaeological research agenda in the early years of excavation and presentation to the public. Arthur, his bones dispersed who knows where, was no longer buried at Glastonbury. And yet by the 1950s Arthur, Avalon and Glastonbury had become a serious matter for both historians and archaeologists.

There were far more people interested in Arthur in the twentieth century than could be accommodated by a small academic community. New genres emerged in which these people could express their own ideas, like the historical novel and the fantasy novel, in both adult and children's forms, a transatlantic phenomenon that takes in authors such as Rosemary Sutcliff (1920–92), Mary Stewart (1916–) and Marion Bradley (1930–99). However, in parallel with it there was a renewed interest in the mythological aspects of Glastonbury's past on the part of archaeologists, led by the independent scholar Geoffrey Ashe, who described this loose movement as a modern Quest for Arthur. The search for a historical Arthur did not suit everybody's tastes, largely because the figure of medieval chivalry had to give way to a Dark Age warrior king, a much more hairy, rough-and-ready character than the romantics liked to portray. If Arthur really was a historical figure he would have been alive in the aftermath of Roman Britain, and his lifespan could reliably be placed in the period approximately 470–540.

Luckily this modern Arthurian quest found a champion in Ralegh Radford (1900–1999), who directed an intermittent programme of excavations at Glastonbury Abbey from 1951 to 1964. Radford was an acknowledged expert on church history and the Dark Ages. He had already dug successfully at Tintagel Castle, where he discovered shards of a rich Mediterranean pottery of the fifth and sixth centuries, similar to pottery later found in Somerset on Glastonbury Tor and at South Cadbury. And luckily for Radford there were funds available for excavation at the abbey. In 1926 Bond had emigrated to America, where his work at Glastonbury became known through lecture tours. He befriended a wealthy couple from Minnesota, George and Blanche Van Dusen, who were prepared to sponsor further excavations, focusing on the area of the early Christian settlement at the abbey. Applications to excavate at the abbey were rejected by the Abbey trustees, however, irrespective of whether they knew that Bond was lined up to direct them. After Bond died in 1945 the campaign to re-start excavations continued. After several rejections, the widowed Mrs Van Dusen finally agreed to sponsor excavations unconditionally. The archaeologist would decide what and where to excavate and that was Ralegh Radford.

Archaeology in the two decades after the war was confident and ambitious, involving itself in excavations of nationally important sites, often with widespread and welcome publicity. But many of these digs did not deliver the rigorous and thorough scientific analyses that they promised. Alas, Glastonbury Abbey, like Stonehenge, was among them. Radford, like Peers, was interested in the early history of Glastonbury and concentrated his efforts on the Anglo-Saxon churches on the site, considerable evidence for which survived at the west end of the medieval abbey church. He also claimed to have discovered a timber building of the fifth century, which would have proved that the monastery was a Celtic foundation, but the dating evidence for this was later found to have been flawed. Radford was minded to extend Glastonbury's sacred history back to pagan times. To the south east of Glastonbury, built across the access to the peninsula, is a bank and ditch just over a kilometre (1,100 yards) long. It looks at first like a defensive structure, but it would be easy to round it at the ends and so probably had some other purpose. Radford thought it was the boundary of a Celtic sacred enclosure, or *temenos*. However, excavation across the bank has been unable to explain why or exactly when it was raised. The evidence suggests that is most likely to have been raised in the Dark-Age or Anglo-Saxon periods. But it was enough for Radford to start thinking of the abbey as a site of pre-Christian sanctity.

In 1962 Radford discovered what he deduced was the excavation made in 1191 in the search for Arthur's grave. He could be sure that it was of this date because when it had been backfilled the fill included small chips of Doulting stone. This was a type of limestone quarried from near Wells which was first used at Glastonbury Abbey for the rebuilding of the Lady Chapel after the fire of 1184. It was a thrilling discovery, to have found evidence of an event reported in contemporary literature, but it did not prove that the skeletal remains removed from the grave in 1191 were those of Arthur and Guinevere. Radford nevertheless credited it as a distinct possibility, as well as the possibility that Glastonbury could have been the Isle of Avalon after all. He had been swept up by the wave of enthusiasm for Arthur.

Other archaeologists were cooler on the subject. Excavations were also undertaken at Glastonbury in the 1960s at the Chalice Well and at Glastonbury Tor, all directed by Philip Rahtz (1921–2011) of Birmingham University. The Chalice Well Trust sponsored a season of excavations at the Chalice Well in 1960, although it uncovered little evidence of activity in Roman times, and nothing that would clinch a connection with Arthur. In fact the importance of the Chalice Well in Glastonbury mythology is the work of successive owners from the late nineteenth century onwards. Excavations on the Tor proved more interesting, even if no Arthurian connection was proved. The summit is now dominated by the tower, all that remains of the medieval chapel of St Michael. Before the chapel had been built, Rahtz was able to show that there had been a settlement of some sort in Arthurian times, and that between the tenth and the twelfth centuries there was a monastic settlement, presumably a small cell of the abbey. The Dark Age remains on such a prominent hilltop seemed to Rahtz to be an eyrie-type fortress of some local chieftain. He wondered initially whether it could be Melwas, the chieftain besieged at Glastonbury by Arthur, according to the *Life of St Gildas* written by Caradog of Llancarfan, although he later revised his interpretation in favour of it being an early monastic site.[21]

The flagship project in this 1960s Quest for Arthur was the excavation of the hillfort of South Cadbury in south Somerset. It was this site that Leland commented upon as the historical Camelot. How the site should be tackled was the responsibility of the Camelot Research Committee, founded in 1965, with Geoffrey Ashe prominent. Today its constituents seem unlikely bedfellows. They included the Society of Antiquaries, the universities of Wales and Bristol, the Honourable Society of Knights of the Round Table and the Pendragon Society. Sir Mortimer Wheeler, by then a grand old man of British archaeology, became its president, and its sponsors included the British Academy, Bristol United Press and the BBC. Excavations, led by Leslie Alcock, took place between 1966 and 1970. *The Observer* newspaper sponsored some of the work in return for exclusive rights, and the BBC made a film of it.

The results, needless to say, were an anti-climax. A report on the excavations was entitled *Cadbury–Camelot*, but it was more publicity than substance. The excavations were hardly a failure—they established a sequence of occupation beginning in the Neolithic period, followed by the Iron Age fort that was re-occupied in Dark-Age times, right through to the possibility that there was a mint there in the eleventh century—but there was no Arthur. Alcock was undeterred and continued to argue for an historical Arthur, as did another eminent historian of the period, John Morris, who published the *Age of Arthur* in 1973. Four years later a young scholar, David Dumville, wrote a savage critique of the quest for a historical Arthur. He pointed out the essential unreliability of the early sources as historical documents, and that to look for a figure on the basis that there is 'no smoke without fire' was an inadequate justification for all the resources that had been thrown at it. It seems to have brought many academics to their senses, including Leslie Alcock, who retreated from his earlier position.

It is in their contribution to our understanding of Glastonbury Abbey that the archaeologists have been least impressive. Even so, the careers of Charles Peers and Ralegh Radford did not suffer for their Glastonbury shortcomings. Both were pillars of the archaeological establishment. Peers was knighted and in 1929 was made President of the Society of Antiquaries; Radford was awarded the gold medal of the Society of Antiquaries in 1972, and to celebrate his ninetieth birthday a volume of essays in his honour was published by leading scholars.[22] The biggest loser in the emergence of establishment, or professional, archaeology was Frederick Bligh Bond. His psychic experiences put him beyond the pale of archaeology and he never received much credit for the good work that he performed there. He was criticised for tailoring some of his evidence to suit his pet theories, particularly regarding the Edgar Chapel and the overall length of the abbey church. But Peers and Radford also tailored their interpretations to their reading of medieval literature, and look naïve in retrospect. If there is any consolation, it is Bond's work that is still talked about.

Since the flurry of excitement died down, Arthur has disappeared from the discussion of Britain in the centuries following the withdrawal of the Roman imperial army in 410. Even the term Dark Ages has fallen out of favour. Visitors to the abbey are still reminded that it was Arthur's reputed burial place, but then Arthur has commercial merit irrespective of his historical merit. When Somerset County Council re-opened the county museum in Taunton in 2011 it was able to tell the story of early medieval Somerset using the evidence of archaeology alone. Arthur is not even mentioned. The historical Arthur has been cast out, like Joseph of Arimathea, and his natural home is now among the unorthodox thinkers.

9

And Did Those Feet ...?

Joseph returned to favour at Glastonbury during the period of Christian revival at the abbey, but in the twentieth century he emerged as quite a different person to the Joseph of the apocryphal literature, the Grail romances or John's official monastic history. The rise of history and archaeology as intellectual disciplines had created a body of local expertise on the subject of Glastonbury's early history, but people outside of this emerging establishment wanted to contribute too. Like most theories about Glastonbury, the new theory of Joseph's visit to Britain was formulated well beyond the boundary of Somerset, and takes us initially on a detour to Cornwall.

We have come across popular culture before, specifically in gatherings at the Glastonbury thorns from the seventeenth century onwards. By the nineteenth century rural Britain was undeniably changing and the beliefs and traditions of its natives seemed to be in a steep and terminal decline. Rural culture was romanticised under a new umbrella term Folklore, and a conscious effort was made to collect up material and make sense of it before it vanished altogether. Contemporary authors believed that they were recording aspects of country life that belonged to a time out of mind but, as we will see, traditions are not always as old as they seem.

One of the most prominent of Victorian folklorists was Sabine Baring-Gould (1834–1924). Devonian by birth, for much of his career he was vicar of Lew Trenchard in Devon. It allowed him plenty of time to indulge his interests, writing novels and hagiographies, pursuing archaeology and collecting folk songs and traditions in the west of England. He wrote the hymn 'Onward Christian Soldiers'. One of his largest projects was a multi-volume hagiography published in the 1870s, in which he first encountered Joseph of Arimathea. The author referred to the 'many strange traditions' associated with Joseph and Britain but dismissed them as 'wholly worthless'.[1] Two years after these words had appeared in a revised edition of the work in 1897 Baring-Gould had reversed this view in a conversion of Damascene proportions. What was perhaps to be his most significant piece of writing was a seemingly innocuous passage in the *Book of Cornwall*, published in 1899, where he describes the culture of the tin miners.

> Another Cornish story is to the effect that Joseph of Arimathea came in a boat to Cornwall, and brought the Child Jesus with him, and the latter taught him how to extract the tin and purge it of its wolfram. The story possibly grew out of the fact that the Jews under the Angevin kings farmed the tin of Cornwall. When the tin is flashed, then the tinner shouts, 'Joseph was in the tin trade', which is probably a corruption of 'S. Joseph to the tinner's aid!'[2]

What sounds like an ancient Cornish tradition was in fact less than ten years old. It originated from the Chief Bard of Cornwall, Henry Jenner (1848–1934), who worked at the British Museum. He heard the phrase 'Joseph was in the tin trade' at a metal casting shop in London in the 1890s, where workmen were making tin sheets for organ pipes. He did not know to which Joseph it referred and had no reason to suppose that it referred to any of the Biblical characters of that name. Cornwall had its tin trade, but Joseph was not the patron saint of tin miners, an honour that went to St Piran. It was Jenner who told Sabine Baring-Gould, who made the link between tin and the Cornish mines and then added a new twist to the story—that Joseph had brought Jesus with him. Strange, then, that no previous author had ever heard such a story emanating from the county's mines.

Cornwall seems to have been an especially fertile place to capture popular culture. The mineral geologist Robert Hunt published in 1881 his *Popular Romances of the West of England*, an encyclopaedic (although not necessarily exhaustive) study of Cornish traditions. He makes no mention of Joseph or Jesus; nor did other active Cornish folklorists of the period such as William Bottrell or Margaret Courtney. Likewise, the eighteenth-century antiquary William Borlase, vicar of Ludgvan in the heart of Cornish mining country, made a lot of use of local superstition in his studies, but never mentioned Joseph. One of the problems of folklore studies, however, was that the people who published works of popular superstition did not always engage directly with their subject matter. Sabine Baring-Gould is guilty in this instance. Even Robert Hunt employed a postman to seek out tales from the inhabitants of Cornwall's western tip. Perhaps the traditions they collected were only of the type that they asked for.

There was circumstantial evidence that kept alive the possibility of a connection between the Bible lands and Cornwall. It was a popular belief that Jewish merchants had engaged in the Cornish tin trade, although not earlier than the medieval period. An old Cornish song told of a time before King John, when:–

... that red-robed sinner
Robb'd the Jew of the gold he had made as a tinner.[3]

By the end of the sixteenth century, when Richard Carew was writing his *Survey of Cornwall* (1602), there were mining remains beyond memory that were ascribed to the Jews. In the nineteenth century Marazion was still referred to as Market-Jew, old smelting works were known as Jew's Houses, a spoil heap was an *Atall Sarazin* (Saracen was another Cornish term for the Jews), and old specimens of metal were Jew's Tin. Ghosts of old Jewish miners were known as Knockers, Knackers or Buccas, 'sent for slaves by the Roman emperors to work the mines' as a punishment for crucifying Jesus. There was a tradition that St Paul came to Cornwall to buy tin from Creekbraws mine and preached at nearby Gwennap Pit, the natural amphitheatre in which John Wesley would preach in the eighteenth century. So there were already sufficient Biblical associations with Cornwall to ensure that Sabine Baring-Gould's claims were not dismissed out of hand.

Most of this material was taken up by John Taylor (1851–1910) in his book *The Coming of the Saints* (1906). By day Taylor was professor of gynaecology at Mason College in Birmingham (now part of Birmingham University), and he was the founder of the hospice in Birmingham that still bears his name. But he was an Edwardian Renaissance man with literary and religious leanings, and who believed in 'plain living, high thinking and holy aspiration'. *The Coming of the Saints* was his chief literary achievement, a labour of love written in the intervals in his busy professional career, and would be much quoted. In it is the first detailed exposition that combined the myths of Joseph in Cornwall and in Glastonbury. The tin traders' route described by Diodorus of Sicily allowed Taylor to propose a detailed itinerary by which Joseph the tin merchant could have travelled up the Rhone valley from Marseilles, across France via Limoges to Brittany, and across the sea to Cornwall, landing at St Michael's Mount.

Taylor also revived the cult of Joseph at Glastonbury, which had been made to seem more convincing by the emergence of the Cornish material. He resurrected early writings, such as those of Gildas, William of Malmesbury and the Grail romances, and incorporated Welsh sources into his story of how Joseph came to Britain, and how his descendants became British nobility and royalty. At Glastonbury he noted that the dimensions of the *vetusta ecclesia* were preserved inside the walls of the Lady Chapel, completed in 1186, and thought he knew why. The little wattle church had been built by Joseph 60 feet long and 24 feet wide, which computations by the Reverend W. S. Caldecott had purportedly shown were the exact dimensions of the Jewish Tabernacle, built to specifications revealed to Moses by God himself.

John Taylor noted but was not especially interested in the idea that Jesus had come to Britain. That particular strand of the myth was to receive an extra boost from an unexpected quarter. William Blake's short poem 'Jerusalem', published in 1808, had appeared in the preface to his poem *Milton*, but without the title that it later acquired (it has nothing to do with Blake's longer poem called *Jerusalem*). The four verses attracted little notice at the time, but found an audience when they appeared in 1916 in an anthology of patriotic verse, *The Spirit of Man*, edited by the Poet Laureate, Robert Bridges. It aimed to rouse the nation's spirit that had been dented by increasingly grim news from the Western Front. Its inspiring language certainly elevated England as an especially sacred place, although Glastonbury is not mentioned:

> And did those feet in ancient time
> Walk upon England's mountains green?
> And was the Holy Lamb of God
> On England's pleasant pastures seen?
>
> And did the Countenance Divine
> Shine forth upon our clouded hills?
> And was Jerusalem builded here
> Among these dark Satanic mills?

Robert Bridges asked Hubert Parry to set the poem to music, to be sung like a hymn at a meeting of Fight for Right, a group that campaigned for an all-out victory against Germany and urged against making any kind of accommodation with the enemy. Parry converted Blake's four stanzas into two verses, sung with organ accompaniment for the first time at the Queen's Hall in London in March 1916, less than two weeks after it was composed. Parry was uncomfortable with the Fight for Right movement, but by the time he withdrew his support for it in 1917 the hymn was attracting wider interest. It had been taken up by the Suffragette movement in 1917 and Millicent Garrett Fawcett asked Parry if it could be performed at a Suffragette Demonstration Concert in 1918. Parry was much more in sympathy with Suffragette aims and obliged them by providing an orchestrated arrangement of it. It was at this concert that the original title, 'And did those feet in ancient time', was replaced by 'Jerusalem'.

Parry assigned the copyright of 'Jerusalem' to the National Union of Women's Suffrage Societies. It became the official Women Voter's Hymn. When the NUWSS was wound up in 1928 the copyright passed to the Women's Institutes. By the time it came into the public domain fifty years after Parry's death, in 1968, it had achieved the status of an alternative national anthem. Blake's words had proved to be as protean as any Glastonbury myth. George V believed that the hymn, as it had now become, could be a more rousing national anthem than the dreary dirge God save the King. England (as opposed to Britain) has no official national anthem, but Jerusalem has become the unofficial anthem in the world of English cricket, Rugby League and at the Commonwealth Games. Politicians of the right and left, and conservative and radical factions of British society, have also appropriated the lines to their own causes. Jarrow hunger marchers sang it in the 1930s. Clement Attlee promised to build a New Jerusalem in the 1945 General Election. Labour, Conservative and Liberal parties have sung it at their annual conferences. Edward Elgar's orchestration of it is performed at the Last Night of the Proms and it has been recorded by such diverse modern acts as the new-age Tim Blake (erstwhile member of the hippy group Gong), the hard rock of Bruce Dickinson and the Baroque strains of Emerson, Lake & Palmer. The words are open to interpretation, which is both a blessing and a curse.

One place where Blake's words have not found universal approval is the Church of England. True, the hymn is sung in many churches and cathedrals, but there have been dissenting voices among the clergy who have pointed out that, for all its rousing patriotism, it speaks less of God than with its author's revolutionary spirit. Blake's language is notoriously abstruse and so a literal interpretation of the poem is naive. The poem is a kind of word-music, rich and suggestive, with the potential to conjure different images and meanings in everyone who reads or hears it. For most people the words invoke a mystical sanctity to the land of England, and to a lot of people it is a poem of revolution, but Blake was never a nationalist. The lines were written in London in defiance of British patriotic fervour against republican France. It was a time of war, when the ideals of liberty, equality and fraternity were threatened with extinction from tyrants and warring nations. Blake was perhaps conjuring an idealised England of peace and love, a purer world that existed before the world of mechanisation overtook it, exemplified by modern weapons of war. Blake was perhaps resisting the pressure to become cynical and worldly in the second half of the second verse, when he vows:–

I will not cease from mental fight:
Nor shall my sword sleep in my hand
Till I have built Jerusalem
In England's green and pleasant land.

Contrary to what is widely assumed, it seems very unlikely that, when he wrote it, Blake knew of any tradition that Jesus had visited Britain. Nor is there any evidence of him having visited either Glastonbury or Cornwall. But the twentieth century made of it what it wanted to. The most popular interpretation of it is that it refers specifically to a visit to Britain by Jesus, during the lost years between the ages of twelve and thirty about which the Bible is silent. However, when it was written in 1804 there was no tradition that Jesus came to Britain. Supporters of the theory have pointed out that Blake's earliest known engraving is of 'Joseph of Arimathea among the rocks of Albion', made in 1773. It suggests that Blake was abreast of popular culture, and it is quite likely that he had read pamphlets such as *The Holy Disciple, or, The History of Joseph of Arimathea*. The image in question, however, is copied from a figure painted by Michelangelo in the Pauline chapel at the Vatican. Joseph does not carry a staff, or lead a band of disciples, but is a draped and hooded figure at the sea's edge. There is a caption that describes him as 'one of the Gothic artists who built the cathedrals in what we call the Dark Ages'. It was the lot of early Christians to be 'wandering about in sheep skins & goat skins of whom the world was not worthy'. Joseph and his association with Britain may have been widely known, but Blake produced his own version that pays little heed of the details of that tradition. There is no evidence that he knew of another tradition linking Joseph with the young Jesus. Blake's suggestive words gained a popular profile just when the story of Joseph of Arimathea trading tin in Cornwall emerged. The Bible and the apocryphal literature say nothing to suggest that Joseph and Jesus were related, but the inference was quickly made. So instead of Blake's words drawing on a tradition of Jesus visiting Britain, they actually helped to create that myth in the first place. Soon 'Jerusalem' would find yet another new title as 'the Glastonbury hymn'.

The Jesus connection was not wholly embraced in Glastonbury itself. Glastonbury's Christian myths enjoyed a renaissance from the end of the nineteenth century. Charles Marson (1859–1914), vicar of Hambridge near Taunton, noted in 1909 that cuttings from the holy thorn in the churchyard of St John had adorned the altar of the church at Christmas for fourteen of the previous seventeen years. In his own history of Glastonbury, Marson credited Joseph as the founder of Christianity in Glastonbury and was prepared to reconsider the historical value of the Grail romances. By 1926, in his book *The Glories of Glastonbury*, Armine le Strange Campbell noted that while the legends are not facts, the existence of ancient legends is a fact, and argued that Glastonbury's traditions, including the eloquent verses of William Blake, are 'stories to cherish'. The possibility that Christ had come to England as a boy seemed improbable but not impossible.

The man who did most to revive Glastonbury traditions was the Reverend Lionel Smithett Lewis (1867–1953), who became vicar of St John in Glastonbury in 1921. Lewis, originally from Kent, did nothing by halves. He had previously been vicar of St Mark in Whitechapel, where he was an active member of the Church Anti-Vivisection League. When he moved to Somerset he immediately found a new cause and immersed himself in Glastonbury's history. A year after his arrival he published the first edition of his successful book *St Joseph of Arimathea at Glastonbury*. Fifteen years later its sixth edition was published and there were 24,000 copies of the book in print. It was, therefore, demonstration that history had acquired a popular audience. In 1925 he followed it with another successful book, *Glastonbury 'the mother of saints'*, an account of every saint with Glastonbury associations.

Lewis relied heavily on John Taylor's work and quotes or refers to his book extensively. But Lewis added his own new material. Contrary to received wisdom, Lewis claimed that evidence of Joseph's grave at Glastonbury had survived. In the churchyard of St John was a medieval tomb chest, decorated with quatrefoils and with a panel inscribed 'J. A.'. This was traditionally associated with a man named John Alleyn. Charles Marson had not mentioned it in his earlier account of Glastonbury, noting that Glastonbury Abbey never claimed to have found the grave of Joseph. But Lewis argued that John Blome had dug for and found Joseph's grave in 1345, citing the Lincolnshire monk who claimed in 1367 that the grave had been found. According to the tradition cited by Lewis, the tomb was made for the abbey's shrine to St Joseph, and was seen there among the ruins in 1662 by John Ray. Fearing its destruction by Puritan fanatics (who were in fact by now in retreat with the collapse of the Commonwealth and the restoration of Charles II) it was moved by the parishioners out of the abbey ruins and into the parish churchyard. The name John Alleyn was apparently invented to ward off hostile enquiries as to its provenance. In 1928 the vicar had it moved inside the church, where it remains, ostensibly to prevent its further deterioration, but surely mainly to afford it due reverence. It stands in the chapel St Katharine in the parish church. In 1935 a new stained glass window for the chapel was provided by A. J. Davies, of the Bromsgrove Guild of glass painters. Several of the glass panels narrate the story of Joseph of Arimathea, protesting about the crucifixion of Christ, laying him in the tomb, and his arrival and settlement in Glastonbury with the two cruets, and placing his staff in the ground on Wearyall Hill. The guiding hand of Lewis is all too obvious.

For Lewis, the possible visit of Christ to Britain was only peripheral to his interests. Most of his work was a re-statement of earlier authors on the subject of Joseph. His original contribution, or accretions to the legend if you prefer, is that the tomb in the church of St John, as described above, was made for the bones of Joseph, and that the Virgin Mary had also died and been buried at Glastonbury. These were largely speculative, but the evidence for Christ's visit was provided not from the authority of ancient authors, but the alternative receptacle of ancient knowledge, folklore. The tradition that Jesus came to Britain was found among the 'hill-folk' of Somerset and Gloucestershire (from information supplied by the Archdeacon of Wells), and apparently in the west of Ireland too. The argument, however, was centred upon traditions at Priddy, a village in the former lead-mining district of the Mendip Hills. A tradition that Christ had been at Priddy was apparently known in the neighbourhood by a popular saying 'as sure as Our Lord was at Priddy', but its origin was disputed. Dean Robinson of Wells, following Beatrice Hamilton Thompson, countered that the tradition had a much more mundane origin. The story was invented by the village schoolmistress to provide the plot for a school play. Nevertheless, the tradition of Christ in Somerset was developed by two other outsiders, the Reverend Henry Ardern Lewis (1879–1957) of Talland in Cornwall, later of St Martins in the Isles of Scilly, and the Reverend Cyril Comyn Dobson (1879–1960), vicar in Paddington, London, and later of St Mary in the Castle, Hastings.

Cornwall was the place first identified with the myth of Christ in England. Henry Lewis, while he was vicar of Talland in south Cornwall, went in search of folklore of the south Cornish coast that might have been missed by previous fieldworkers, simply because they had never thought to ask about it. Lewis was well rewarded, although some of his informants initially claimed to know nothing of the legend. The Reverend Hammond, of neighbouring St Just-in-Roseland, told him that there was a tradition of Christ in his parish, which Lewis then visited for himself. One man even told him that Christ's party had anchored at St Just creek. An old man said that Christ had landed at Falmouth, while other vague memories of Christ's visit to Cornwall were found on the coast at Looe Island, Talland and Polperro. Inland, Lewis also found rich pickings in the mining districts. A Falmouth person told him that Christ had been at Creekbraws mine, presumably confused with the story of St Paul unearthed in the previous century by Robert Hunt, and another suggested he had been to Ding Dong, another supposedly ancient mine, after landing at Mounts Bay near Penzance. One person in Redruth, in the heart of mining country, claimed to know the song 'Joseph was a tin man', but Lewis was unable to extract from him, or anyone else, anything beyond the first line.

Lewis was especially interested in Looe Island, sometimes known as St George's Island, off the south coast of Cornwall. Islands such as this and St Michael's Mount were thought to have been the main ports trading with the Middle East, and on Looe Island was a small monastery. This was a Celtic monastery founded in the sixth century, then re-founded as a Benedictine cell of Glastonbury Abbey by 1114. Later in the twelfth century a new chapel, known as Lammana, was built on the mainland to make it easier for pilgrims to visit. Glastonbury had sold Lammana in the late thirteenth century but the association of the two was suggestive. Lewis met a woman, nearly 100 years old, who told of him of piece of cloth which was part of Christ's shroud, and which Lewis interpreted as folk memory of one of the relics at Lammana chapel. Not everyone agreed with Lewis' claims for Looe Island, but a Mrs Jeffrey wrote to the *Cornish Times* in 1948 that an old couple at Looe had kept alive the story but never spoke of it for fear of ridicule. It was acknowledged that the tradition, which had been passed down through the generations for nearly 2,000 years, had died out during Lewis' research into the subject. It had been found in the nick of time, a familiar claim made by folklorists in the nineteenth and early twentieth centuries. One man at Port Looe initially denied any knowledge of such a legend but after persistent questioning eventually conceded that he had heard his wife speak of such things. This can be taken two ways. Did he not want to confess hearing about the legend for fear of ridicule? Or did he just confess because the vicar was a man of obvious authority in matters biblical and must therefore have been speaking of something that the man ought to know? Sadly, in the folklore of this period the authentic voice of the folk is all too often lost. It is only the author we hear.

Cyril Comyn Dobson began his researches independently and was the first to publish on the subject of Christ's visits to both Cornwall and Somerset (for some reason Dobson was at pains to point out that Christ never visited Devon). He was already a prolific enquirer into biblical mysteries, having written books on the Ark of the Covenant and *The Story of the Empty Tomb as if told by Joseph of Arimathea* (1920). Dobson's Christianity had acquired a patriotic and imperial flavour. In 1917 he published a pamphlet *God, the War and Britain*, in which he argued that 'Britain, or rather the Christian church in Britain, is the instrument God wants to use' to ensure worldwide Christianity, to be achieved through missionary efforts across the Empire.[4] It would culminate in the restoration of Jerusalem to the Jews, a real possibility toward the end of the First World War. Undeterred that these predictions did not come to pass after 1918, in a later book, *Britain's Place in History* (1936), he argued that Britain was chosen by God to prepare for the Second Coming, and therefore that the Empire was established with God's blessing in order that the truth of Christianity could be disseminated. Dobson seems to have relished the kind of historical enquiry that thrived on uncertainty. His earlier work on Joseph of Arimathea was inspired by the discovery of the Garden Tomb in the Holy Land, which some antiquaries argued had been the Joseph's tomb in which Jesus was laid and was resurrected. Dobson used an imaginary conversation as the vehicle for telling his story, but his Joseph resided and died in the Holy Land and was a follower of, rather than a blood relation of, Jesus.

This interpretation changed completely when it came to considering Jesus and Joseph in Britain, in a pamphlet published in 1936 as *Did our Lord visit Britain as they say in Cornwall and Somerset?* Having set out his arguments regarding the visit of Jesus to Glastonbury, he concluded by suggesting that 'it is perhaps best that its truth should not be definitely established, lest the place should become the scene of superstitious veneration', an ambition that was comprehensively unfulfilled.[5]

Blake, Baring Gould and the Reverend Morgan's influential book *St Paul in Britain* (1861) were his starting points. Suggestive place names were the bedrock of Somerset's claims that Jesus had been there. A tradition, the source of which is not identified, is that Joseph and Jesus came 'in a ship of [the Mediterranean port of] Tarshish to the Summerland and sojourned in a place called Paradise'.[6] Summerland is Somerset and Paradise is a district around Burnham-on-Sea that survives in the name of Paradise Farm. It subsequently emerged that there is also a Paradise near Glastonbury Tor. Godney, a village on the Somerset Levels between Burnham and Glastonbury, was interpreted as meaning 'God-marsh-island'. Dobson envisaged the party from Palestine landing near Burnham and taking a river boat across the marshes to Glastonbury, over land to Priddy in the Mendips, and then returning from Priddy on the River Axe.

That Jesus was a relative of Joseph was a Byzantine myth, although Dobson had to admit that 'the source of this Eastern tradition the Author has been unable to elicit'.[7] In fact the argument that they were related was based on speculation. The Jewish tradition was that the eldest relative of a dead person was responsible for organising the burial, which is why Joseph pleaded with Pilate for the body of Christ. It is an odd argument because the Gospels surely intend to suggest that he buried Jesus because he was his devoted follower, believed in his teachings, and was brave enough to stand out from the crowd and give the crucified Jesus the dignified burial he deserved. If he was simply doing his family duty then Joseph seems far less admirable. Christ's sojourn in Britain was easy to accommodate with the narrative of his life in the Bible, because nothing of his life is mentioned between the ages and twelve and thirty. He could have been anywhere and doing anything.

That Jesus had been absent from Palestine is implied because, on his return, John the Baptist seems not to know his own cousin. Dobson and others thought they knew where he was—travelling with Joseph and then, as a young man, settling in Glastonbury where he built a small retreat of wattle and daub. This was not on the site of the later abbey, but beside the Chalice Well. Here Jesus drank 'the purest crystal water' from a spring in which Joseph would later submerge the holy chalice, and by which Joseph and his companions would later erect their houses. The hermitage of Jesus was later consecrated as a chapel when it was found by the Pope Gregory's missionaries. Its discovery was purportedly recorded in a letter from St Augustine to the Pope, although Dobson was mistaken and was merely misquoting William of Malmesbury, who said it appeared in an unknown history of the Britons. Joseph then built a church for his group of disciples, the *vetusta ecclesia* that William of Malmesbury saw in the twelfth century, and which was destroyed by fire in 1184. That a hermitage was built by Christ himself is the reason, never before explained, why Gildas had claimed that Christianity was founded in Britain during the reign of Emperor Tiberius (i.e. before AD 37), before Joseph's supposed arrival in AD 63, and before the Roman

Empire invaded in AD 43. Why Glastonbury? Glastonbury was thought to be a centre of Druid religion, which Dobson portrays as a kind of proto-Christianity.

This trio of antiquarian vicars was mindful of the criticisms that it received. L. S. Lewis admitted that his work was written 'afar from great libraries' and yet the substance of his book is almost entirely founded upon the authority of ancient authors. These were the same authors that had been found wanting in previous centuries. Scholarship in the 1920s was beset with many practical difficulties, however. Even works published during the era of printing, such as James Ussher and Sir Henry Spelman, were difficult to access beyond the old universities. Today these works can be found in the special collections departments of many university libraries, or can be read on-line, but a century ago they were still largely in private collections and therefore very time-consuming to track down and study. Predictably, therefore, Lewis' history was called into question. His nemesis was Dr Armitage Robinson (1858–1933), Dean of Wells, who published *Two Glastonbury Legends* in 1926, refuting the legends of both King Arthur and Joseph of Arimathea. What irked Lewis most was the accusation that he had misread William of Malmesbury. Robinson was the first to notice, not only that the earliest extant copy of William of Malmesbury was a thirteenth-century work written by another hand, but that it included material, specifically the legend of Joseph of Arimathea, that was not the work of the original author. If the legend of Joseph was a later interpolation it would undermine the authenticity of his legend at Glastonbury. Lewis of course was having none of it: 'if he had produced a [manuscript] in a different handwriting we would accept it'.[8] The dispute between the freethinking and enthusiastic outsider and the learned but sceptical establishment man prefigured many of the archaeological disputes of the twentieth century.

L. S. Lewis, as well as Cyril Dobson, was especially aggrieved at the condescending tone adopted by the establishment, implying that thinking on these matters was best left to wiser heads. Of course, the pedagogic approach to history has long been set aside, but for most of the twentieth century the don was a figure of real intellectual authority. Cyril Dobson met his nemesis in Beatrice Hamilton Thompson. Dobson's book was published in 1936 and by 1940 four editions had been printed, but a curt refutation was published by Beatrice Hamilton Thompson in 1939 as *Glastonbury: Truth and Fiction*. Thompson was a Reformation historian and she upset Cyril Dobson, so much so that he could not bring himself to utter her name: 'I deeply regret the tone in which [*Glastonbury: Truth and Fiction*] is written, and its lack of literary taste and courtesy'.[9] Lewis, Lewis and Dobson all rejected the cool analyses they were up against, that historical sources could be categorised either as fact or fiction. Although their factual content could not be established, it seemed unfair to brand oral traditions and legends as fiction. For a start, much the Holy

Bible is tradition. Christopher Hollis livened up the debate following Robinson's criticism of L. S. Lewis by arguing that all worthwhile history is written from one standpoint or another, and therefore that history is not a question of fact or fiction, but is either theist or atheist, in the broad sense of those terms. 'The impartial historian is simply an atheist without the courage of his convictions'.[10]

The success of this generation of authors, who had all died by 1960, can be seen in the modern stained-glass windows in the parish churches of Glastonbury and Street, and in St Patrick's chapel in Glastonbury Abbey. A new generation succeeded them, amplifying the original claims a little, but not really adding any new compelling evidence. Joseph has now been re-interpreted as the uncle rather than great-uncle of Christ, younger brother of Joseph of Nazareth. Britain has a long tradition of independent historians, some of whom have been interested in Joseph and Jesus at Glastonbury, such as Glyn Lewis' *Did Jesus come to Britain?* (2008), Dennis Price's *The Missing Years of Jesus: the extraordinary evidence that Jesus visited Britain* (2010) and Arthur Eedle's *Albion Restored* (2013). Dr Gordon Strachan (1934–2010) was a Church of Scotland minister and erstwhile academic at Edinburgh University. In his book *Jesus the Master Builder* (1998) he argued that Christ had come to Britain to learn from the Druids. He maintained that Jesus led a peripatetic life between the ages of twelve and thirty, travelling in search of the wisdom of the world. Jesus had apparently become interested in Pythagorean mathematics while working on the building of the town of Sepphoris in Greece. It led him to visit the Druids, who were themselves adepts at mathematics and astronomy. The idea that Druids were like the Jews, both waiting for the emergence of the promised Messiah, is an attractive one for the heritage of the Celtic west. Strachan may have modernised the work of L. S. Lewis but, like his contemporaries, sheds no new light on his visit to Glastonbury, and is content to re-state the well-worn previous material on the subject.

The cult of Joseph of Arimathea has become a transatlantic phenomenon. Books have poured forth from America, including historical enquiries like Justin Griffin's *Glastonbury and the Grail: Did Joseph of Arimathea Bring the Sacred Relic to Britain?* (2012) and Robert Cruikshank's narrative *Joseph of Arimathea: The Man who Buried Jesus* (2011). Then there are the fictionalised accounts, like Brian Mellor's *Joseph of Arimathea—The Forgotten Man* (2012) and M. E. Rosson's *Uncle of God: The Voyages of Joseph of Arimathea* (2010). Another American novelist with a lifelong fascination for things Arthurian is Donna Crow, author of *Glastonbury: The Novel of Christian England* (1992), which tackles the more conventional legend of Joseph and the Holy Grail. Sceptics would argue that the proper place for stories about Joseph and Jesus at Glastonbury is found here, on the fiction shelf.

10

The Immemorial Mystery
of Glastonbury

In the early twentieth century Glastonbury became a go-to place, something that had not really happened in the railway age, but which gathered momentum in the age of the motor car. The town's reputation for alternative lifestyles really began in Edwardian England and not the 1960s. Something of its mix of upright Christianity, mysticism and commercial exploitation is captured in the 1933 novel *A Glastonbury Romance*, by John Cowper Powys. The novel explores the effect of a special myth on the inhabitants of a small town, in which the Grail represents the spiritual powers that continuously interact and influence life on Earth. Glastonbury seemed an ideal location to set the novel. 'There are only about a dozen reservoirs of world-magic on the whole surface of the globe', including Jerusalem, Rome and Mecca, 'and of these Glastonbury has the largest residue of unused power. Generations of mankind, aeons of past races, have—by their concentrated will—made Glastonbury miraculous'.[1] The plot of the novel centres around John Geard, an evangelical lay-preacher, who wants to restore Glastonbury as a centre of pilgrimage, vowing to organise a Religious Fair and to build a shrine for the 'holy spring'. His rival is John Crow, who has different vision for Glastonbury, based on industry and tourism, and is contemptuous of Glastonbury heritage. In fact he is warned in advance: 'you'll hate the senti-mentality that has been spread over everything there, like scented church-lamp oil'. Centres of pilgrimage breed cynicism. 'You'll hate the visitors. You'll hate the tradesmen catering for the visitors; you'll hate the sickening superstition of the whole thing'.[2] The novel could not have been set in Glastonbury without the author's belief that it can carry these epic personal experiences, and can be the holy city and the Waste Land all at once. The most important character in the novel is the place itself, setting a marker which has been followed by numerous incomers throughout the twentieth century—the so-called Avalonians.

For a while, Glastonbury was best known to a wide audience as a place of music and theatre, but there were also Arts-and-Crafts idealists, spiritualists and dreamers there, which make the Avalonians a diverse but tightly-knit group of people. The attraction of Glastonbury was instinctive. As Dion Fortune later wrote, the place 'seems to radiate a strange and potent influence', even if it defies explanation.[3]

Glastonbury's cultural landscape was changing. The Chalice Well only fully enters the story of Glastonbury mythology in 1886. That was the year in which it was first identified as the place where the Holy Grail was buried, in the inaugural journal of the Glastonbury Antiquarian Society. It was also the year when the well became the property of the Roman Catholic Church. The French Order of Missionaries of the Sacred Heart of Jesus established a missionary college at the adjoining Tor House. Its primary purpose was not to revive the cult of the Grail but to send missionaries to the far reaches of the Pacific. Tor House had previously been the Anchor Inn, so named, according to a modern tradition, because it was built on the site of anchorites' cells. Now it was re-imagined as the last place in which the Holy Grail was seen on Earth. The Sacred Heart Fathers traded bottled water in exchange for a contribution to the school there. They moved out in 1912, by which time it was established on the map of mythological Glastonbury.

The London-based playwright Alice Buckton (1867–1944) purchased Tor House and the Chalice Well in 1912. She was a socialist with Arts-and-Crafts tastes, and was an active campaigner on the part of women and children. At what was now named Chalice Well House she opened a School of Pageantry. She also made it the headquarters of the Glastonbury Crafts Guild and the Folk Play and Festival Association, and planned to host the first Glastonbury Festival in 1914. This was for a 'Festival Production of the Birth of Arthur', a choral drama by Rutland Boughton with libretto by Reginald Buckley, under the stage direction of Alice Buckton herself. A prospectus promised lectures, concerts and picnics and pilgrimages to the many romantic and historic places in the neighbourhood. A public appeal for funds stressed that Glastonbury was the ideal place for staging an English Music Drama, being the burial place of Arthur and the Holy Grail, and the place where Joseph of Arimathea had built the first church in Christendom.

Rutland Boughton (1887–1960) was a rising figure in English contemporary music who had his own ideas for a festival of music and drama, the English answer to Bayreuth, in which Boughton would play the role of his hero, Richard Wagner. Through Philip Oyler, who was headmaster of a Nature School that Boughton's son attended, the idea of Glastonbury as a possible venue was first mooted. Oyler even obtained an option to purchase Tor House and the Chalice Well grounds, although nothing came of it. He also introduced Boughton to the Reverend Charles Day, vicar of St John's, which facilitated Boughton's entrée into Glastonbury society when he performed at a concert of the town's choral society in 1913. Here he came into contact with Alice Buckton.

Alice Buckton gave a 'dramatic reading' of the *Birth of Arthur* at the Chalice Well in 1913—it was so oversubscribed that she gave a second performance—but longer-term plans to collaborate with Boughton did not work out. She staged her own Midsummer Festival at Chalice Well in 1914, but the venue for Boughton's festival was to be the town's Assembly Rooms. The timing of his first performance, on 5 August 1914, the day after Britain entered the First World War, could not have been worse. Boughton lost the services of the Beecham Symphony Orchestra and other key performers, and premiered his opera, *The Immortal Hour*, to the backing of a grand piano. The festival overcame this initial setback, grew in confidence over the next two years, and received positive reviews from the likes of George Bernard Shaw. Boughton established a Glastonbury Festival School in order that the small parts and chorus could be performed by local talent, leaving the lead parts to professional performers. Costume and stage design was largely the work of his erstwhile lover and chief collaborator, Christina Walshe.

The festival survived a two-year break, enforced when Boughton was called up for army service, but the festival school was revived in 1919 and the festival continued until 1926, for which Boughton composed many works, including *The Queen of Cornwall*, based on a play by Thomas Hardy. Increasingly, however, the festival found it hard to make ends meet and Boughton found it difficult to attract sponsors. His bohemian lifestyle was not to the taste of provincial grandees, among whom his reputation as an adulterer was not helpful. Nor were his political sympathies. The final straw came in 1926, the year of the General Strike, when he staged in Bristol and London a socialist version of his nativity opera *Bethlehem*, performed entirely by the Glastonbury Players. Boughton was never invited back and the Glastonbury Festival Players went into liquidation with debts of over £1,300. It also happened to be the end of the most successful period of his life, principally achieved through the critical and popular acclaim of *The Immortal Hour*. Boughton's work was performed in Glastonbury again in 1958 to mark his eightieth birthday and the festival was revived briefly in 1964 and 1965, but has long since been overshadowed by the festival near Pilton.

Alice Buckton, meanwhile, built an open-air theatre in the valley above the Chalice Well, where she staged performances with her Guild of Glastonbury and Street Festival Players, a rival to Boughton's ensemble. Homespun productions involving amateur players still needed funds to make them viable and in the 1920s this proved more and more difficult. In 1922 Alice made a silent film about Glastonbury history, which was the last notable work of her players. She maintained her opposition to the commercial exploitation of Glastonbury, and was active in persuading the National Trust to acquire Glastonbury Tor. She also established a Chalice Well Trust to ensure the long-term future of the Chalice Well. In the event it was sold in 1949 to the Glaston Tor School, on condition that the public should have access to the well.

Alice Buckton was a well-known local character and, predictably, acquired a reputation for eccentricity. She was once rumoured to have conducted Holy Communion on Glastonbury Tor. But her memorial service was conducted in St John's church by the Reverend L. S. Lewis. Alice Buckton's poem 'Glastonbury' appeared as the preface of Frederick Bligh Bond's *The Gate of Remembrance*. Bond was a friend and supporter of her work at the Chalice Well and in 1919 he designed the ironwork cover for the well head. It features two interlocking circles, representing the coming together of spirit and matter, creating a pointed oval called the *vesica piscis*. Keen Avalon watchers would have recognised this sign, since it was derived from Bond's researches at Glastonbury Abbey and had only just come to light. In the Chalice Well cover the *vesica* is bisected by a spear which, according to Bond, had a double meaning. The spear penetrating the *vesica* had an obvious sexual connotation, but the weapon was also a symbol of Christ's crucifixion, the fifth of his five wounds.

Frederick Bligh Bond was much more at home with the Avalonians than he was with the archaeologists. Unknown to the committee that appointed him to conduct excavations at Glastonbury Abbey, Bond had long been interested in the paranormal and was an active member of the Society for Psychical Research. From the very beginning he resolved to be guided by psychical methods during his work at the abbey. Through the Society for Psychical Research he had come into contact with Captain John Allen Bartlett, who had discovered that he had the unbidden facility of automatic writing. Bartlett became Bond's collaborator, but his identity was protected by the pseudonym John Alleyne, or 'J. A.'. Their psychic sessions took place in Bristol and Glastonbury, in which Bartlett held a pencil over a sheet of paper and Bond placed the fingers of his right hand lightly on his collaborator's writing hand. They asked questions and waited to see what scripts would be delivered in return. Many of them were incoherent or referred to matters on other subjects. On one occasion a poem emerged from Bartlett's hand, which could not have come at a more opportune moment. When the Prince and Princess of Wales came to Glastonbury in the summer 1909 they were presented with an illuminated parchment manuscript that included these very same lines.

Bond began with a specific research agenda. He wanted to find out about the chapel built in memory of King Edgar by Abbot Richard Bere in the early sixteenth century. It was known to have existed, but because the foundations were no longer visible, its location in relation to the rest of the abbey church was uncertain. The dimensions and details of the Edgar Chapel, and its position at the east end of the abbey church, were communicated to them in words by Johannes Bryant and in a drawing signed by Gulielmus Monachus. Subsequent excavation duly revealed the foundations of the chapel, although not without an element of controversy, as we will see later. Its position at the east end of the chancel was hardly unexpected and therefore the chapel could have been discovered by conventional powers of deduction. This could also have been said of other information communicated by four of the abbeys brothers. These were Gulielmus of the fourteenth century, Rolf, Camilus Thesiger, who was purser to Abbot Bere in the early sixteenth century, and Johannes Bryant, a monk and stonemason who had died in 1533. Johannes could even describe Arthur's shrine:–

> On ye south side, as we deeme it, ye will find most of ye pieces and even ye tombs of Arthur and of ye two saints Edgar [i.e. Edmund] all black stone with much guilding and ye effigies of ye Kinge and ye Queene in black stone—nay, rather, ye Lyons were in light stone like ye bases of ye tombes.[4]

Less obvious was the other chapel built by Abbot Bere, dedicated to Our Lady of Loretto, which had been built following Bere's visit to Italy in 1503. A shrine at Loretto, in Italy, had a miracle-working image of the Blessed Virgin Mary and her cult was very much in fashion in the late fifteenth century. Abbot Bere's Loretto chapel was discovered attached to the north transept of the abbey church, although not in quite the same position as Bond was led to believe, a fact he was at pains to acknowledge.

Despite appearances, Bond and Bartlett did not think that they were communicating with individual monks. Instead, Bond envisaged their enquiries as opening a channel through which 'a larger field of memory, a cosmic record latent, yet living, and able to find expression in human terms' could enter.[5] In order for this to succeed, the contents of the enquirers' minds were actively engaged, if only unconsciously. They were tapping the power of a timeless Universal Spirit. Even the Society for Psychical Research distanced itself from some of this. The Reverend F. T. Fryer of Bath reported back to the Society on meetings he had with Bond, and concluded that Bartlett's jottings were telepathic communications picking up all sorts of thoughts in Bond's head. In other words, Bartlett was amanuensis to Bond's subconscious. Only in the 1920s, when he was working with other psychics, did Bond come round to the idea that the communications they received came from a fraternity of departed souls that he called The Company of Avalon. But by this time he was already *persona non grata* at Glastonbury Abbey.

The temporary cessation of fieldwork during the war years gave Bond lots of thinking time. It was in this period that the boldest of his theories emerged and his subconscious thoughts fed into his sessions with Captain Bartlett. In one of these sessions, in August 1917, Abbot John of Breynton (1334–42) was described by Camilus Thesiger as 'Geomancer to ye Abbey of old tyme'. It encouraged Bond to focus his efforts on elucidating the thinking behind the ground plan of Glastonbury Abbey, which would take him on a quest far beyond straightforward archaeology. Excavations of the early twentieth century were largely directed towards revealing the ground plan, from which the appearance of the abbey could reasonably be recreated. It is hardly a coincidence, therefore, that the most startling of Bond's discoveries at Glastonbury concerned the two-dimensional form of the plan. Camilus Thesiger enlightened him even further: 'our Abbey was a message in ye stones. In ye foundations and ye distances be a mystery—the mystery of our Faith, which ye have forgotten and we also in ye later days'.[6] There was apparently a hint of this in the words of William of Malmesbury, who described the floor of the *vetusta ecclesia* as 'artfully interlaced in the forms of triangles or squares'.[7] But that may be an over-interpretation of William. Nevertheless Bond believed that the geometry laid out on the floor of the Lady Chapel by Abbot Breynton was lost when the abbey fell into ruin. 'All ye measures were marked plaine on ye slabbes in Mary's Chappel, and ye have destroyed them.' The floor was also laid with the signs of the zodiac 'that all might see and understand the mystery'.[8] Bond had to figure out what these measurements were and what they meant. He calculated that the abbey buildings had been built in squares of 74 feet. The outer measurement of the length of the abbey church was 592 feet, or eight squares long, and the nave and chancel were one square wide. The Lady Chapel was a half square wide but the more intriguing question was the nature of the measures on its floor.

Bond noticed some remarkable geometry at work and linked it with the practice of gematria, the Jewish system of assigning numerical values to letters, the most well-known example of which is the number of The Great Beast—666. Gematria had been quite fashionable in the early years of the twentieth century, in the wake of a successful book, *The Canon*, by William Stirling, that appeared in 1897. Bond figured that if he could elucidate the mathematical principles by which the Lady Chapel had been built he could reveal its underlying secret code. The Lady Chapel is enclosed within a hexagon, of which the sides are 37 feet long and the east and west walls form two of those sides. From a plan of the Lady Chapel, Bond was able to draw two examples of a *vesica*, a pointed oval shape composed of the arcs of overlapping circles. One is inside the building and spans two thirds the length of the chapel. The other is 37 feet wide and 64 feet long, i.e. the width and length of the Lady Chapel respectively. The area of the building was 2,368 square feet which, by gematria, is the equivalent of ΙΗΣΟΥΣ ΧΡΙΣΤΟΣ (Jesus Christ) or Ὁ ἍΓΙΟΣ ΤΩΝ ἉΓΙΩΝ (The Holy One of Holy Ones).

The cardinal points of the *vesica* form the points of two symmetrical equilateral triangles, creating a rhombus with an area of 1,184 square feet, which Bond concluded memorialised the date when the Lady Chapel was begun.

Bond's geometry and calculations are very impressive, but fall apart if there are any inaccuracies in the measurements. When he excavated the Edgar Chapel, attached to the east end of the abbey church, which was in any case not added until the last years of the abbey, he claimed that it had an apsidal end, as opposed to the square end that would be expected in late Gothic architecture. Later investigators agreed that Bond gave the impression that there was an apse simply by the way he cleared the rubble from the site, and it seems that Bond was influenced by the psychic directions rather than the evidence of his own eyes. (Bond was defiant, however, and remained adamant of his discovery until the day he died.) Once the Edgar Chapel is a given a square end Bond's measurements change and the whole thesis collapses. His own admission that the Lady Chapel was only 'about 64 feet' long was an inner doubt that he evidently managed to accommodate. In fact he was convinced that he had revealed the 'sacred mystery' that William of Malmesbury said was beneath the floor of the *vetusta ecclesia*, although William was referring to a different building with different dimensions. Moreover, the Lady Chapel to which Bond referred was built after William of Malmesbury had died. In subsequent years Bond's interpretation would be picked apart, not least by John Michell who added new interpretations. For most people the more ways in which a building can be interpreted geometrically the less convincing any of them are, but to Michell they prove that the *idea* of it is a valid one.

Bond continued his Glastonbury researches after he was excluded from its archaeology, a time when, understandably, his interest turned more to the mystical than the practical. In 1921 he met a psychic lady, known only by her initial S, whose automatic scripts put Bond on to another line of thought: that Joseph's original chapel was circular and was surrounded by twelve hermits' cells in a perfect circle. Another automatic script gave the dimensions of this plan, which Bond would eventually decide gave a circumference of 888 Roman feet. In gematria, the number 888 spells the name of Jesus. Bond also caught the Arthurian bug and in 1925 had his blank verse *The Story of King Arthur* privately printed.

The late Victorian period was a golden age of mysticism and spiritualism and Bond was a man of his time. European imperialism had exposed to the west traditions of wisdom and spirituality seemingly more ancient than their own. Out of interest in scientific discoveries, psychology, ancient civilisations, paranormal and magical phenomena emerged the Theosophical movement, first in America and soon in the remainder of the western world. It aimed at a universal knowledge of God that drew something from all religions, especially through the techniques of Hinduism and Tibetan Buddhism. Knowledge of Oriental religions inspired spiritually restless people to explore mysticism and esoteric religion at home, which spawned the revival of ancient traditions like Rosicrucianism. It also encouraged experimentation in different techniques such as meditation and altered states of consciousness, to achieve a higher form of mental awareness. Some of the people drawn to these challenges came to Glastonbury, but they were not initially interested in history as we might understand it today. They were on a spiritual quest in which Glastonbury offered possibilities of fulfilment.

Many of their experiences, including bizarre coincidences, a histrionic sense of self destiny and wish-fulfilment would no longer be taken very seriously—in fact there were plenty of sceptics at the time. Nevertheless the possibilities of the unseen and the power of the mind were an open subject in the early decades of the twentieth century. But at this period mysticism was not incompatible with Christianity and most of the protagonists in this phase of Glastonbury history were, like Frederick Bligh Bond, Christians. Glastonbury Abbey and the holy thorn played only a bit part. There were universal truths to uncover, one of which was the supposed discovery of the Holy Grail.

One of the people with psychic abilities who gravitated to Glastonbury was Dr John Goodchild (1851–1914). He had a medical practice serving the expatriate community in the resort of Bordighera on the Italian Riviera. Here, in 1885, he purchased a curious glass bowl, or cup, that had caught his eye, the date and provenance of which defeated the experts to whom he showed it, including Sir Augustus Franks at the British Museum. A date in New Testament times was suggested as a possibility. Nothing happened with regard to the cup for another twelve years. In the meantime Dr Goodchild, who was a minor author of the Celtic revival, became captivated by the East and became convinced that a world of enlightenment and wisdom existed before Christianity. The locus of this thinking was not England but Ireland, where he argued that there was a cult worshipping the female aspect of the Deity, venerating a High Queen who was later manifested in the Irish saint Bride or Bridget, before the knowledge declined with the march of Rome.

After his book expounding these ideas, *The Light of the West*, was written, Goodchild started hearing voices. They told him that the cup had been held by Jesus and that after his father died Goodchild should take it to Bride's Hill near Glastonbury, where ultimately it would pass into the care of a young woman. Goodchild's sojourn in Glastonbury in 1898 was a protracted one because he waited three weeks for further instructions, which told him to take the cup to St Bride's Well, where he concealed it in its then murky waters. Goodchild had plenty of time to think about the meaning of the cup. For a while he was in correspondence with Fiona Macleod, author of *The Immortal Hour* that Rutland Boughton would later set to music, unaware that this was a pseudonym used by William Sharp for writing that he was not entirely in control of. The two men met in Glastonbury, and in the abbey grounds Sharp found himself writing some lines that Goodchild saw as prophetic.

> From the Silence of Time, Time's Silence Borrow.
> In the heart of To-day is the word of Tomorrow.
> The Builders of Joy are the Children of Sorrow.[9]

Goodchild's reading of it was that the cup he had buried was a Cup of Sorrow, which would be transformed into a Cup of Joy when it was retrieved by its next, female keeper. In the late summer of 1906 Goodchild saw visions in the sky on two separate occasions, one that of a sword in the eastern sky, followed by a cup in the western sky. He interpreted these as portents, respectively the Sign of the East and Sign of the West.

Goodchild's latter vision coincided with the visit to Glastonbury of two sisters from Bristol, Janet and Christine Allen. A friend of theirs and fellow Bristolian, Wellesley Tudor Pole (1884–1968), had received a psychic intimation that they should search the waters of St Bride's Well where they found, but did not take home, the glass bowl. By coincidence, or perhaps not if you are of a sceptical cast of mind, Goodchild and Tudor Pole were already acquainted. Goodchild had sent to Wellesley Tudor Pole a drawing of the cup in the western sky and it was through him that Goodchild came to meet the two sisters. It became clear to Goodchild that they were to be the heirs of the cup that had been spoken of many years previously. In due course Wellesley's sister, Katharine, returned to Glastonbury, rescued the bowl and took it to Bristol. The Tudor Pole and Allen families were convinced that they had recovered the Grail cup, and their attempts to date it came to the attention of the national press, which ran the story as the discovery of the Holy Grail. Dr Goodchild was less convinced and stuck to his original understanding that it was only a cup that Jesus had carried.

All of the people involved in the discovery of the cup were prone to paranormal experience. On their first ever visit to Glastonbury in 1905 the Allen sisters had sat in their boarding house and achieved communication with a medieval monk through automatic writing. He told them their destiny was to 'heal and uplift humanity' and 'the Kingdom of your Father is in Nature, and in your inmost self', a manifesto in miniature of twentieth-century New Ageism.[10] Their pilgrimages therefore had a purpose and the cup appeared to be fulfilment of it. A room in the Tudor Pole household was converted to a shrine in which the vessel was placed on an altar, and devotees were invited to meditate or receive healing. It became a focus of female spirituality. The presence of the cup was the source of many supposed cures and mystical revelations. Later the cup would return to Glastonbury, at the Chalice Well, by which time the Holy Grail and the whole historical landscape of Glastonbury was a very different place.

Alternative history was the making of modern Glastonbury. Its origins lie not with mystics and spiritualists, however, but in the timescale of the past. The combined efforts of archaeology and geology had given the Edwardian generation a much deeper sense of time than the Georgians ever imagined, and people sought connections not with their immediate ancestors but over a much longer time span. Where once there had been only pagans before the arrival of Christianity, now there were ages of Stone, Bronze and Iron before the Romans. One of the mediums through which deep time could be appreciated was through places. Some places were found to have had a much longer time span than had once been thought.

Ideas about the continuity of British history were shot through in early twentieth-century landscape history, notably in Walter Johnson's *Byways in British Archaeology* (1917), H. J. Massingham's *Downland Man* (1926) and especially in Alfred Watkins' study of leys, *The Old Straight Track* (1925). In these works was a tendency to see sites of churches as ancient places of sanctity, chosen for Christianity precisely because they had been revered in previous times. There was even some credible supporting evidence of the idea, in the form of a letter quoted by the Venerable Bede. Written in 601, Pope Gregory the Great urged Abbot Mellitus, one of the missionary group sent with Augustine to convert the pagan Anglo-Saxons of England, not to destroy the native temples, but to convert them to Christianity. For antiquaries thirteen hundred years later, the argument followed that wherever there was a church there was likely as not an older place of sanctity. Alfred Watkins used this argument a lot, and in Glastonbury the temptation to think about a pre-Christian past was irresistible. Paganism and Christianity have had an uneasy co-existence at Glastonbury ever since.

The question naturally arose, that if Glastonbury had enjoyed special sanctity in Christian times, could have it have done so in earlier periods too? Is Glastonbury an archetypal sacred place, of which the Christian churches are only just the latest manifestations? Within a few years Glastonbury's portfolio of special places had grown beyond the traditional abbey, thorns and Tor to encompass the Chalice Well, St Bride's Well and, in different guises, the whole of the surrounding landscape. The conventional disciplines of history and archaeology did much to advance the idea of pre-Christian Glastonbury. The Glastonbury Antiquarian Society sponsored excavations of the Iron Age 'lake villages' at Glastonbury and Meare by Arthur Bulleid from 1892 onwards. These excavations are widely regarded as being exemplary work for the time, even if the connotation of prosperous and settled communities is no longer accepted. Historians could point to Caradog's twelfth-century Life of St Collen, who set up his hermit's cell on Glastonbury Tor. Here he heard men talking about Gwyn ap Nudd, who dwelt there as king of Annwn, the Celtic underworld, clear indication for some that Glastonbury Tor had a pagan Celtic heritage.

John Cowper Powys described it as the 'immemorial mystery of Glastonbury', and believed he was contemplating a power 'older than Christianity, older than the Druids, older than the gods of the Norsemen or the Romans, older than the Gods of the Neolithic men'.[11] For Dion Fortune, the pen name of Violet Mary Evans (1890–1946), Glastonbury was a timeless sacred centre, as alive in the ancient past as it was in the middle ages, and by the same token spiritually alive in her own day. She could point to the revival of the Chalice Well as evidence of a Glastonbury renaissance and speculated that there was once a stone circle on the summit of the Tor that was overthrown when it was replaced by the church.

Patterns in the landscape had interested scholars long before the twentieth century. In 1574 John Dee is said to have made a map of Glastonbury in which the heavenly constellations were plotted on the ground, but this work has not survived, assuming that it ever existed. For the next three centuries this category of ideas was more or less exclusive to Stonehenge. In 1777 a Mr Waltire argued that the landscape around Stonehenge was a planisphere in which the barrows accurately represented the position and magnitude of the fixed stars and in 1846 Edward Duke argued that the major earthworks of Wiltshire formed an accurate planetarium, with Stonehenge at the centre. There was also interest in hill figures, like the Long Man of Wilmington and the Cerne Abbas Giant, cut into the chalk downlands in southern England. Perhaps there were other figures carved out into other landscapes that had not hitherto been recognised.

Some people saw patterns in the landscape that they interpreted as deliberate symbolic constructions. Publication of the county series of Ordnance Survey maps from the 1870s onwards greatly aided this kind of endeavour. Dr John Goodchild had detected the shape of a giant fish in the landscape below Wearyall Hill. In 1909 Reverend F. G. Montagu Powell suggested in *The Spectator* magazine that it represented the wise salmon in the early Welsh tale of 'Culhwch and Olwen', although Goodchild preferred to think of it as the Irish Salmon of Wisdom. It convinced Goodchild that Glastonbury was a Druid centre and that it was long a place of special sanctity before the Christians arrived. The ground in question, known as Beckery (also known as Little Ireland), included Bride Hill, in which the eye of the fish was the well of St Bride, a place that would figure prominently in the saga of the cup.

In 1918 Frederick Bligh Bond, in his capacity as an architect, was commissioned to design alterations for a country retreat on the Polden Hills in Somerset, known as Chilton Priory. It was not a monastic building, but had been built in the early nineteenth century as a fashionable Gothic conceit. Its new owners were John Maltwood, a very wealthy businessman, and his wife Katharine Maltwood (1878–1961), who had made a name for herself as a sculptor and was a regular exhibitor at the Royal Academy and other London galleries.

Katharine Maltwood's interest in Arthurian mythology had been awakened by an interest in Pre-Raphaelite artists. In 1925 she was studying the *High History of the Holy Grail*, trying to track the quests of the knights in the Somerset countryside, on the assumption that the work had been written at Glastonbury Abbey. While she was staying at Chilton Priory she became intrigued by the patterns in the landscape marked by hills, field boundaries, roads and streams. Although the house was in an elevated position that invited her to look out over the Somerset Levels, the materials to unlock the secret of the landscape were laid out on her desk. Like her contemporary, Alfred Watkins, the mystery could not have been revealed to her without Ordnance Survey maps. But she later went further and contracted Hunting Aerosurveys to photograph the landscape from the air. Aerial photography was then a new and cutting-edge technique in archaeology. Only in 1928, O. G. S. Crawford and Alexander Keiller published *Wessex from the Air*, a revelation of how aerial photography could render large archaeological sites with clarity and eloquence. From the evidence of maps and aerial photography Maltwood was convinced that the she had discovered a zodiac, or Temple of the Stars as she preferred to call it, in the Somerset landscape and took for granted that it was older than Christianity.

The zodiac covers an area of approximately ten miles diameter between Glastonbury in the north and Somerton in the south. Glastonbury Tor and the Chalice Well fall within the head of Aquarius. The outline of Wearyall Hill forms one of the two fish of Pisces, and is one of the most convincing, if fortuitous, shapes. The guardian of this Temple of the Stars was a dog further to the west, the nose of which is the prominent hill Burrow Mump. She calculated that the zodiac was constructed about 2,700 BC by Sumer-Chaldean priests on land already dedicated to the Egyptian god of the dead, Osiris. Like many of her contemporaries, Maltwood was influenced by Theosophical thinking, which held that the wisdom of the ages is concealed in allegorical mysteries, to be revealed when the time was right. Maltwood's discovery showed that the time was now. The temple explained symbolically the processes of nature in the seasonal cycle of death and rebirth, pre-Christian stories later woven into the Grail legends. And she concluded that her beloved Grail knights were Christian reincarnations of the old gods—hence King Arthur is Hercules, Sir Lancelot is the Lion and Sir Gawain the Ram. Her Temple of the Stars was a Paradise Garden, the 'oldest scientific heirloom of the human race'.

Katharine Maltwood made strenuous efforts to interest professional archae-ologists in her discovery, but they did not think it worthy of serious enquiry. She even tried to enlist the support of The National Trust, the Royal Astronomical Society and the Royal Society of Arts, but to no avail. Having emigrated to Canada hardly helped her, but not for the last time a theory of Glastonbury received a more sympathetic hearing in North America than in England. Her scheme is easy to criticise. For example, Cancer is represented as a ship repre-senting Argo Navis (a constellation not visible at northern latitudes) rather than the traditional crab, but is made up of straight ditches, or rhynes, dug in the post-medieval period to drain the levels. Even as late as the medieval period this part of the landscape was featureless marshland. Goodchild's salmon is nowhere to be seen, so either one of them had to be wrong, or there were two landscape designs of different dates.

Maltwood had her supporters by the 1960s, including influential figures like John Michell, while even sceptics like Colin Wilson were prepared to con-sider the zodiac a possibility. The Glastonbury zodiac inspired the search for other zodiacs in various parts of the country. In the late 1940s Lewis Edwards reported to the Avalon Society that he had found a zodiac temple at Pumpsaint in Carmarthenshire. Other examples were claimed in the 1960s, by Mary Caine at Kingston-upon-Thames, and at Nuthampstead in Hertfordshire by the author and geomancer Nigel Pennick. In 1969 Mary Caine tweaked Maltwood's orig-inal scheme: she turned Scorpio upside down, altered the wings of the dove representing Libra, added a meditating monk next to Gemini, and changed the outlines of Pisces, Virgo and Sagittarius. It was an exercise that fatally under-mined the project. If the lines could be so easily re-drawn, then the shapes on the map offered an interesting game but did not represent anything authentically ancient. Other people disagreed because, although the details may be faulty, she had at least lifted the cloak of invisibility from the landscape. John Michell, who did much to make the original scheme widely known, decided that many of the shapes were simulacra, the tendency of the eye to see all sorts of like-nesses in random phenomena like clouds and rocks. It was the *idea* of a symbolic landscape for which he gave her credit. It inspired him to look for his own inter-pretation and in due course he found it. The positions of the stars of the Great Bear constellation were marked out on islands in the Somerset Levels, part of a solar zodiac in the Somerset countryside.

After Katharine Maltwood and Frederick Bligh Bond, the other influen-tial figure in the new Glastonbury mythology was Dion Fortune. Born into a Christian socialist family, her interest in the hidden forces that govern life led her first to psychology and then to occultism. Like so many Christians of the period, she was drawn to more mystical forms of Christianity and was influenced by

eastern religions as well. She has been described as a spiritual pragmatist, taking
something from the Rosicrucians, the Theosophical Society and the Christian
Mystic Lodge. In 1919 she was initiated into the Alpha and Omega Temple of the
Hermetic Order of the Golden Dawn. She made her name as a writer in London
but inevitably felt the gravitational pull of Glastonbury, where she stayed at Alice
Buckton's Guest House at the Chalice Well and acquired a property in 1924 that
became the Chalice Orchard Club. *Avalon of the Heart* is her personal view of
Glastonbury and its spiritual history, and was published in 1934. It is a view of
Glastonbury from the city, from London.

For Dion Fortune, even the name Great West Road has a magical ring to it
and her book begins with a journey on it, described like a pilgrim gradually
shedding the trappings of modern life and entering a world ever more harmoni-
ous yet mysterious. Away from the 'narrow and difficult streets of the city' and
'the heavy traffic of Chiswick', into the Thames valley where the old market
gardens are gradually giving way to suburban housing developments, she heads
westwards to a more unsullied world. Here 'smoke hangs over the clustering
hamlets that lie thick in this rich land', beyond which the sea is 'hidden by the
grey mist of difference' and the great beacon of her destination comes into
view—Glastonbury Tor.[12] Thousands of people continue to make such a journey
every year. For Dion Fortune, Glastonbury provided a rural retreat that allowed
her to re-charge herself before she plunged herself back into London life. In
that sense she was ordinary rather than extraordinary. She performed one of
the balancing acts of modern life. Dion Fortune's pragmatic and unprejudiced
approach to spiritualism also informs her appreciation of Glastonbury's history
as a sacred place. Here the forces of the pagan and Christian Gods seemed to
be in equilibrium, existing in a harmony that she continued to need. *Avalon of
the Heart* makes passing reference to ideas that would be revived in the 1960s
and 1970s—that the summit of the Tor has a spiral, processional way, and that
Glastonbury's sacred origins lie with refugees from Atlantis.

Dion Fortune was also ahead of her time in the sense that she found in
Glastonbury and its ancient traditions an essential ingredient of modern life. For
all her worldly achievements and activities she needed to stay in touch with more
spiritual things, a need that demanded a place to embody them. Here Fortune
is with John Cowper Powys, and with Wellesley Tudor Pole, who combined his
spiritual quest with a successful career in business. They lived in a triumphalist
age of technological progress and yet remained in thrall to the world's ancient
mysteries. In a world that was killing off the Gods, they realised that they needed
them after all. Glastonbury was henceforth no longer just, or in many people's
minds even, a place of Christian sanctity, but a place that now belonged to Gods
of all time.

11

New Jerusalem

The counter-cultural spirit of 1960s Glastonbury was made in the 1950s. The Chalice Well had emerged as an important sacred place through its promotion by Alice Buckton and others, which has continued since the Chalice Well Trust purchased it in 1959. The prime mover in ensuring the long-term future of the place was Wellesley Tudor Pole. He had become the keeper of the cup brought to Glastonbury by Goodchild, and after the second war took it on many pilgrimages to hilltop sites dedicated to St Michael, hoping to reawaken these ancient sacred shrines (on the basis that all of these hilltops are Christianised pagan centres). Since his death in 1968 the cup has been in the possession of the Chalice Well Trust. Although is no longer regarded as ancient, its power to inspire people in their own spiritual quests is widely acknowledged.

In 1957 Geoffrey Ashe published his *King Arthur's Avalon*, in which the prehistory of Glastonbury as a sacred centre was readily incorporated into the history of the place, in a way that the professional archaeologists had not hitherto done. Ashe, born in London and brought up in Canada, was to be as accessible to alternative thinking as he was to orthodox archaeology, and was to be far more influential than any archaeologist at Glastonbury. Although he is best known for reviving the subject of a historical Arthur at Glastonbury, his interests have been wide ranging. In 1973 he published a novel, *The Finger and the Moon*, in which Avalon was the figure of a divine woman, her body fashioned from the contours of the landscape. It was only a short step to the concept of Avalon as a centre of ancient Goddess worship, an idea that has been realised since that time.

There were other stirrings of original thinking by the 1960s. The terraced sides of Glastonbury Tor give the hill a distinctive profile. They were long presumed to be natural, or to be the terraces that form naturally when cattle graze on steep hills. In 1964 an Irishman, Geoffrey Russell, suggested that they are a deliberate feat of engineering to produce a three-dimensional maze, or labyrinth. In effect it meant that if a person followed the line of the terraces from the bottom it would lead eventually to the summit, turning the Tor into a great processional way. If so, then the construction was probably undertaken in the Neolithic period of prehistory, before 2,000 BC, when other comparable earthworks were created. While it is archaeologists who are best equipped to find answers about the distant past, Russell is a good example of how it is often amateurs who ask the best questions. Not all archaeologists were dismissive. Philip Rahtz, who excavated on the summit of the Tor in the 1960s, thought it worthy of serious consideration. In his final thoughts on the subject Rahtz suggested that the stepped profile was of Neolithic origin and was similar to the original stepped profile of Silbury Hill in Wiltshire. Evidence of prehistoric wooden trackways across the Somerset Levels shows the area to have been well populated, so such a large feat of engineering was entirely possible at that time. Russell also found an ally in Geoffrey Ashe, who mulled over the subject for a decade and published his own version in *The Glastonbury Tor Maze* in 1979. Russell and Ashe drew attention to the Welsh *Caer Sidi*, which they translated as 'spiral castle', said to house a fruitful fountain (shades of the Grail cup) and to have been associated with Annwn, the Celtic underworld. This chimed in nicely with the medieval tale of St Collen, who made a hermit's cell near the Tor and had a vision of Gwyn ap Nudd, the king of the Underworld. By original thinking and openness to a diverse range of evidence, many new possibilities emerged to explain the sanctity of Glastonbury. It brings us neatly to the work of John Michell.

John Michell (1933–2009) was the key figure in the emergence of Glastonbury as the capital of New Age culture. He described himself as a radical traditionalist, enjoyed the benefit of an Eton and Oxbridge education, but shunned the obvious doors that such a background could have opened for him. He was a well-connected figure in trendy 1960s London and was one of the prominent voices of late sixties counter-cultural thinking. Michell had an omnivorous appetite for knowledge and the ability to absorb disparate theories from a wide range of authors, who otherwise seemed to have little in common, and then to re-interpret and mould their findings into a new and unified vision of the past. To his detractors, it should be pointed out, he was the worst kind of dilettante, the pied-piper of pseudo-mysticism. At the onset of the Age of Aquarius, however, Michell was in the right place at the right time. He wrote about Glastonbury in his first book, *The Flying Saucer Vision* (1967), and returned to the subject of Glastonbury throughout the remainder of his writing career.

Michell's own quest went far beyond antiquarianism or personal spirituality. It was about the state of the world. Civilisation seemed to have reached a critical stage where further development seemed unlikely. 'To many people our only hope of development and even survival seems to lie in the achievement of a new, higher vision, whatever form this may take'.[1] Michell looked to the past for a way out of the present, exactly as Katharine Maltwood had done when she railed against the 'callous materialism and indifference' of the modern world.[2] Like many of his contemporaries, Michell followed closely reports of UFOs. So did Carl Jung, who published in 1959 *Flying Saucers: a myth of things seen on the sky*, in which he interpreted these unknown aerial phenomena as a portent of great changes. Michell agreed. That human developments had been influenced by extra-terrestrial forces was revealed in ancient religious practices. Contemporary interest in the possibility that Earth had been visited from space also ensured that he had an audience. This was the 1960s, the decade of the space race, the same decade in which Gerald Hawkins decoded the astronomical computer we know as Stonehenge and when Erich von Daniken saw evidence of extra-terrestrial visitors in the ancient civilisations of the world. Von Daniken's evidence was global and sensational (and long forgotten), whereas Michell's work was more tightly focused. His interest in Glastonbury was fundamentally about the Tor. This and other hills were interpreted as the places where God and men interacted, on the basis that sun worship and the cult of St Michael are both derived from worship of a sky god. Further, when Abbot Whiting was executed on Glastonbury Tor in 1539 Michell felt sure that it had happened there because it had retained a reputation as a place of sacrifice. 'So Glastonbury Tor became another of the sacred high places where the erection of a gibbet perverted the old practice of offering men to the gods from the sky'.[3]

Michell continued to develop his Glastonbury theories for the rest of his life, although the extra-terrestrial aspects of his thinking shrank from view in his later work. *The Flying Saucer Vision* now reads like a period piece, another contribution to a decade when space heralded great possibilities that would be unfulfilled.

John Michell's most widely quoted theory is that of leys, set out in his work *The View over Atlantis*, first published in 1969. Leys were lines of earthly power that the ancients knew about and manipulated. Arthur Lawton had first suggested as much in a book published in 1939, but at that time he was a lone voice. In the early 1960s Michell had been one of the early recruits in the revival of Alfred Watkins' theory of old straight tracks. By this time researchers such as the French ufologist Aimé Michel and an ex-RAF pilot Tony Wedd had developed new areas of research. The most significant of them was that leys, or straight lines across the landscape, were used by extra-terrestrial craft as a navigational device, or were lines of magnetic current by which means extra-terrestrial craft could channel the Earth's energy.

Michell knew about a lot of other related things. He was familiar with the work of Wilhelm Teudt, who had argued that German 'holy lines' linking ancient sites were set up to mark important astronomical events. (Teudt's subsequent membership of the Waffen SS put these ideas beyond the pale in the years following the war.) He was also abreast of developments in astro-archaeology and was quicker than archaeologists to assimilate the arguments of an Oxford professor of engineering, Alexander Thom, who argued that megalithic monuments were constructed using precise engineering and complex trigonometry. Michell embraced folklore, the Chinese art of Feng-shui, claims made by psychometrists such as Iris Campbell who thought that Glastonbury Tor was an 'epicentre of magnetism', the orgone accumulator theory of Austrian psychologist Wilhelm Reich, and more. He argued that, although individual researchers could be wrong, the cumulative effect of their labours was compelling. The ley system was integral to a global civilisation in which spirit, energy, or indeed spiritual energy is transmitted across the land. It was 'a fusion of the terrestrial spirit with the solar spark, by which this energy could be disposed to human benefit'. The golden age was a reality.

Two of the most remarkable leys passed through Glastonbury. The well-known alignment of the abbey church, its major chapels and St Benedict's church was claimed to be a ley that, further east, passed through Stonehenge. The other significant ley is sometimes called the St Michael's Line. Its axis is the two Somerset hills Glastonbury Tor and Burrow Mump. Although they are both natural hills, Michell argued that the alignment was formalised by the geomancers who created and maintained the ley system. To the south west it passes over Brentor on Dartmoor, and then over a sequence of notable Cornish landmarks—the natural rockpile on Bodmin Moor known as the Cheesewring, Roche Rock, Carn Brea and terminates at St Michael's Mount. To the north east the line is less exciting, although it passes through Roystone Cave and Bury St Edmunds Abbey before terminating in the North Sea near Lowestoft. In its course across Wiltshire it passes through Avebury, where the absence of a world-centre mountain was rectified by the construction of Silbury Hill. Critics have pointed out that these landmarks and constructions do not fall in a straight line and therefore cannot have the significance he claimed for them. But the St Michael's Line has retained its devotees. In the 1980s Paul Broadhurst and the dowser Hamish Miller embarked on a journey along the line (pilgrimage is just as apt) to establish whether it was still charged with energy. They claimed to have discovered two lines of current spiralling around the main axis of the line (they call them Michael and Mary lines). The line forms the backbone, the principal axis of southern England and people were traditionally drawn to its nodal points where the current was strongest. Already in prehistory Glastonbury was the holiest earth of England.

Michell was more generous to Christianity than some of his contemporaries. The twenty-first Book of Revelation describes a vision of New Jerusalem, a future that he saw was on the verge of being realised on Earth. Industrial and technological society was hostage to finite resources, and 'there is no reason to doubt that within the next few years the earth will die of plague, poison, burns or wounds'.[4] Nuclear Armageddon was an imminent possibility. Michell had explored the sacred geometry of Glastonbury in *The View over Atlantis*, in which the forgotten work of Frederick Bligh Bond was revived, and expanded on it in a later book about sacred mysteries, *City of Revelation* (1972). In later editions of these books, culminating in various editions of *New Light on the Ancient Mystery of Glastonbury* (1990 and later), he compared Glastonbury with New Jerusalem. In Revelation an angel described New Jerusalem as square in plan, each side being 12,000 stadia in length (about 1,400 miles or 2,300 kilometres), with walls 144 cubits (approximately 200 feet or 65 metres) high or thick. It had twelve gates, one for each of the Tribes of Israel. Glastonbury, like Stonehenge, Chartres, the Egyptian pyramids and the Temple of Jerusalem, were all based upon the cosmic proportions found in the Book of Revelation.

Assuming a hide to be 120 acres and to be one furlong wide, Michell calculated that their total area of the Twelve Hides of Glastonbury was 1,440 acres and superimposed a square of these dimensions on a map of Glastonbury, with the site of Joseph's wattle church at the centre. The eastern side of the grid was a north-south ley discovered in the 1970s by Paul Devereux and Ian Thomsom that passes through Glastonbury Tor. Glastonbury was therefore planned following the relative proportions mentioned in the Bible. However, the medieval Twelve Hides were scattered to the west and north of Glastonbury and bear no relation to the grid that Michell created for it.

Bond's excursions into gematria were reworked by Michell. In gematria the number 1,665 spells out the Spirit of the Earth, and the area of Joseph's first church was calculated to be 166.5 megalithic yards diameter, the unit of measurement (2.72 feet) determined by Alexander Thom in the 1960s. Nobody would make that calculation now, of course, but Michell excludes nothing. The megalithic yard, the foot and the cubit are all valid units of measurement. By adding an eighth 74-foot grid square to Bond's original scheme the length of the abbey was extended from 582 feet to the highly significant 666 feet (never mind that the abbey was not 666 feet long). It also gave him an area of 66,600 cubits. For John Michell there is no such thing as coincidence, and if little details can be nit-picked they do not undermine the cumulative evidence for his principal claim that Glastonbury encodes the dimensions of paradise.

Michell had a lot of fun drawing lines and circles on a map. For all his belief that great leaps forward in knowledge come from revelation, at the expense of toil, Michell was quite absorbed in longer processes of research. He drew two intersecting circles, centred on sites of supposedly ancient sanctity—the abbey and the late-nineteenth century Roman Catholic church. It replicates Frederick Bligh Bond's intersecting-circle design on the cover of the Chalice Well. But only one of Michell's cardinal points is ancient, the abbey, but not the original part of it. The site of the old church is within it but not in a significant position.

The significance of these perceptions is debatable, but they capture his love of the mysteries of geometry and mathematics. Keith Critchlow also had a go at reinterpreting Bond's scheme, in search of 'a buried science of cosmic harmonies'. From Bond's survey, 'we have found evidence of the Golden Mean system $\sqrt{5} + \frac{1}{2}$ inherent in the plan'.[5] Later, Nigel Pennick extended this idea and claimed that the abbey's ground plan incorporated both of the Masonic systems of sacred geometry—Ad Triangulum and Ad Quadratum—which was extended outwards to determine key landmarks in the town like the market cross. At its heart, these schemes present places as pre-determined, which clashed with the conventional view that the abbey and the town grew slowly over hundreds of years and, especially in the case of the town, in an unplanned manner.

The impact of *The View Over Atlantis* was significant, but it only amplified ideas that had gained currency in the underground movement. John Michell's first writings on leys and Glastonbury appeared in the magazine the *International Times*. 'The rediscovery of a lost source of inspiration on earth, can only take place in a land where the *genius loci*, the native spirit, is still capable of being evoked'. It was a call to arms for an imminent, peaceful revolution: 'For just such a moment, we are told, the gods of Britain have been waiting, sleeping beyond the apple trees of Avalon, the spiritual twin of Britain'.[6] All of this was an inspiration to young radical minds. Another London magazine, but a much more occasional one and the outlet of a mystical group, was *Gandalf's Garden*. Only six issues were ever produced, although one of them, published in 1969, features Glastonbury strongly. 'The Glastonbury Mystique: Jesus and the Druids' was written by 'Meiwana', an example of the passing fashion for far-out pseudonyms. It presented the theories of unfashionable old vicars like Lewis and Dobson, but in a new guise following a vision experienced at the Chalice Well, in which Jesus was initiated as a member of the highest order of Druids. It invited new pilgrims to meditate at Glastonbury, so that the 'old, divisive, demanding ego' could be cast off and the liberated individual could be 'born into Freedom, Love, Wisdom and Joy'.[7]

In this new age of Aquarius it seemed that there was something stirring in Glastonbury, a lost knowledge that would point the way to the future. Mary Caine and John Michell both cited Katharine Maltwood's zodiac and the concept of a hidden message left in the landscape by an ancient civilisation. It encouraged people to visit it for themselves. Mary Caine's enthusiasm was infectious. On the basis that 'it's a marvellous idea, and if it's not there, it ought to be', she reinterpreted the Glastonbury zodiac, the oldest and biggest of Britain's antiquities and ultimate source of Glastonbury's mystique. The twelve hides given to Joseph were now the signs of the zodiac. Critics might have argued that the roads defining the zodiac were modern, but she was having none of it: 'all were prehistoric paths leading to prehistoric camps and holy places in prehistoric times when people were more beautiful than they are now, and did beautiful crazy, corporate things like Stonehenge and Silbury Hill and huge White Horses'.[8] The hippies arrived in Glastonbury and have never left. The most prescient comments of the time were perhaps those of Geoffrey Ashe, also writing in *Gandalf's Garden*, who sensed that Glastonbury's time was nigh. When Glastonbury awoke, summoned by Albion's sons and daughters inside the enchanted boundary, an enduring community of Avalon would be created. 'The time to found that community is drawing near.'

So the trio of Michell, Caine and Ashe represented a view of the past that went beyond an intellectual puzzle. It made the confines of academic archaeology look narrow by comparison. Even as history it had a liberating and energising effect on so many of its readers. Here was history that had never been taught in schools, about epic events that had taken place in rural England. It was history that could not be learned by rote as a sequence of dates marking the deeds of great men, together with the accompanying moral certainties. Moreover, this generation was not deferential to the professionals. Far from it, they were determined to think for themselves, confident that they could explain the world just as well as the academics, simply because they were unencumbered by academic strictures and protocols. It was the beginning of the democratisation of the past, although it would be a long time before the professionals became comfortable with that idea. They portrayed a world where life was not determined by material well-being and status, but in which an inner spiritual life was even more fulfilling. It is not hard to see the appeal for anyone of a yearning or inquisitive disposition, or just felt stifled by a safe, predictable job.

The best-known long-term legacy of the informal manifesto in *Gandalf's Garden* has been the Glastonbury Festival, which takes place at the summer solstice five miles away from Glastonbury at Worthy Farm near Pilton—in fact just by the posterior of Katharine Maltwood's Sagittarius. The festival started in 1970, but the following year best summed up its early ethos and was the most legendary festival of the early years. It was a free festival held at the solstice, where the right vibes were ensured by setting the stage on the ley between Glastonbury and Stonehenge, and where music was mixed with dance, poetry and theatre. It was this festival that yielded the live album *Glastonbury Fayre* in 1972 and Nic Roeg's film of the same name.

Many of Michell's detractors were people who had already studied the material closely for themselves. Some of his greatest admirers, on the other hand, were inspired to settle in Glastonbury and make their own investigations. One of these was the Londoner Anthony Roberts (1940–1990), who moved to Glastonbury in 1981 and later died of a heart attack on Glastonbury Tor. He had already brought minds together in an eclectic collection of different approaches. The

1970s was the ley decade and they were found across the Glastonbury land-scape—one links the churches of St John and St Benedict with Wells Cathedral to the north east and the hillfort at Castle Neroche to the south west.

In the opinion of Anthony Roberts, the zodiac was laid out at some time between 10,000 and 2,700 BC, followed by astronomer priests 2,000 BC, who put up standing stones, developed the Chalice Well and dug the local earthwork known as Ponter's Ball. Druids followed, making a spiral maze around the Tor. His view of recent centuries is entirely negative. If the zodiac is now difficult to see on the ground it is simple because the 'landscape has been systematically violated over the last few hundred years'. The chief villain is Christianity, which usurped and destroyed the ancient sacred landscape. To give any credit to Christians it is first necessary to establish for them some non-Christian credentials. Hence St Dunstan is redeemed in Roberts' mind because he was an 'astrologer, alchemist and magician'. To cleanse the world of the ills of modern society it was therefore necessary to sweep away the accretions of Christianity to find the purity of the pagan spirit that it supplanted. It is a curious argument but one that reveals the prejudices of early counter-cultural Glastonbury. It seeks to celebrate seekers after spiritual fulfilment who came and made their lives at Glastonbury, but excludes a community that prospered there for, at the most conservative estimates, over 800 years. To exclude the church is as futile as pretending that the history of Glastonbury can be written without its myths. But this new generation of thinkers is predominantly pagan, and therefore it is apt that their chief source of inspiration was Katharine Maltwood rather than Frederick Bligh Bond.

The architect and art historian Keith Critchlow was a significant influence on John Michell. Critchlow developed Bond's idea of an original round chapel with twelve satellites and suggested that the ground plan of the original Glastonbury settlement was laid out to the same plan as Stonehenge. Critchlow pursued the idea of sacred geometry throughout his career, notably in the study of Islamic art, and it was a scheme behind his major architectural works like the Sri Sathya Sai hospital in India. Michell incorporated Critchlow's ideas into his own work. Both Glastonbury and Stonehenge, according to Michell, had been set out according to a traditional plan. It could have been passed down over two millen-nia from the building of Stonehenge, or it may have been revealed at Glastonbury by a revelation, a favourite Michell topic. Joseph's cell and its twelve satellites were the 'thirteen spheres' of Melkin's prophecy. He argued that the sites of some of these satellite hermit cells were preserved by later features, specifically St Dunstan's Chapel, the Galilee attached to the east end of the Lady Chapel, one of the pyramids on the south side of the Lady Chapel, and the tomb of Arthur. All this allowed Michell to loosen Glastonbury from its historical Christian setting and to perceive instead a universal legend. 'Glastonbury Abbey was built as the spiritual successor of Stonehenge ... and for the same purpose, the distillation of solar energy and its fusion with the terrestrial current or life essence.'[9]

A new generation of authors overlapped with Michell and have taken the baton into the twenty-first century. Nicholas Mann has written several Glastonbury books, focusing on the Tor and Glastonbury's springs. There are shades of Michell in his portrayal of the Tor as a world mountain, natural temple and cosmic axis, and interpretation of Christianity and mythology as manifestations of the same ancient Order of Avalon. So too the belief that humanity is on the brink of a great leap forward in consciousness. His language is sometimes baffling. An aquifer in the Tor is apparently the source of quite specific energies in its springs: the white spring (adapted to supply the town in 1870) and the red spring (i.e. Chalice Well):–

> this unusual two-layer geophysical system causes the atomic and ionic bonds of the elements dissolved in the water within it to hold a polarity of electromagnetic forces in a flux capable of interacting with and influencing the subtle energies of the human psychophysical system.[10]

Is he putting non-scientists in their place or just having us on? But Avalon people were also midwinter sky watchers, gaining the knowledge that made Newgrange, Stonehenge and Avebury possible. From St Edmund's Hill, about a mile north west of the Tor, the midwinter sunrise can be observed ascending the northern flank of the Tor, but in 1,600 BC Mann contends that the rising sun would have flashed at each of the terraces. So the Tor was cut partly for astronomical purposes.

Kathy Jones, a Priestess of Avalon, was co-founder of the Glastonbury Goddess Temple which opened in 2002. She and others see the form of the Goddess in the landscape itself, and these shared beliefs have now become a community. It is easy to think that they live in a different world to the rest of us. The community's 2013 newsletter remarks that:–

> the mists of Samhain are faintly swirling, drifting off the lake in this warm autumn. As the moon waxes and wanes—Ceridwen and Arianrhod, in their dance of dark and light—regardless of the unseasonal weather, I feel deep down the need to move into the Dark.

But the Goddess Temple has a retail arm, where you can stock up on essentials such as a Crone goddess banner, Spirit of Avalon incense, and a 'Wise Woman' deck of oracle cards.

Glastonbury may have attracted a permanent settlement of consumer-society refuseniks, but a walk around the town today reveals that many of them have an astute business sense. There are shops for books (Glastonbury has far more bookshops per head than it ought to have), crafts and clothes, and adverts for every form of alternative therapy and medicine you can think of. There are centres for Christian healing and holistic retreat. Glastonbury is also the place for shamanic healing, Qi Gong, craniosacral therapy, creative kinesiology, crystal sound activation, the place to learn Stargaia or Lomi Lomi massage and so on. It is a town of goods and services. Pagans and Christians will all find their place there. Glastonbury's protean myths have spawned numerous other avenues of research—it has become a centre for modern druidry, for green-man research, shamanism and pagan deities.

Glastonbury is very much a town for modern times, providing a niche market for a place in which we can interpret the world in any way that suits us. The downside is that people can come here seeking themselves and not each other, and create a community that is not judgmental, but that does not challenge either. The National Trust, anxious not to offend, does not tell visitors to the Tor what they think its significance was, whether or not the terraces are natural, and why alternative theories might be wrong. That is up to the visitor to decide. The Church of England is likewise happy to accommodate alternative ideas and beliefs. In 2007 Sig Lonegren laid out a non-Christian labyrinth in the churchyard of St John. It commemorated the tercentenary of Glastonbury receiving a Royal Charter from Queen Anne in 1705, which implicitly accepts that Glastonbury could flourish spiritually if it could do so economically.

Glastonbury was re-cast in the late twentieth century. Joseph and the thorn have declined in importance at the expense of the Tor and Chalice Well. This shift in emphasis has long been part of Glastonbury's history. Once, its claim to importance was founded upon the relics of Celtic and Anglo-Saxon saints. But they were superseded by Arthur in the late twelfth century and he in turn was eclipsed by Joseph in the fifteenth and sixteenth centuries. The abbey had been the focus of all of these cults but, when it was closed, attention switched to the thorn tree on Wearyall Hill and the walnut tree in the abbey grounds. The demise of these trees, having been destroyed by unchecked enthusiasm and by wanton vandalism, shifted the focus back again to the abbey, which remained at the heart of Glastonbury mythology until, ironically, it was saved for the nation and dressed up as a heritage attraction. But in the twentieth century the scope of Glastonbury mythology broadened considerably and it is unlikely to shrink again in the future. A nostalgic longing for a lost world runs through Glastonbury's history—of the monks for the heroic deeds of saints and King Arthur, for devotees of the thorn to the lost monastery, of antiquarians for the middle ages, and of New Age devotees for a pre-industrial and pre-Christian world.

End Notes

The Holiest Earth in England

1. Chesterton, *A short history of England* (1917), p. 26.
2. Powys, *A Glastonbury Romance* (1975), p. 125.
3. Hollis, *Glastonbury and England* (1927), p. 11.
4. Rahtz & Watts, *Glastonbury: Myth and History* (2003), p. 54.
5. Doel, Doel & Lloyd, *Worlds of Arthur* (1998), pp. 85, 87.

The Richest Monastery in England

1. Brereton, *Travels in Holland, United Provinces, England, Scotland and Ireland 1634–1635* (1844), p. 172.
2. Rahtz & Watts, *Glastonbury* (2003), pp. 77-78.
3. Morland, 'Glaston's Twelve Hides', *Proceedings of the Somerset Archaeological and Natural History Society* 128 (1984), p. 41.
4. Gildas, *Ruin of Britain*, chapters 8, 12.2.
5. Scavone, 'Joseph of Arimathea, the Holy Grail and the Edessa Icon', *Arthuriana* 9.4 (1999), p. 13.
6. Hutton, *Witches, Druids and King Arthur* (2003), p. 72.
7. Southern, 'Aspects of the European tradition of historical writing', *Transactions of the Royal Historical Society* 23 (1973), pp. 249-50.
8. Morland, 'Glaston's Twelve Hides', p. 41.
9. Scott, *The early history of Glastonbury: an edition, translation and study of William of Malmesbury's De Antiquitate Glastonie Ecclesie* (1991), p. 157.
10. *Ibid.*
11. *Ibid.*, p. 41.
12. *Ibid.*, p. 43.
13. *Ibid.*, pp. 123, 125.
14. *Ibid.*, p. 51.
15. *Ibid.*, p. 53.
16. *Ibid.*, p. 67.
17. *Ibid.*
18. *Ibid.*
19. *Ibid.*

Avalon

1. Scott, *The early history of Glastonbury: an edition, translation and study of William of Malmesbury's De Antiquitate Glastonie Ecclesie* (1991), p. 157.
2. Lloyd-Morgan, 'From Ynys Wydrin to Glasynbri: Glastonbury in Welsh vernacular tradition', in Abrams & Carley, eds., *The archaeology and history of Glastonbury Abbey* (1996), pp. 306-11.
3. .Higham, *King Arthur: myth-making and history* (2002), p. 170; Luke xxiii.26.
4. Geoffrey of Monmouth, *History of the Kings of Britain*, translated by Lewis Thorpe (1966), p. 261.
5. Carley & Townsend, *The Chronicle of Glastonbury Abbey: an edition, translation and study* (1985), p. 181.
6. Doel, Doel & Lloyd, *Worlds of Arthur* (1998), p. 86.
7. Scott, *Early History of Glastonbury*, p. 83.
8. Malory, *Le Morte d'Arthur* (1969), p. 4.
9. Lloyd-Morgan, 'From Ynys Wydrin to Glasynbri', pp. 304, 308.

Joseph and the Holy Grail

1. Matthew xxvii. 57-60; Mark xv. 43-46; Luke xxiii. 50-55; John iii. 1-21, vii. 50-51.
2. Luke x.
3. Nicodemus xii.1, in *New Testament Apocrypha* (1965), pp. 513-14.
4. *Ibid.*, xv.6, p. 518.
5. Lagorio, 'The evolving legend of Joseph of Arimathea', in Carley, ed., *Glastonbury Abbey and the Arthurian tradition* (2001), pp. 60-61.
6. Littleton & Malcor, *From Scythia to Camelot* (1994).
7. Barber, *The Holy Grail* (2004), p. 39.
8. *Ibid.*, p. 129.
9. *Ibid.*, p. 94.
10. Scavone, 'Joseph of Arimathea, the Holy Grail and the Edessa Icon', *Arthuriana* 9.4 (1999), pp. 15-16.
11. de Boron, *Merlin and the Grail* (2001), p. 22.
12. *Ibid.*
13. *Ibid.*, p. 119.
14. Barber, *Holy Grail*, p. 132.

First Among Christian Nations

1. Carley & Townsend, *Chronicle of Glastonbury Abbey* (1985), pp 34-35.
2. *Ibid.*, p. 55.
3. Acts xii.2.
4. John of Fordun, *Chronicle of the Scottish Nation* (1872), p. 70.
5. Loomis, *Council of Constance* (1961), pp. 323, 324.
6. Crowder, *Unity, heresy and reform* (1977), p. 119.
7. Carley, 'A grave event: Henry V, Glastonbury Abbey and Joseph of Arimathea's bones', in *Glastonbury Abbey and the Arthurian tradition* (2001), pp. 301-2.
8. *Ibid.*, p. 301.
9. Watkin, 'Last glimpses of Glastonbury', *Downside Review* 67 (1949), p. 83.

10. *Ibid.*, p. 86.
11. *Ibid.*, p. 84n.
12. Ellis, ed., *Chronicle of John Hardyng* (1812), p. 85.

Protestants and Pilgrims

1. Brereton, *Travels in Holland, United Provinces, England, Scotland and Ireland 1634-1635* (1844), p. 173.
2. Chisholm Batten, 'The holy thorn of Glastonbury', *Proceedings of the Somerset Archaeological and Natural History Society* 26 (1880), p. 118.
3. Camden, *Britannia* (1695), p. 64.
4. Chisholm Batten, 'The holy thorn of Glastonbury', p. 119.
5. Broughton, *The Ecclesiasticall Historie of Great Britaine* (1633), pp. 110-11.
6. Brereton, *Travels*, p. 174.
7. Broughton, *Ecclesiasticall Historie*, p. 137.
8. Walsham, 'The holy thorn of Glastonbury', *Parergon* 21.2 (2004), p. 13.
9. Broughton, *Ecclesiasticall Historie*, p. 138.
10. Symmons, *A vindication of King Charles* (1648), p. 76.
11. Exodus iii, 2-4; Numbers xvii.
12 .Baxter, *The certainty of the world of spirits* (1834), p. 80.
13. *Ibid.*, p. 81.
14. *Ibid.*, pp. 78-79.
15. Fuller, *The Church History of Britain*, i (1837), p. 16.
16. Aubrey, *The Natural History of Wiltshire* (1847), p. 57.
17. Krikler, 'The foxglove, "the old woman from Shropshire", and William Withering, *Journal of the American College of Cardiology* (May 1985), pp. 3a-9a.
18. Browne, *Pseudodoxia Epidemica* (1658), p. 112.
19. Camden, *Britannia*, p. 63.
20. Spenser, *The Faerie Queene*, book II, canto 10, verse 53.
21. Champion, *The pillars of priestcraft shaken* (1992), p. 56.
22. Spelman, *Concilia, Decreta, Leges, Constitutiones* (1639), pp. 6-12.
23. Stillingfleet, *Origines Britannicae* (1840), pp. 6-14.
24. Collier, *Ecclesiastical History of Great Britain*, i (1708), pp. 7-12, quote at p. 10.
25. Burgess, *Tracts on the Origin and Independence of the British Church* (1815), pp. 97n, 56.

Vulgar Errors

1. Chandler, ed., *Travels through Stuart Britain* (1999), p. 227.
2. Wickham Legg, ed., 'A relation of a short survey of the western counties ... in 1635', *Camden Miscellany* 52 (1936), p. 80.
3. Aubrey, *Natural History of Wiltshire* (1847), p. 57.
4. Morton, *In search of England* (1932), p. 134; *Journal of the New York Botanical Garden* 42.2 (1941), p. 5.
5. Stukeley, *Itinerarium Curiosum* (1724), p. 146.
6. Broughton, *The Ecclesiasticall Historie of Great Britaine* (1633), pp. 127-28, 136.
7. Walsham, *The Reformation of the Landscape* (2011), pp. 496-97.
8. Eyston, *A Little Monument to the once famous Abbey and Borough of*

Glastonbury, in Hearne, *History and Antiquities of Glastonbury* (1722), pp. 1-2.
9. *Ibid.*, p. 109.
10. Defoe, *A Tour Through the Whole Island of Great Britain* (1971), pp. 256-57.
11. *Gentleman's Magazine* 23 (1753), p. 49.
12. Mullan & Reid, *Eighteenth-Century Popular Culture* (2000), p. 217.
13. *Ibid.*, p. 222.
14. *Ibid.*, pp. 222-23.
15. *Ibid.*, p. 218.
16. Saunders, *A Description of the Curiosities of Glastonbury* (1781), p. 38.
17. Stout, *The Thorn and the Waters* (2008), p. 29.
18. Mullan & Reid, *Eighteenth-Century Popular Culture*, p. 230.
19. *Ibid.*, p. 235.
20. *Ibid.*, p. 236.
21. Kilvert, *Kilvert's Diary 1870-1879* (1999), p. 324.
22. *Ibid.*
23. Hunt, *Popular Romances of the West of England* (1881), p. 389.
24. Inhabitant of Bath, *Wilt thou be whole?* (1751), p. 68; II Kings v.
25. *Gentleman's Magazine* 23 (1753), pp. 578-79.

The Fall and Rise of Glastonbury Abbey

1. Carley, *Glastonbury Abbey* (1988), p. 169.
2. Drayton, *Poly-Olbion* (1613), song 4.
3. Brereton, *Travels in Holland, United Provinces, England, Scotland and Ireland 1634-1635* (1844), p. 173.
4. Wickham Legg, L. G., ed., 'A relation of a short survey of the western counties made ... in 1635', *Camden Miscellany* 52 (1936), p. 79.
5. Morris, ed., *Journeys of Celia Fiennes* (1949), p. 242.
6. Wickham Legg, 'A short survey of the western counties', p. 79.
7. Grose, *The Antiquities of England and Wales*, v (1785), pp. 37-38.
8. Saunders, *A Description of the Curiosities of Glastonbury* (1781), p. 41.
9. Willis, *An History of the Mitred Parliamentary Abbies*, ii (1719), p. 197; Grose, *Antiquities of England and Wales*, p. 35.
10. Stukeley, *Itinerarium Curiosum* (1724), p. 145.
11. Sweet, *Antiquaries* (2004), p. 298.
12. *Avalonian Guide to the Town of Glastonbury* (1814), p. 47.
13. Saunders, *A Description of the Curiosities of Glastonbury* (1781), p. 33.
14. Freeman, 'Glastonbury British and English', in *English Towns and Districts: a series of addresses and sketches* (1883), p. 82.
15. *Ibid.*, p. 92.
16. Ashe, 'Arthur and English history', in *The Quest for Arthur's Britain* (1968), p. 242.
17. Tennyson, 'The Holy Grail', lines 50-66.
18. Hawker, *The Quest of the Sangraal*, lines 98-106.
19. de Vere, 'King Henry II at the tomb of King Arthur', part 2, verses 7, 9, 10.
20. Morton, *In Search of England* (1932), p. 131.
21. Rahtz, 'Glastonbury Tor', in Ashe, ed., *The Quest for Arthur's Britain* (1968), p. 148; Rahtz & Watts, *Glastonbury; Myth and History* (2003), p. 78.
22. Abrams & Carley, eds., *The Archaeology and History of Glastonbury Abbey: Essays in Honour of the Ninetieth Birthday of C. A. Ralegh Radford* (1996).

And Did Those Feet ...?

1. Baring-Gould, *Lives of the Saints*, iii (1897), p 284.
2. Baring-Gould, *The Book of Cornwall* (1906), p. 57.
3. Hunt, *Popular Romances of the West of England* (1881), p. 341.
4. Dobson, *God, the War and Britain* (1917), p. 23.
5. Dobson, *Did our Lord Visit Britain, as they say in Cornwall and Somerset?* (1947), p. 43.
6. *Ibid.*, p. 31.
7. *Ibid.*, p. 15.
8. Lewis, *St Joseph of Arimathea at Glastonbury* (1937), p. 7.
9. Dobson, *Did our Lord Visit Britain*, p. 7.
10. Hollis, *Glastonbury and England* (1927), p. 10.

The Immemorial Mystery of Glastonbury

1. Powys, *A Glastonbury Romance* (1975), p. 285.
2. *Ibid.*, p. 86.
3. Fortune, *Avalon of the Heart* (1986), p. 57.
4. Bond, *The Gate of Remembrance* (1921), pp. 56-57.
5. *Ibid.*, p. 39.
6. *Ibid.*, p. 147.
7. Scott, *The Early History of Glastonbury: An Edition, Translation and Study of William of Malmesbury's De Antiquitate Glastonie Ecclesie* (1991), p. 67.
8. Bond, *Gate of Remembrance*, p. 147.
9. Benham, *The Avalonians* (2006), p. 39.
10. *Ibid.*, p. 48.
11. Powys, *Glastonbury Romance*, p. 125.
12. Fortune, *Avalon of the Heart*, pp. 1-6.

New Jerusalem

1. Michell, *Flying Saucer Vision* (1974), p. 11.
2. Brown, *Katharine Emma Maltwood* (1981), p. 42.
3. Michell, *Flying Saucer Vision*, p. 162.
4. Michell, *City of Revelation* (1973), p. 166.
5. Critchlow, 'Introductory notes on a new theory of proportion in architecture', in Williams & Jackson, eds., *Glastonbury: A Study in Patterns* (1969), p. 30.
6. Michell, 'Centres and lines of latent power in Britain', *International Times* 19 (1967), p. 5.
7. Benham, *The Avalonians* (2006), p. 171.
8. Caine, 'The Glastonbury giants', *Gandalf's Garden* 4 (1969), online at http://www.users.globalnet.co.uk/~pardos/GGZodiac2.html.
9. Michell, 'Glastonbury Abbey: a solar instrument of former science', in Williams & Jackson, eds., *Glastonbury: A Study in Patterns* (1969), p. 31.
10. Mann, *Energy Secrets of Glastonbury Tor* (2004), p. 8.

Bibliography

Abrams, L., *Anglo-Saxon Glastonbury: Church and Endowment* (Woodbridge: Boydell Press, 1996)

Abrams, L. and Carley, J., eds., *The Archaeology and History of Glastonbury Abbey: Essays in Honour of the Ninetieth Birthday of C. A. Ralegh Radford* (Woodbridge: Boydell Press, 1996)

Annand, W., *Mysterium Pietatis, or The Mysterie of Godlinesse* (London: Robert Boulter, 1671)

Ashe, G., *King Arthur's Avalon* (London: Collins, 1957)

Ashe, G., ed., *The Quest for Arthur's Britain* (London: Pall Mall Press, 1968)

Ashmole, E., *Theatrum Chemicum Britannicum* (London: Nathaniel Brooke, 1652)

Aubrey, J., *The Natural History of Wiltshire* (London: Wiltshire Topographical Society, 1847)

Avalonian Guide to the Town of Glastonbury, 2nd edition (Glastonbury: J. Wakefield, 1814)

Barber, R., *The Holy Grail: Imagination and Belief* (London: Allen Lane, 2004)

Baring-Gould, S., *Lives of the Saints*, vol. 3, revised edition (London: John Nimmo, 1897)

Baring-Gould, S., *The Book of Cornwall*, new edition (London: Methuen, 1906)

Barrow, J., and Brooks, N. P., eds., *St Wulfstan and His World* (Aldershot: Ashgate, 2005)

Baxter, R., *The Certainty of the World of Spirits Fully Evinced* (London: Joseph Smith, 1834)

Benham, P., *The Avalonians*, 2nd edition (Glastonbury: Gothic Image, 2006)

Bond, F. B., 'Glastonbury Abbey: report on the discoveries made during the excavations of 1908', *Proceedings of the Somerset Archaeological and Natural History Society* 54 (1909), pp. 107-30

Bond, F. B., 'Glastonbury Abbey: sixth report on the discoveries made during the excavations', *Proceedings of the Somerset Archaeological and Natural History Society* 59 (1913), pp. 56-73

Bond, F. B., 'Glastonbury Abbey: eighth report on the discoveries made during the excavations', *Proceedings of the Somerset Archaeological and Natural History Society* 61 (1916), pp. 128-42

Bond, F. B., *An Architectural Handbook of Glastonbury Abbey*, 3rd edition (Glastonbury: Central Somerset Gazette, 1920)

Bond, F. B., *The Gate of Remembrance*, 4th edition (Oxford: Basil Blackwell, 1921)

Boron, R. de, *Merlin and the Grail*, translated by Nigel Bryant (Woodbridge: D. S. Brewer, 2001)

Brereton, Sir W., *Travels in Holland, United Provinces, England, Scotland and Ireland 1634-1635* (London: Chetham Society, 1844)

Broadhurst, P., and Miller, H., *The Sun and the Serpent* (Launceston: Pendragon Press, 1989)

Broughton, R., *The Ecclesiasticall Historie of Great Britaine* (Douai: Mark Wyon, 1633)

Brown, R. A., *Katharine Emma Maltwood: Artist 1878–1961* (Victoria, Canada: Sono Nis Press, 1981)

Browne, Sir T., *Pseudodoxia Epidemica, or Enquiries into Very Many Received Tenets and Commonly Presumed Truths*, 4th edition (London: Edward Dod, 1658)

Burgess, T., *Tracts on the Origin and Independence of the British Church* (London: F. C. and J. Rivington, 1815)

Caine, M., 'The Glastonbury Giants', *Gandalf's Garden* 4 (1969)

Caine, M., *The Glastonbury Zodiac: Key to the Mysteries of Britain* (Torquay: Grael Communications, 1978)

Camden, W., *Britannia, Newly Translated into English*, edited by E. Gibson (London: Swalle & Churchil, 1695)

Carley, J., 'Melkin and the esoteric tradition at Glastonbury Abbey', *Downside Review* 99 (1981), pp. 1-17

Carley, J., *Glastonbury Abbey: The Holy House at the Head of the Moors Adventurous* (Woodbridge: Boydell Press, 1988)

Carley, J., ed., *Glastonbury Abbey and the Arthurian Tradition* (Cambridge: D. S. Brewer, 2001)

Carley, J., and Townsend, D., *The Chronicle of Glastonbury Abbey: An Edition, Translation and Study of Glastonbury's Cronica sive Antiquitates Glastoniensis ecclesie* (Woodbridge: Boydell Press, 1985)

Chambers, E. K., *Arthur of Britain: The Story of King Arthur in History and Legend*, (London: Sidgwick & Jackson, 1966)

Champion, J. A. I., *The Pillars of Priestcraft Shaken: The Church of England and its Enemies, 1660–1730* (Cambridge: Cambridge University Press, 1992)

Chandler, J., ed., *Travels through Stuart Britain: The Adventures of John Taylor, the Water Poet* (Stroud: Sutton Publishing, 1999)

Chesterton, G. K., *A Short History of England* (London: Chatto & Windus, 1917)

Chisholm Batten, E., 'The holy thorn of Glastonbury', *Proceedings of the Somerset Archaeological and Natural History Society* 26 (1880), pp. 117-25

Collier, J., *Ecclesiastical History of Great Britain*, vol. 1 (London: Samuel Keeble, 1708)

Collinson, J., *The History and Antiquities of the County of Somerset*, vol. 2 (Bath: R. Cruttwell, 1791)

Crawford, D., 'St Joseph and Britain: the old French origins', *Arthuriana*, 11.3 (2001), pp. 1-20

Crowder, C. M. D., *Unity, Heresy and Reform, 1378–1460: The Conciliar Response to the Great Schism* (London: Edward Arnold, 1977)

Davies, Rev J., *A Short Description of the Waters at Glastonbury* (Exon: Andrew Brice, 1751)

Defoe, D., *A Tour through the Whole Island of Great Britain* (Harmondsworth: Penguin, 1971)

Dobson, C. C., *God, the War and Britain* (London: Elliot Stock, 1917)

Dobson, C. C., *The Story of the Empty Tomb as if told by Joseph of Arimathea* (London: Charles Thynne, 1920)

Dobson, C. C., *Did our Lord Visit Britain, as they say in Cornwall and Somerset?*, 5th edition (Glastonbury: Avalon Press, 1947)

Doel, F. and G., and Lloyd, T., *Worlds of Arthur: King Arthur in History, Legend and Culture* (Stroud: Tempus, 1998)

Dunning, R., *Somerset Monasteries* (Stroud: Tempus, 2001)

Ellis, H., ed., *The Chronicle of John Hardyng* (London: F. C. and J. Rivington, 1812)

Farmer, D., *Oxford Dictionary of Saints*, 4th edition (Oxford: Oxford University Press, 1997)

Fiennes, C., *The Journeys of Celia Fiennes* (London: Cresset Press, 1949)

Finke, L. and Shichtman, M., *King Arthur and the Myth of History* (Gainesville, USA: University of Florida Press, 2004)

Fortune, D., *Avalon of the Heart*, revised edition (Wellingborough: Aquarian Press, 1986)

Freeman, E., *English Towns and Districts: A Series of Addresses and Sketches* (London: Macmillan & Co, 1883)

Fuller, T., *The Church History of Britain*, new edition vol. 1 (London: Thomas Tegg & son, 1837)

Genet, J. P., 'English nationalism: Thomas Polton at the Council of Constance', *Nottingham Medieval Studies* 28 (1984), pp. 60-78

Geoffrey of Monmouth, *History of the Kings of Britain*, translated by Lewis Thorpe (Harmondsworth: Penguin, 1966)

Gillingham, J., *Richard I* (London: Yale University Press, 1991)

Gransden, A., 'Antiquarian studies in fifteenth-century England', *Antiquaries Journal* 60 (1980), pp. 75-97

Grose, F., *The Antiquities of England and Wales*, vol. 5, new edition (London: S. Hooper, 1785)

Hamilton Thompson, B., *Glastonbury, Truth and Fiction* (London: Mowbray & Co, 1939)

Harriss, G. L., ed., *Henry V: the Practice of Kingship* (Stroud: Alan Sutton, 1993)

Hearne, T., *The History and Antiquities of Glastonbury* (Oxford: printed at the theatre, 1722)

Higham, N. J., *King Arthur: Myth-Making and History* (London: Routledge, 2002)

Highley, C., *Catholics Writing the Nation in Early Modern Britain and Ireland* (Oxford: Oxford University Press, 2008)

Hollis, C., *Glastonbury and England* (London: Sheed & Ward, 1927)

Hopkinson-Ball, T., *The Rediscovery of Glastonbury: Frederick Bligh Bond, Architect of the New Age* (Stroud: Sutton Publishing, 2007)

Hunt, R., *Popular Romances of the West of England* (London: Chatto & Windus, 1881)

Hutton, R., *Witches, Druids and King Arthur* (London: Hambledon and London, 2003)

Hurd, M., *Rutland Boughton and the Glastonbury Festivals* (Oxford: Clarendon Press, 1993)

Inhabitant of Bath, *Wilt thou be whole? or, the virtues and efficacy of the waters of Glastonbury* (London: Benjamin Matthews, 1751)

John of Fordun, *Chronicle of the Scottish Nation*, translated by W. F. Skene

(Edinburgh: Edmonston and Douglas, 1872)

Jones, K., *In the Nature of Avalon: Goddess Pilgrimages in Glastonbury's Sacred Landscape* (Glastonbury: Ariadne Publications, 2000)

Jones, K., *The Ancient British Goddess: her Myths, Legends, Sacred Sites and Present Revelation*, 2nd edition (Glastonbury: Ariadne Publications, 2001)

Kilvert, F., *Kilvert's Diary 1870–1879: Selections from the Diary of the Rev. Francis Kilvert* (London: Pimlico, 1999)

Lewis, H. A., *Christ in Cornwall? Legends of St Just-in-Roseland and Other Parts* (Falmouth: J.H. Lake, 1939)

Lewis, L. S., *St Joseph of Arimathea at Glastonbury, or the Apostolic Church of Britain*, 6th edition (Wells: Cathedral Press, 1937)

Littleton, C. S., and Malcor, L., *From Scythia to Camelot: A Radical Reassessment of the Legends of King Arthur, the Knights of the Round Table, and the Holy Grail* (London: Garland, 1994)

Loomis, L. S., *Council of Constance: Unification of the Church* (London: Columbia University Press, 1961)

Mabey, R., *Flora Britannica: The Definitive New Guide to Wild Flowers, Plants and Trees* (London: Sinclair-Stevenson, 1996)

Malory, Sir T., *Le Morte d'Arthur*, vol. 1 (Harmondsworth: Penguin, 1969)

Maltwood, K., *A Guide to Glastonbury's Temple of the Stars: Their Giant Effigies Described from Air Views, Maps and from 'The High History of the Holy Grail'* (London: Women's Printing Society, 1934)

Mann, N. R. *Energy Secrets of Glastonbury Tor* (Sutton Mallet: Green Magic, 2004)

Mann, N. R, *Isle of Avalon: Sacred Mysteries of Arthur and Glastonbury* (Sutton Mallet: Green Magic, 2008)

Mann, N. R, *Glastonbury Tor: A Guide to the History & Legends*, revised edition (Glastonbury: Temple Publications, 2010)

Mann, N. and Glasson, P., *The Star Temple of Avalon: Glastonbury's Ancient Observatory Revealed* (Glastonbury: Temple Publications, 2007)

Mann, N., and Glasson, P., *The Red & White Springs of Avalon: A Guide to the Healing Waters of Glastonbury* (Glastonbury: Temple Publications, 2010)

Mantle, George, *Recent Discoveries at Glastonbury Abbey* (Glastonbury: Gazette Printing Co, n. d.)

Marson, C., *Glastonbury, or the English Jerusalem* (Bath: George Gregory, 1925)

Michell, J., 'Centres & lines of the latent power in Britain', *International Times* 19 (1967), p. 5

Michell, J., *The View over Atlantis* (London: Abacus, 1972)

Michell, J., *City of Revelation: On the Proportion and Symbolic Numbers of the Cosmic Temple* (London: Abacus, 1973)

Michell, J., *The Flying Saucer Vision* (London: Abacus, 1974)

Michell, J., *New Light on the Ancient Mystery of Glastonbury* (Glastonbury: Gothic Image, 1990)

Miller, P., *The Gardener's Dictionary*, vol. 2, 4th edition (London: author, 1754)

Morgan, Rev. R. W., *St Paul in Britain, or the Origin of British as Opposed to Papal Christianity* (Oxford: J. H. Parker, 1861)

Morland, S., 'Glaston's Twelve Hides', *Proceedings of the Somerset Archaeological and Natural History Society* 128 (1984), pp. 35-54

Morton, H. V., *In Search of England* (London: Methuen, 1932)

Mullan, J., and Reid, C., eds., *Eighteenth-Century Popular Culture: A Selection*

(Oxford: Oxford University Press, 2000)

New Testament Apocrypha, translated by R. M. Wilson (London: Lutterworth, 1965)

Ormrod, W. M., *Edward III* (London: Yale University Press, 2011)

Plot, R., *The Natural History of Staffordshire* (Oxford: printed at the theatre, 1686)

Plot, R., *The Natural History of Oxfordshire*, 2nd edition (London: Charles Brome, 1705)

Poole, R., *Time's Alteration: Calendar Reform in Early Modern England* (London: UCL Press, 1998)

Powys, J. C., *A Glastonbury Romance* (London: Pan Books, 1975)

Quest of the Holy Grail, The, translated by P. M. Matarasso (Harmondsworth: Penguin, 1969)

Rahtz, P., 'Glastonbury Tor: a modified landscape', *Landscapes* 3.1 (2002), pp. 4-18

Rahtz, P., and Watts, L., *Glastonbury: Myth and History* (Stroud: Tempus, 2003)

Roberts, A., *Sowers of Thunder: Giants in Myth and History* (London: Rider & Co, 1978)

Roberts, A., ed., *Glastonbury: Ancient Avalon, New Jerusalem* (London: Rider & Co, 1992)

Robinson, J. A., *Two Glastonbury Legends* (Cambridge: Cambridge University Press, 1926)

Rouse, R., and Rushton, C., *The Medieval Quest for Arthur* (Stroud: Tempus, 2005)

Saunders, S., *A Description of the Curiosities of Glastonbury* (London: J. Mathews, 1781)

Scavone, D., 'Joseph of Arimathea, the Holy Grail and the Edessa Icon', *Arthuriana* 9.4 (1999), pp. 1-31

Scott, J., *The Early History of Glastonbury: An Edition, Translation and Study of William of Malmesbury's De Antiquitate Glastonie Ecclesie* (Woodbridge: Boydell Press, 1981)

Smith, A. W., 'And did those feet ...?: the legend of Christ's visit to Britain', *Folklore* 100 (1989), pp. 63-83

Spelman, Sir H., *Concilia, Decreta, Leges, Constitutiones* (London: Stephen & Meredith, 1639)

Stillingfleet, E., *Origines Britannicae, or the Antiquities of British Churches*, revised edition (London: William Straker, 1840)

Stout, A., *The Thorn and the Waters* (Frome, Green and Pleasant Publishing, 2008)

Stukeley, W., *Itinerarium Curiosum* (London: the author, 1724)

Swanton, M., ed., *The Anglo-Saxon Chronicles* (London: J.M. Dent, 1996)

Sweet, R., *Antiquaries: The Discovery of the Past in Eighteenth-Century Britain* (London: Hambledon and London, 2004)

Symmons, E., *A Vindication of King Charles, or a Loyal Subject's Duty* (1648)

Taylor, B., and Brewer, E., *The Return of King Arthur: British and American Arthurian Literature Since 1900* (Cambridge: D. S. Brewer, 1983)

Taylor, J. W., *The Coming of the Saints: Imaginations and Studies in Early Church History and Tradition* (London: Methuen & Co, 1906)

Taylor, J. W., *The Doorkeeper and Other Poems, With a Memoir by his Wife* (London: Longmans, Green & Co, 1910)

Thomas, K., *Man and the Natural World* (Harmondsworth: Penguin, 1984)

Thomson, R. M., *William of Malmesbury*, revised edition (Woodbridge: Boydell Press, 2003)

Tilton, H., *Discord and Desecration at Esoteric Glastonbury* (unpublished report to the first international conference on Contemporary Esotericism, 2012)

Tongue, R. L., *Somerset Folklore* (London: Folk-Lore Society, 1965)

Vickery, A. R., *Holy Thorn of Glastonbury* (St Peter Port: Toucan Press, 1979)

Walsham, A., 'The holy thorn of Glastonbury: the evolution of a legend in post-Reformation England', *Parergon* 21.2 (2004), pp. 1-25

Walsham, A., *The Reformation of the Landscape: Religion, Identity and Memory in Early-Modern Britain & Ireland* (Oxford: Oxford University Press, 2011)

Warner, R., *A History of the Abbey of Glaston* (Bath: R. Cruttwell, 1826)

Warren, W. L., *Henry II* (London: Eyre Methuen, 1973)

Waters, Brian, *Severn Tide* (London: J. M. Dent, 1947)

Watkin, A., 'Last glimpses of Glastonbury', *Downside Review* 67 (1949), pp. 76-86

Webb, D., *Pilgrimage in Medieval England* (London: Hambledon and London, 2000)

White, G., *The Natural History of Selborne* (Oxford: Oxford University Press, 1993)

White, R., *Britannia Prima* (Stroud: Tempus, 2007)

Wickham Legg, L. G., ed., 'A relation of a short survey of the western counties made by a lieutenant of the Military Company in Norwich in 1635', *Camden Miscellany* 52 (1936)

Williams, G., *Wales and the Reformation* (Cardiff: University of Wales Press, 1967)

Williams, M. and Jackson, J., eds., *Glastonbury: A Study in Patterns* (London: Research into Lost Knowledge Organisation, 1969)

Williams, M. and Jackson, J., eds., *Britain: A Study in Patterns* (London: Research into Lost Knowledge Organisation, 1971)

Willis, B., *An History of the Mitred Parliamentary Abbies*, vol. 2 (London: Robert Gosling, 1719)

Wood, J., *Choir Gaure, Vulgarly called Stonehenge, on Salisbury Plain* (Oxford: printed at the theatre, 1747)

Wood, J., *The Holy Grail* (Cardiff: University of Wales Press, 2012)

Woolf, D., *The Social Circulation of the Past: English Culture 1500–1730* (Oxford: Oxford University Press, 2003)

Wright, G. W., 'The Chalice Well or Blood Spring, and its traditions', *Proceedings of the Glastonbury Antiquarian Society* 1 (1886), pp. 20-36

Index